Alexander Balloch Grosart, John Donne

Complete Poems

Alexander Balloch Grosart, John Donne

Complete Poems

ISBN/EAN: 9783337005627

Printed in Europe, USA, Canada, Australia, Japan

Cover: Foto ©Thomas Meinert / pixelio.de

More available books at **www.hansebooks.com**

The Fuller Worthies' Library.

THE COMPLETE POEMS

OF

JOHN DONNE, D.D.

DEAN OF ST. PAUL'S.

FOR THE FIRST TIME FULLY COLLECTED AND COLLATED WITH
THE ORIGINAL AND EARLY EDITIONS AND MSS.
AND ENLARGED
WITH HITHERTO UNPRINTED AND INEDITED POEMS FROM MSS. ETC.
AND PORTRAITS, FACSIMILES, AND OTHER ILLUSTRATIONS
IN THE QUARTO FORM.

Edited

WITH PREFACE, ESSAY ON LIFE AND WRITINGS, AND NOTES,

BY THE

REV. ALEXANDER B. GROSART,

ST. GEORGE'S, BLACKBURN, LANCASHIRE.

IN TWO VOLUMES.

VOL. I.

PRINTED FOR PRIVATE CIRCULATION.
1872.

TO

ROBERT BROWNING,

THE POET OF THE CENTURY FOR THINKERS,

I DEDICATE

THIS FIRST COMPLETE EDITION OF THE POEMS OF

JOHN DONNE

(BORN 1573, DIED 1631) ;

KNOWING HOW MUCH HIS POETRY,

WITH EVERY ABATEMENT,

IS VALUED AND ASSIMILATED BY HIM :

RIGHT FAITHFULLY,

ALEXANDER B. GROSART.

The Fuller Worthies' Library.

THE

COMPLETE POEMS OF DR. JOHN DONNE.

VOL. I.

SATIRES.   II. THE PROGRESS OF THE SOUL.
III. ELEGIES.   IV. EPITHALAMIUMS.

CONTENTS.

Those marked with a star [*] have not before been printed: those with a dagger [†] have been derived from authoritative MSS.   G.

PREFACE.

I do not hide from myself that it needs courage (though
I do not claim praise for its exercise) to edit and print
the Poetry of Dr. JOHN DONNE in our day. Nor would
I call it literary prudery that shrinks from giving publicity to such sensuous things (to say the least) as indubit-
ably are found therein. Contrariwise the susceptibility
that makes one so shrink is healthy and true, and its
sharp though unvociferous warning may not safely be
stifled. I deplore that Poetry, in every way almost so
memorable and potential, should be stained even to un-
cleanliness in sorrowfully too many places ; and while
I believe Donne might have written over his collected
Poems what Robert Herrick put for epigraph to his
Hesperides, viz.

> ' To his Book's end this last line he'd have plac't :
> Jocond his Muse was ; *but his Life was chast*,'—

I yet fear William Cartwright's hitherto overlooked protest in his tacit allusion probably to these very lines,
in his noble tribute to Ben Jonson, must hold :

> ' No bargaining line there ; no provoc'tive verse ;
> Nothing but what Lucretia might rehearse :
> No need to make good count'nance ill, and use
> *The plea of strict life for a looser Muse.*'

We know too that in later years Donne lamented his
'youthful verse.'

Nevertheless, I take the responsibility of including
Donne in my Series on these grounds :

(a) I do not *publish* or throw open to all, but limit
to fellow-booklovers and fellow-students, by a 'private
circulation,'—a modified publicity.

(b) The poetry of Donne occupies a unique place
in the Literature of the period. This is universally admitted.

(c) To get at 'the form and pressure' of the time,
you must study this Poetry. His 'Satires' and 'Elegies'
carry in them an unwritten chapter of Elizabethan history.

(d.) Those whom these Volumes may be assumed
to reach are 'strong' enough to use them for literary
purposes unhurt; and respect is due to the 'strong'
equally with the 'weak.'

(e.) Only through his Poetry do you come near to
Donne in the fulness of his faculties and in his most
characteristic utterances.

(f) The moral and spiritual study of an intellect
so remarkable and intense, and of an after-life so white
and beautiful, is of profoundest suggestiveness. It is
only truthful too, to give all known materials for right
estimate and right solution of problems started by the
Life and Writings of Donne. Finally,

(g) 'With every abatement'—as I say in my Dedi-
cation—the Poetry of Donne is imperishable in much
of it, and notable in all, and historically and philoso-
phically to be held fast. Granted that as in rose's heart
or lily's chalice you are shocked to find a slug crawl-

ing. Yet none the less is the rose 'a thing of beauty,' none the less the lily of the finest and nicest workmanship of The Gardener; *e. g.* here is one line out of many equally arresting, that springs up first (so to say) not merely from 'reeds and rushes' slime-rooted, but as it were out of ordure such as makes one hold the nose :

'Love built on beauty soon as beauty dies.'

I reserve a Study of the Life and Writings of DONNE for Volume II., that (as in CRASHAW) the completed Poetry may be before the reader in its perusal. There I hope to make good the highest claims that have been advanced in his name, and likewise give a critical account of the original and after-editions of the Poems (1611-1669 onward) and of various MS. collections that have been drawn on by me. I shall also exemplify, by passages strangely neglected, the 'cunning' and subtle faculty of our Singer, without any need of Coleridge's somewhat paradoxical theory of Donne's measures and accentuation. By the way, the name of Coleridge reminds me that even well-informed critics and literary authorities, *e. g.* Mrs. Jameson in her ' Loves of the Poets,' and Lieut.-Col. Cunningham in his edition of the Works of Ben Jonson, and others, continually quote the empty burlesque lines on Donne of *Hartley* Coleridge, as *the* Coleridge's, in the teeth of the latter's abundant expressions of his lofty estimate and love for Donne as a Poet. Perhaps too the perfunctory way in which Donne is ordinarily read can scarcely be more sorrowfully, if also ludicrously, proved than by the habitual treatment of the 'commendatory' poems prefixed to the 'Anatomie' and

the ' 2d Anniversarie,' as though they formed part of
the Poems themselves, instead of having been the af-
fectionate and admiring tribute of (afterwards) Bishop
Joseph Hall (as shown in the place).

For the present it must suffice to state that I have
had ALL the editions of Donne thus far issued before
me while preparing my own; that I have collated and
re-collated the whole with prolonged carefulness; that
in each case the source of the successive poems is recorded in the place, and all noticeable 'various-readings'
in related Notes and Illustrations; that such collating
and utilisation of MSS. public and private have enabled me to correct the swarming errors and bewilder-
ments of previous editions; and that in Notes and Illustrations I have brought together (as in my other
books of the Series) materials that may not prove un-
useful to students of our elder poetic literature at
its best. With reference to these Notes and Illustrations I cannot too emphatically or unreservedly acknow-
ledge my indebtedness to Dr. BRINSLEY NICHOLSON,
for his lavish and suggestive communications toward
these, in common with all the volumes of the Fuller
Worthies' Library, since I had the privilege of his
friendship. I continue to find all friends formerly
named right willing to aid in every possible way.

I feel it to be a singular honour to be the first to
have engraved Oliver's exquisite miniature of Donne.
It seems to me a surpassingly noble face, with genius
stamped on its every line. Nor is the engraver (Mr.
W. J. Alais) undeserving of his meed of praise for his
part. I thank the owner of the original for his kindness in allowing me the use of it. I limit impres-

sions to the one hundred quartos and twenty-five
separately (folio : proofs). For the ordinary large
paper (8vo), by favour of Messrs. Longman and Co.,
I am enabled to furnish Holl's admirable reproduction
of an (alleged) Vandyck, but the authenticity of which
I should scarcely venture to vouch for. It idealises
the homely engraving of Merian in the folio Sermons.
In Volume II. will be found (in the quarto) a photo-
facsimile, by the Woodbury process, of Marshall's celebrated portrait of the Poet in his eighteenth year, from
an unusually brilliant impression; also a facsimile of
Donne's handwriting, &c.

I had prepared my usual Memorial-Introduction,
containing very considerable biographical additions to
Walton and our data hitherto, e. g. a series of important and characteristic Letters in H.M. Record Office,
the Losely Letters — his Will *in extenso* (never before seen apparently)—and other letters and documents
from public and private sources. Some of these I
shall require in part for the already-named Essay; but
finding from my accomplished correspondent, the Rev.
Dr. AUGUSTUS JESSOP (to whom I am indebted for an
unpublished and vivid poem by Donne, which will
appear in Volume II.), that he has long been engaged
upon a really critical and worthy edition of the complete Prose Works of Donne, and that the 'Life and
Introduction' he hopes very soon to put to press, I
forego the pleasure of first printing these various papers,
and gladly hand over the whole to him in faithful
transcripts. Dr. Jessop has given a taste of his quality·
as an editor of Donne in his natty little collection
of the 'Essays' (1855); and I feel sure that a writer

so conscientious, and a critic so open-eyed and scholarly, will make his edition of Donne a real addition to our English classics. The late Dean Alford's edition (6 vols. 8vo) was a literary *fiasco*.

I refer the reader to the several introductory Notes, and Notes and Illustrations, for anything farther requiring to be said. It only remains to be added, that, as in all my Worthies, I reproduce the whole in integrity, and that in the present Volume several important additions to Donne's Poems are given, while in Volume II. there will be considerably more—all as explained in the Contents and in their places.

ALEXANDER B. GROSART.

Park View, Blackburn, Lancashire.

*** It may be needful to note that by the words 'the child-wife' (p. 69), in relation to Mrs. Elizabeth Drury, is meant the ideal child-wife (so too child-woman and child-mother) of the Poet. 'Mrs.' was then and long subsequently used to designate young ladies of quality or gentry marriageable but unmarried. The youthful Elizabeth Drury, it need scarcely be stated, was not married; and as 'Mrs.' (in the modern sense) sounds oddly, perhaps it is well thus to record the fact.

I.

SATIRES.

1593-1602.

VOL. I.

NOTE.

The Satires come first necessarily, inasmuch as the date of the first two, if not three (1593),and internal evidence, through allusions in others pointing to 1597, warrants us to conclude that as they were among the earliest satires in our language, so also they must have been among the earliest of their author's productions of any extent, while they are certainly the most noticeable and characteristic verse of his.

Mr. J. Payne Collier in perhaps his best book, the ' Poetical Decameron' (2 vols. 8vo. 1820, vol. i. 153 *et seqq.*), asserted and established Donne's claim to be regarded as ' the oldest English satirist,' notwithstanding the boast of Bishop Hall in his Prologue to *his* Satires (1597). On this and related points the reader will find more in our Essay on the Life and Writings of Donne (prefixed to vol. ii.).

Our text of the first three Satires is a careful reproduction, even to its somewhat arbitrary capitals, of Harleian MS. 5110. The first and second Satires are in one handwriting, the third in another, and the second and third are occasionally interlined in (apparently) a third handwriting: *e. g.* in the opening of the second:

> ' Sr though (I thank God for it) I do hate
> there is one
> All this toune perfectly, yet in euery state
> In all things, so excellently best .
> There are some found so villanously best,
> that
> As hate towards them [erased] breeds pitty toward the rest.'

So in the third there are marginal alterations as follows:

> ' Graccus Loues all as one, and thinks yt soe
> As women doe in divers fashons goe
> In divers habits yet ar   still are kind.
> So doth, so is Religion ; and this blind-
> nes too mutch. . . .'

The MS. is a small folio, and consists of (*a*) one leaf; on front of which, near top, is written in a different handwriting from any of the others :

> Jhon Dunne his Satires
> Anno Domini 1593

and a former owner has a date above : 16 October 1725. (*b*

Five leaves and a blank leaf. There are scratched arithmetical figures on both fly-leaves.

I do not think this venerable MS. is in the author's autograph: but it is unquestionably as early as 1593, and being so, must be accepted as of great if not absolute authority. Nevertheless, in their places we have pointed out a number of better readings from later MSS. &c.; and in Notes and Illustrations annotated the later variations, printed and MS.; 5110 MS. contains only the first three Satires.

As shown in our Essay, these Satires were probably, indeed certainly, included in that privately-printed volume whose utter loss is so grievous. The earliest printed edition now known and extant is that of the quarto collection of the Poems of 1633 (pp. 325-349), which contains the first five. The sixth was first given in the edition of 1669, the seventh in 1635. Our text of the latter four is based on that of 1669 (on which and other printed texts see our Preface), with various-readings in their Notes and Illustrations. These have been drawn—besides the different printed texts—from a careful collation by myself of the following MSS. in the British Museum:

> Harleian 4955:
> Lansdowne MS. 740: Plut. lxxiv.

The former is very beautifully written in a great folio, and embraces poetry from all the chief Writers of the period: but as neither it nor the other is dated, I have only accepted their readings when self-vindicatory and when confirmed by other authenticated sources. I attach very great weight to a MS. now in the possession of F. W. Cosens, Esq., London. It has the book-plate of 'Thomas Stephens, of the Inner Temple, Esq.,' and is dated '19th July 1620.' It is a singularly rich collection. The prose 'Paradoxes' (showing interesting variations) form the first portion, and exclusive of Donne's—which are nearly complete and with additions—there are poems by Carew, Daniel, King, and others. The utmost 'pains' had evidently been taken by the writer of this precious (quarto) MS. At times he leaves a blank, where he could not make out the word or words, and these are afterwards carefully filled-in. Whoever he was—of Stephens I can gather nothing —he must have been intimate with Donne himself. In the fourth and sixth Satires I owe to this MS. various corrections, albeit the latter's text is still unsatisfactory in parts. Another important

MS. I designate the Hazlewood - Kingsborough MS., as having been in the famous Kingsborough collection, and afterwards owned by Hazlewood.   See more on this in our Preface.

On Pope's so-called 'versifying' of certain of these Satires and Parnell's, and the traditional nonsense of incapable, however high-named critics, about our Worthy's obscurity and so on, I refer to our already-named Essay. ·G.

SATIRE I.

Away, thou changling motley humorist,
Leaue mee, and in this standing woodden chest,
Consoled wth theese fewe bookes, let me ly
In prison, and here be coffind, when I dy.
Here are God's Conduits, graue divines; and here   5
Nature's Secretary, the philosopher;
And iolly Statesmen, wch teach how to ty
The senews of a Cittyes mistique body;
Here gathering Chronicles, and by them stand
Giddy fantastiqe Poets of each land.   10
Shall I leave all this constant Company,
And followe headlong wild uncertaine thee?
First sweare by thy best loue in earnest,
(Yf thou, wch lou'st all, can loue any best,)
Thou wilt not leaue me in the middle street,   15
Though some more spruce Companion thou do meete
Not though a Captaine do come in thy way,
Bright parcel-guilt, wth forty dead men's pay;
Not though a brisk, perfum'd, pert Courtier
Daine wth a nod thy Courtesyes to answer;   20
Nor Come a veluet Justice wth a longe
Great traine of blew coats, 12 or 14 stronge,

Shalt thou grinne or faune on him, or prepare
A speach to court his beauteous sonne and heyre.
For better and worse take mee, or leaue mee :   25
To take and leaue me is adultery.
O monster, superstitious Puritan
Of refind manners, yet Ceremonial man,
That, when thou meet'st one, wth enquiring eyes,
Doth search, and like a needy broker prise   30
The silke and gold hee weares, and to that rate,
So hie or low, doest raise thy formall hat :
That wilt consort none, untill thou haue knowne
What lands hee hath in hope, or of his owne ;
As though all thy Companions should make thee   35
Jointures, and marry thy deare Company.
Why should'st thou that doest not onely approue,
But in ranke itchy lust, desire and loue,
The nakednes and barenes to enioy   barrenness
Of this plumpe muddy hoore, or prostitute boy, whore
Hate vertue, though shee be naked and bare?   41
At birth and death our bodyes naked are ;
And till our soules be unapparellèd
Of bodyes, they from blis are banishèd :
Man's first best state was naked ; when by sinne   45
Hee lost that, yet hee was clothd but in beast's skinne,
And in this course attyre wch nowe I weare,   coarse
With God and wth the muses I Conferre.
But Since thou, like a contrite Penitent,
Charitably warn'd of thy sinne, doest repent   50

Theese vanityes and giddinesses, loe
I shut my chamber dore, and come, let's goe.
But sooner may a cheape hoore, who hath beene   whore
Worne by as many seneral men in sinne,
As are blacke fethers, or muske-Collored hose,   55
Name her child's right true fathcr 'mongst all those;
Sooner may one gues, who shall beare away   guess
Th' infant of London heyre to an India;
And sooner may a gulling-weather-spy,   .
By drawing forthe heauen's Scheme, tell certainly   60
What fashiond hats or ruffes, or suites, next yeare
Our supple-witted antiqe youthes will weare;   [Than
Then thou, when thou departst from hence, can show
Whether, why, where, or wth whom thou wouldst go.
But howe shall I bee pardon'd my offence,   65
That thus have sin'd against my Conscience?
    Now we are in the streete; hee first of all,
Unprouidently proud, creepes to the wall;
And so imprisond and hemd in by mee,
Sels for a little roome his liberty.   70
Yet though he cannot skip forth now to greete
Euery fine silken painted foole wee meete,
He them to him wth amorous smiles allures,
And grinns, smackes, shrugs, and such an itch endures,
As 'prentises or Schooleboyes, wch do knowe   75
Of some gay sport abroad, yet dare not goe;
And as fidlers stop lowest at highest sound,   low'st
So to the most braue stoups hee nighst the ground;

But to a graue man hee doth moue no more
Then the wise politiqe horse would heretofore,   80
Or thou, O Elephant, or Ape, wilt doe,
When any names the k[ing] of Spaine to you.   [see
Now leapes hee upright, ioggs mee, and cryes, 'Do you
Yonder wel-fauourd youth?' 'W^{ch}?' 'Yea! 'tis hee
That dances so diuinely.'   'O,' said I,   85
'Stand still, must you dance to for Company?'   too
He droupt; wee went, till one wch did excell
The Indians in drinking his Tobacco well
Mett us : they talkt; I whisperd, 'let us go;
May bee you smel him not, truly I do.'   90
He heares not mee, but on the other side
A many-colourd Peacock hauing spide,
Leaues him and mee; I for my lost sheepe stay;
He followes, ouertakes, goes in the way,
Saying, 'him, whom I last left, all repute   95
For his deuice, in handsoming a suite,
To iudge of lace, pinck, panes, cut, print, or pleight,
Of all the Court to haue the best Conceit.'
'Our dull Comedians want him, let him go;
But O, God strengthen thee, why stoupst thou so?'   100
'Why, hee hath traueld long; no, but to mee
Which understand none, hee doth seeme to bee
Perfect *french* and *Italian*.'   I replyed,   ·
'So is the Pox.'   Hee answer'd not, but spide
More men of sort, of parts and qualityes :   105
At last his loue hee in a window spyes,

And like light dewe exhal'd hee flinges from me
Violently rauisht to his lechery.

Many were there, hee could comand no more ;
He quareld, fought, bled ; and turn'd out of dore   110
Directly came to mee, hanging the head,
And constantly a while must keepe his bed.

NOTES AND ILLUSTRATIONS.

Heading: there is none in the 1593 MS.; but elsewhere (e. g.
Stephens' MS.) it is written ' Satyra 1;' and so in 1633 and subsequently.

Line 1, ' *changling.*' 1633 ' fondling:' so Stephens' MS. and
Lansdowne MS. 740. As ' changeling' is ambiguous, being used
for fairy changelings, and as ' motley' expresses the various
picked costumes of different customs which the foppish Eng-
lishman was supposed to delight in, probably ' fondling' was
the author's revised word.

Line 2, ' *standing woodden chest.*'   Books were kept in
' chests ;' but query, Is the poet not here humorously likening
his little study-closet to such a chest ? Cf. Marvell's ' Flecknoe,'
lines 10-14.

Line 3, ' *consoled :*' 1633 ' consorted ;' and so usually. As
before he says ' away,' &c., there was no need of consolation:
and this doubtless Donne saw, and therefore wrote in later revision ' consorted.'

Line 6. In '69 the reading is ' *Is* Nature's . . .' which re-
places ˉ˘ by the proper ˘ˉ.

Line 7, ' *iolly.*' 1635, 1639, 1669, &c. ' wily.' It is ' jollye'
in Stephens' MS. and Harleian MS. 4955. On ' jolly,' see relative note on ' Progress of the Soul' (line 294). But ' wily' is
the revised and preferable word.

Line 9, ' Chronicles :' 1633 and usually ' Chroniclers,' which
again seems the revised and better word.   Stephens' MS.
' Heer's' for ' Here.'

Line 13. Even when first written, in e|arnest| would be
harsh ; but it would be far more harsh at a later date, when pro-

nunciation was more slurring, and when this license of increasing the syllables of a word had greatly gone out. 'Here is your present best love in this town or place:' and the 'here' was thus probably our author's later insertion.

Line 15, 'middle street'=middle of the street: Latinate, *in media via.*

Line 18, '*parcel-guilt*' = part-gilded. So in Christopher Brooke's Richard III. 'percell guylt' (our edition, page 60, line 14). So too in Shakespeare, 'parcel-gilt goblet' (2 Henry IV. ii. 1).

Ib. '*forty dead men's pay.*' Cf. Elegy vii. line 9. There, as here, 'dead names' are names which carry no service, the phrase being adopted from the very common custom of carrying dead men's names on the companies' muster-rolls, and thereby drawing pay in excess of the true numbers.

Line 22, '*blew coats*,' the livery of the lower retainers and servitors, and in especial of those in and from the country.

Line 23, '*Shalt:*' in 1633 and usually 'Wilt:' Stephens' MS. 'shalt.' 'Thou shalt swear thou wilt not,' is the better English; but 'shalt' expresses the repetition of the oath to him.

Ib. '*or*,' written with a long 'r,' which gives it the appearance of 'of.'

Line 25, '*and:*' 1633 and usually 'or.' When you are impressing on one the conditions, as Donne is here, the 'or' is the more emphatic—remember you take me for better or for worse; that is, for worse when the worse comes. 'Or' probably our author's later word.

Line 27, '*monster:*' so Harleian MS. 4955: 'monstrous' in 1633 and Lansdowne MS. 740, and Stephens' MS. 'Monster' is the better word, but I remove the usual comma (,) after Puritan. Donne does not call him a Puritan, but a Puritan of manners; where Puritan is used metaphorically, or for the sake of the paradoxical point, instead of Purist.

Line 30, '*doth:*' Stephens' MS. 'dost.'

Ib. '*prise*'=price or set at value.

Line 32, '*raise:*' Stephens' MS. 'vaile'=(nautical) to lower, not the flag, as some writers have said, but the topsails, in token of submission or courteous recognition of authority, the vessel being thus placed at the mercy of the other. Hence it was applied metaphorically to any such act. We have the word 'vail' used as above in Marlowe (T. the Great, ii. 1), '. . . shall vail to us.' So too Hall (Satires, book iii. v.), 'his bonnet *vail'd.'* Probably *'vail'* was our author's variation, set aside on observing the word 'high.'

Line 33. In Stephens' MS.

'That wilt consort with none, untill t⁰ [= thou] hast knowne.'

,, 40, *'this;'* usually 'thy,' and so in Stephens' MS.; and as 'this' is a relative, and there is no antecedent, the sense requires 'thy' or 'a.'.

Ib. *'muddy.'* I have not met the word so applied, but it is stronger than the nearest synonym 'filthy.' Allan Ramsay is perhaps unjustly censured by Burns for using *'muddy'* in his well-known song.

Line 44, *'Our:'* 1633 and usually *'of bodies:'* so all British-Museum MSS. and Stephens' MS.; and I accept 'Of.'

Line 45, *'best:'* so Stephens' MS.: but 1633 and B.-Museum MSS. 'blest.' 'Blest' is stronger, as implying the state before the Fall. Man's first state might have been 'best' without being 'blest.'

Line 46, Stephens' MS. 'that, yet he, . .' Stephens' MS. line is a foot too long, showing either that the transcriber had by an error written y⁴ as that and yet, or that it was taken from a copy where the author had doubted of his word, and accidentally left both. The 'but' seems preferable, for he says even when he had sinned, still he required only, &c.

Line 47. I prefer 'which Ĭ [nŏw wĕar], because the emphasis is thrown on the 'I,' in contradistinction to the previous 'he:' 'which nŏw [Ĭ wĕar]' would be right if he were speaking of a former time—'when I wore something else.' I make these remarks, as elsewhere, though from the authority of the MS. of 1593 it be adhered to.

Line 50. Usually 'sins:' and as penitents as a rule confess their sins, not their sin, and as previously Donne has charged him with no one sin in particular, but with several sins, the plural was doubtless our author's revised word.

Line 54, *'Worne:'* Stephens' MS. and usually 'worne *out'*—the latter probably our author's revised word.

Line 55, *'muske-Collored:'* 1633 'musk-colour.'

,, 58. 1669 reads badly 'The infantry of London, hence to India.' Stephens' MS. 'The Infant of London, th' heire to rich India.' Some lost local allusion, corresponding with the 'Child of Hale,' near Liverpool=a giant.

Line 60, *'Scheme:'* so Stephens' MS.: 1633 'sceanes:' 1639 and 1669 'scheme.'

Line 62, '*supple-witted :*' so Stephens' ms. : 1633 'subtile-witticd :' 1669 'giddy-headed.' These variations, 'subtile-wittied,' 'supple-witted,' 'giddy-headed,' I take to be successive revisions in the order enumerated. 'Giddy-headed' is an allusion to their wits being as giddy as the feathers that covered them.

Line 63, '*hence :*' so Stephens' ms.: 1633 and usually 'mee.' It is 'hence' in Harleian mss.; and 'hence' seems the better.

Line 68. '*Unprouidently :*' 1633 and usually 'Improvidently.'

Line 70, '*roome :*' 1633 and usually 'state;' also 'high' for 'his.' We have here, in the variations of 'roome' and 'state,' one proof among many that the ordinary text gives the author's own revision of the earlier form as represented by the ms. of 1593. The fellow takes the wall-side as the more honourable, and is thereby closed-in more than Donne, who is on the outside. Hence Donne wrote, 'he sells his liberty for a little room,' using 'room' in the sense of state or station, as he uses it in Progress of the Soul, xl. line 8; but on revision he saw that the word was here so ambiguous that at first sight it expressed the contrary, so he altered it to 'state.'

Line 71, '*skip :*' Stephens' ms. 'cannot now step forth to greet.'

Line 72. Query, fine, silken, painted?

,, 80, '*horse.*' Cf. our Sir John Davies (p. 334). Banks' horse Morocco (a horse alluded to by almost every writer of the day) and asses, and, as would appear from the text, elephants, were taught to bow and leap, or go over, on naming the sovereign or the like, but to pay no heed or turn their backs when the Pope or King of Spain (enemy of England) was mentioned. Shakespeare names the 'wonderful horse' (Love's Labour Lost, i. 2). See Peter Hall's ed. of Bp. Hall, vol. xii. pp. 221-2, for curious details.

Lines 81-2. This couplet not in 1633.

,, 82. I print 'k[ing]' simply to show that here the ms. has 'k' only=a contraction for 'king,' as in the usual printed texts.

Line 83, '*and cryes :*' 'and' is omitted sometimes : read 'mee, and.'

Line 84, '*Yea :*' 1633 and usually 'Oh.'

,, 85. Sometimes 'yea' for 'oh,' which would agree best with 'must you,' but not with 'stand still.' Being probably regarded as too puritanic, it was no doubt deleted, and the original 'Oh' is 'O' replaced.

Line 86, '*to :*' ib. 'here.'

  ,,   87, '*wee :*' Stephens' ms. 'he.'

  ,,   88, '*drinking.*' The common phrase for smoking. Cf. Sir John Beaumont's Metamorphosis of Tobacco (our edition).

Line 90. 1633 ''T may be.'

  ,,   90, '*smel.*' The frequent allusions to this in Elizabethan times are very extraordinary. One must suffice:

Scene. *The Duke's Palace.*

Rosaline. Faugh, what a strong sent's here! some body useth to weare socks.

Bal. By this fair candle light 'tis not my feet; I never wore socks since I suckt pappe.

Marston, Antonio and Mellida, act ii. circa 1598.

Cf. Elegy v. line 45.

Line 93, '*stay.*' American edition misprints ' stray.'

  ,,   94, '*in :*' probably a mere clerical error for the usual ' on.'

Line 97. The British-Museum mss. nearly correspond; but ' pinck' is also written ' pinckt.' Stephens' ms. ' To judge a lace, pinck, pains, print, cut, or plaite.' Of the different terms here, *pinck* is = eylot-holes ; *panes* = slits or openings, through which the net lining was seen or pulled out. *Print :* the instances are common which prove that ' in print' meant in regular or apple-pie order. But the use of the word here, and its cognate use as meaning impressions of various kinds, and some of the examples where it is used in speaking of ruffs, lead me to conclude that it meant such frilling or crimping as is done with an Italian iron. Thus when Bp. Earle, in his Microcosmography, speaks of the preference of the Puritan dame for small Geneva print, I apprehend he speaks not of the regularity so much as of the small and formal frilling they wore, in opposition to the large crimpings of people of fashion. As regularity was an essential in ruffs, and could only be attained by a machine ' print' or impression, so I think the general sense of exactness and precision is more likely to have been taken from such printing than from the regularity of type over manuscript.

Lines 100-104. I find a difficulty in the allocation of the different parts of the dialogue. ' I reply'd' shows that ' he doth seem .. Italian' is spoken by the Macaron. Hence I take it that ' Why ?' is most probably the absent and unattending exclama-

tion of the same, who is intent on his courtesy to the stranger;
'He hath travelled long?' the query of Donne; the 'No, but'
part of the Macaron's answer, 'No, but he doth seem,' &c.;
while the phrase 'to me . . . . none' is Donne's parenthetical
clause, meaning [said he] to me, which understood none of
these things, or as humorously explanatory of his pretended
blunder—So is the pox—[said he] to me, which understood not
his affected lingo.

Line 102. Stephens' ms. 'understood nought.'

,, 107, 'light dewe :' Stephens' ms. has 'might ;' but as
there is nothing in the man to recall 'night,' and nothing in
the incident to bring up the image of day after night, the fop
is better characterised by ' light dew.'

Line 108, 'lechery :' 1633 'liberty.' G.

SATIRE II.

Sr, though (I thank God for it) I do hate
All this toune perfectly, yet in euery state
There are some found so villanously best,
That hate towards that breeds pitty toward the rest.
Though Poetry indeed be such a sinne   5
As I ame afraid brings dearths and Spaniards in ;
Though like the Pestilens or old-fashiond loues,
It rydes killingely, catcheth men, and removes
Neuer till it bee staru'd out ; yet their state
Is poore, disarm'd, like Papists, not worth hate.   10
One like a wretch (wch at bar iudg'd as dead,
Yet prompts him wch stands next, and cannot reade,
And sau's his life) giues Idiot Actors means,
Staruing himselfe, to liue by his labourd Sccanes ;

As in some Organs Puppets dance aboue,   15
And Bellowes pant belowe wch them do moue,
One would moue loue by rhimes; but witchcraft's charms
Bring not now their old fears, nor their old harms.
Rams and slings nowe are silly Battery,
Pistolets are the best Artillery.   20
And they who write to lords, rewards to get,
Are they not like Boyes singing at dore for meat?
And they who write, because all write, haue still
That 'scuse for writing, and for writing ill.
But hee is worst, who beggerly doth chawe   25
Others' wits' fruits, and in his rauenous mawe,
Ranckly digested, doth those things out spue,
As his owne things; and they are his owne, its true;
For if one eate my meate, though it bee knowne
The meate was mine, the excrement's his owne.   30
But those do mee no harme, nor they wch use
To outdoe Dildoes or 'out-usure Jewes,
To 'outdrinke the sea, outsweare the letany,
Who wth sins, all kinds, as familiar bee
As Confessors, and for whose sinfull sake   35
Schoolemen new tenements in hel must make;
In whose strange sins Canonists could hardly tell
In which commandement's large receit they dwell.
But these punish themselues.   The insolence
Of Coscus onely breeds my great offence,   40
Whom tyme, wch rots al, and makes Botches Pox,
And plodding on must make a Calfe an Oxe,

Hath made a Lawier, wch was alas of late

But a scarse poet; iollyer of that State   scarce a

Then are new benefic't Ministers, hee throwes   than   45

Like nets or lime-twigs, wheresoe're hee goes,

His title of Barrister on euery wench,

And woes in language of the Pleas and bench.   woos

'A motion, Lady :'—speake Coscus.—' I haue beene

In loue e're sinc 3mo of the Q[ueen.]   tricesimo   50

Continuall claymes I haue made, Iniunctions got

To stay my riual's suite, that hee should not

Proceede;'—spare mee,—' In Hillary terme I went ;

You said, yf I returnd this 'sise in Lent,

I should bee in remitter of your grace ;   55

In th' Interim my letters should take place

Of Affidauits.'   Words, words, wch would teare

The tender Labarinth of a soft maid's eare

More, more then ten Slauonians' scolding, more

Then when winds in our ruin'd Abbeys rore.   60

When sicke with Poetry and possest wth Muse

Thou wast, (and mad, I hop't;) but men wch chuse

Lawe practise for mere gaine, hould sole repute,

Worse then Imbrotheld strumpet's prostitute.

Now, like an Owl-like watchman, hee must walke, 65

His hands still at a bill ; now hee must talke

Idly, like prisoners, wch hole monthes will sweare, whole

That onely suretyship hath brought them there,

And to euery suitor ly in euery thing,

Like a king's fauorite, yea like a kinge :   70

Like a wedge in a blocke, wringd to the bar,
Bearing like Asses, and more shameles farre,
Then Carted whores, ly to the graue Judge ; for   than
Bastardy abounds not in k'gs' titles, nor
Symony and Sodomy in Churchmens' liues,   75
As these thinges do in him; by these hee thriues.
Shortly, as the' sea, hee 'will compas all our Land,
From Scots to Wight, from Mount to Dover Strand,
And spying heyres melting wth Gluttony,
Satan will not ioy at their sins, as hee :   80
For as a thrifty wench scrapes kitchin stuffe,
And barelling the droppinges, and the snuffe
Of wasting Candles, which in 30 yeare,
Relique-like kept, perchance buyes wedding-geare,
Peecemeale hee gets lands, and spends as much tyme. 85
Wringing each acre, as men pulling prime.
In parchments then, large as his feelds, hee drawes
Assurances ; big as glos'd Ciuil lawes,
So huge, that men in our tyme's forwardnes
Are fathers of the Church for writing les.   90
Theese hee writes not ; nor for theese writings payes,
Therefore spares no length, as in those first dayes,
When Luther was profest, hee did desire
Short Paternosters, saying as a frier
Each day his beades; but hauing left those lawes, 95
Adds to Christ's prayr the Pow'r and Glory clause.
But when he sells or changes lands, hee impaires
His writinges, and unwatchd leaues out his heyres,

As slyly, as any Commenter, goes by
Hard words or sense; or in Divinity   100
As Controverters in voucht Texts leaue out
Shrewd words, wch might against them cleare the doubt.
Where are those spred woods wch cloth'd hertofore
These bought lands? not built, nor burnt w^{thin} dore.
Where the old landlord's troups and almes? In hals
Carthusian fasts and fulsome Bacchanals   106
Equally I hate. Meanes bles[t]. In rich men's homes
I bid kil some beasts, but no hecatombs;
None sterue, none surfet so: but O, w' allow
Good works as good, but out of fashion now,   110
Like old rich wardroabs : but my words none drawes
Within the uast reach of th' huge statute jawes.

NOTES AND ILLUSTRATIONS.

Heading: in 1593 MS. 'Sat. 2da;' Stephens' MS. 'Satyra Secunda.'

Lines 1-5. See introductory Note to the Satires for the interlineations of 1593 MS. here, which correspond with 1633, &c. Stephens' MS., as 1633, in line 3 reads 'In all ill things soe excellently best;' and line 4, 'to the rest;' line 1, the second form is the more emphatic, viz. 'perfectly all this town,' as 'perfectly' follows the verb, and is not relegated to the end of the sentence; is also more quaint. Line 2: it will be noticed that in the two forms, 'yet in every state,' and 'yet there's one state,' there is a complete change of idea. 'In every state' means in every kingdom, and is therefore vague ; but 'there's one state' means one position in this town, viz. that which he satirises, the state of Coscus. As this brings the object of the Satire more distinctly before us, it may be regarded as a revised emendation. The bad things he pities are, poetry on

which there is a discursus, and all those things enumerated in
ll. 31-39. Line 3, the form 'In all things,' &c. seems to be an
elaboration of the other, seeing it is stronger and more neatly
put, and, above all, there is that conceit of expression in it
which was then sought after, and the antithetical apposition of
'ill' and 'best.' Farther on, line 4, as between 'that' and
'them' (as usually), 'that,' no doubt, refers to the state; but
'them' is preferable, as more subtle, because it is the 'all ill
things' in the state, or that go to make it up, that he says he
hates.

Line 6. 1633 'As I thinke that . . .' So usually, and in Stephens' MS. 'As I think might.' 1633 is the more humorously
exaggerative.

Lines 7-8. I have accepted in the text the Stephens' MS.
here. In the 1593 MS., and usually, it runs,

'Loue
It ridlingly catch men, and doth remove.'

1669 is 'ridlingly it.' It is just possible that 'ridlingly' may be,
after all, the author's own word, used as in Progress of the
Soul, st. xliv. l. 7, 'ridling lust;' and in Donne's Paradox, vii.
'and that *ridling* humour of jealousie which seeks and would
not find, which requires and repents his knowledge.' This makes
me hesitate as to 'killingly.'

Line 11. '*One.*' Stephens' MS. reads 'Or;' but this is an
error, seeing the sense is not, as at first sight appears, 'their
state is like a Papist's, or like.' At 'hate,' l. 10, end the general remarks on poetry and poets, and so I have put (.) instead of
the usual (:). Then he says, l. 11, 'One [kind of, viz. the play-
writing] poet (like, &c.) gives idiot actors means. One, the
writer of love-poems, would more love by rhymes; another
writes to lords for rams and slings; others write because all
write; and he is worst,' &c. See our Essay for a probable allusion to Shakespeare in this passage.

Lines 12-14, '*cannot read*,' &c. Cf. our SIBBES, under
'break-neck verse,' for illustrations of the text.

Line 17, 'rhimes:' Stephens' MS. 'rythmes:' 1633 'rithmes:'
from Greek.

Line 19, '*silly :*' Stephens' MS. 'symple.' Cf. our long note
on 'silly' in SOUTHWELL, pp. 174-6.

Line 20, '*pistolets.*' A pun = (Spanish) money, and from
French small pistols.

Line 22. 1633, and usually, 'like singers at doores.' Indifferent, except that 'boys' introduces an unnecessary distraction, without adding to the thought.

Line 24. ‘ *That 'scuse :*’ Stephens' MS. ‘A 'scuse.’

„ 27. ‘ *Ranckly :*’ Stephens' MS. and Harleian MS. 4955 ‘ Rawly.’ ‘ Rankly' is clearly an improvement on ‘ rawly;' and it may be added that, looking to the meaning of Dildo, and to the particular sense in which ‘ do' was used in that age, ‘ out-do' seems more correct than ‘ outswiue' (as below), besides being more alliterative.

Line 32. ‘ Dildoes :' 1633 leaves the word blank = mentula succedanea; Coles and Cotgrave, *s. v.* In Harleian MS. 4955 and Stephens' MS. instead, is ‘ outswiue'=out-prostitute.

Line 33, ‘ *letany :*’ 1633 leaves blank.

Ib. Usually ‘ to outsweare;' but our MS. deletes ‘ to.' The elision of the ‘ to' requires the ‘ *or* outusure' to be ‘ *and ;*’ and, indeed, even with ‘ to,' the ‘ and' is preferable; not that he means that each does all, but he lumps these different classes in one as doing him no harm.

Line 34. 1633 supplies ‘ *of* all.'

„ 40, ‘ *great :*’ so Stephens' MS. 1633 and usually ‘ just.' Here ‘ my offence' is the offence to me or in my eyes; and therefore ‘ just' is far stronger than ‘ great.'

Line 44, =[was] scarcely a poet. Could Sir John Davies be intended? See our Essay on this. This is rendered the more probable by the squib Catal. Librorum; where the 16th is ‘ Justitia Angliæ vacationis. So Davis, De Arte Anagrammatum, &c.' At first sight, ‘ that' looks more correct, and so it is, verbally looked at; but the lawyer state is both the main idea and also Coscus present, (and therefore ‘ this') state jollier of this [new] state he throws.

Line 49, ‘ A motion, lady.'—Speake, Coscus.—‘ I haue . . . Proceede.'—Spare me—[this being the lady's exclamation, as before, and meaning ‘ allow me to leave']. Cf. Satire iv. 1. 143.

Line 50. 1633 and usually ‘ *tricesimo*' (as in margin). See our Essay for this date, and its significance. ‘ In Hilary, &c. . . . affidavits.'

Line 54, ‘ *this :*’ so Stephens' MS. 1633 and usually ‘ next.' She could not have said ‘ this,' and therefore it is better to understand the lawyer as quoting her words, viz. ‘ *next* 'size,' more especially when he follows it with the rest of the quotation, ‘ *In* th' *interim.*’

Line 58. As between ‘ A soft maid's eare' of our MS. and

the usual 'maid's soft ear,' the maid was not soft to him; but the inner labyrinth of the ear is most delicate, and one beauty of a woman's outer ear is its softness; and Donne thus speaks in the revised form of the whole organ as tender.

Line 59. 1633 'Sclavonians:' so Stevens' MS.

,, 63, '*hould sole.*' Once more I have had no difficulty in accepting from the Stephens' MS. 'hould sole' for 'bold souls' of 1593 and usually, which seems meaningless. Query, is it a slip for '*foule*'?

Lines 69-70. This couplet left blank in 1633, and so ll. 74-5.

,, 71. 1633 and usually 'wring:' Stephens' MS. and Harleian MS. 4955 'wrung.' I do not know the carrier's or ostler's phrase 'wring to the bar,' but I take it that 'bar' has here the double sense of bar and bar of a court of justice; that,' wring' is used in a combination of its senses of twist and pinch; and that the meaning is, that he twists close up to the bar, and squeezes as close as a wedge in wood the bearing-like Asses his clients, and to the judge lies, &c.

Line 75, '*and:*' Stephens' MS. 'nor.'

,, 78, '*Mount*'= Mount St. Michael, Land's End, Cornwall. He seems to omit all the Irish Channel coast as not compassed by a sea.

Line 79, '*gluttony:*' so Stephens' MS.: 1633 and usually 'luxurie.' As between 'gluttony' and 'luxury' the latter is by far the more general, and therefore the more appropriate term; for heirs were not supposed to get rid of their estates by mere gluttony, a vice of older age, but by debauchery generally; and the especial sense in which luxury was frequently then used, and which the mere mention of the word would bring up, agrees best with the word 'melting,' whether applied to their estates or to themselves: 'lean as a rake' is an old saying.

Line 82, '*droppinges*'= the present drippings [from roast meat].

Ib. '*snuffe.*' Judging by the examples given, I do not see the difference between Johnson's second sense, 'the useless excrescence of a candle,' and his fourth, 'the fired wick.' But his example from Donne,

'For even at first life's taper is a *snuff*,'

is properly an example of sense third: 'A candle almost burnt out.' And the derivation of the word, and its use in the present passage, show that it meant the 'droppings from a candle, the result of guttering; inclusive, probably, of the candle-end embedded in the outspread mass.' It was probably from the candle-end thus forming one with the true snuff, and becoming a part of the kitchen-maid's prerogative, that 'snuff' came, in a secondary sense, to mean a candle-end nearly burnt out.

Line 84, '*geare :*' so Stephens' ms.: 1669 'chear :' 1633 'Reliquely.'

Line 86, ' *Wringing*' == twisting out, extorting.

Ib. '*prime :*' Stephens' ms. reads 'as men pulling for prime.' ' Prime,' in primero, is a winning hand of different suits [with probably certain limitations as to the numbers of the cards, since there were different primes], different to and of lower value than a flush or hand of [four] cards of the same suit. The game is now unknown, but from such notices as we have, it would seem that one could stand on their hands, or, as in écarté and other games, discard and take in others (see Nares, *s. v.*). From the words of our text, the fresh cards were not dealt by the dealer, but 'pulled' by the player at hazard, and the delays of maidish indecision can be readily understood; albeit, as above, the Stephens' ms. substitutes ' men' for ' maids' —the latter probably our author's later correction.

Line 87, '*his :*' usually 'the ;' the latter our author's revision, seeing the fields when the parchments were drawn were not ' his,' but the heir's.

Line 91. The usual verbal form 'written' as opposed to ' writings' of our ms. is neater, because it agrees better with the verb form in previous clause, ' he writes.'

Line 96, '*Pow'r and Glory :*' close of the Lord's Prayer, 'for Thine is the Kingdom and the Power and the Glory.'

Line 98, ' *his heyres :*' in 1593 ms., Lansdowne ms. 740, and printed editions, ' *ses heyres ;*' but I accept ' his heyres' from Stephens' ms. and Harleian 4955.

Line 99, '*As :*' 1593 ms. misreads '*And :*' I accept 'As' of 1633.

„ 105. Our ms. reads 'great halls,' but that doesn't scan: rejected.

Line 107, ' Meanes bles [t]. As between the text of our ms. and ' Mean's bless,' means then, as now, meant riches, possessions, but never the mean or middle. ' Mean' is here the middle between waste and avarice, and he explains the means a mean corresponding to one's station, by In rich men's, &c.

Line 112, '*jawes :*' I prefer this reading to ' lawes' of the ms. Cf. Sat. iv. line 132. G.

SATIRE III.

KIND pity choakes my spleen ; braue scorne forbids
Those teares to issue wch swell my eye-lids.
I must not laugh nor weepe sinnes, but be wyse :
Can rayling then cure these worne malladyes?
Is not ower Mistris, fayre Religion,   5
As worthy of ower sowles deuotion,
As Vertu was to the first blinded Age?
Ar not Heauen's ioyes as valient to assuage
Lusts, as earth's honnor was to them?   Alasse,
As we doe them in means, shall they surpasse   10
Vs in the end? And shall thy father's spirit
Meete blinde philosophers in Heauen, whose merrit
Of strict lyfe may be imputed fayth, and heare
The[e], whome he taught so easy wayes and neere
To follow, damm'd? O, if thow darst, feare this :   15
This feare great courage, and high vallor is.
Dar'st thow ayde mutinous Dutch? and darst thou laye
The[e] in ships, wooden sepulchers, a praye
To leaders rage, to Stormes, to Shott, to dearth?
Dar'st thow diue Seas, and daungers of the Earth?   20
Hast thow couragious fyer to thaw the Ice
Of frozen North-discoueryes ; and,—thryce

Colder then Sallamanders—like deuine
Children in the Ouen—fyers of Spayne and the lyne—
Whose cuntryes, Limbecks to ower bodeyes bee—   25
Can'st thou for gayne beare? and must euery hee
Which cryes not, goddes, to thy Mistris, drawe,
Or eate thy poysonous wordes?   Courage of strawe!
Oh desperate Coward, wilt thow seeme bold, and
To thy foes and his who made the[e] to stand   30
Sowldyer in this world's garrison, thus yeeld,
And for forbid warres leaue the appointed feelde?
Know thy foes : The fowle deuell whome thow
Striuest to please, for hate, not loue, would allowe
The[e] fayne his whole relme to be ridd ; and as   35
The wo[r]ld's all parts, wither away and passe,
So the wo[r]ld's selfe thy other lou'd foe, is
In her decrepid wayne, and thou, louing this,
Doest love a witherd and worne strumpet ; last   39
Flesh (it selfe's Death), and ioyes which flesh can tast,
Thou louest ; and thy fayre goodly sowle, which doth
Giue this flesh power to tast ioy, thow dost lothe.
Seeke trew Religion : oh whear?   Mireus,
Thinking her vnhows'd heere, and fled from vs,
Seekes her at Roome ; Ther, becaus he doth know   45
That she was thear a Thousand yeare agoe ;
He loues her ragges, so as we heere obey
The state-cloth wher the prince sat yesterday.
Grants to sutch braue loues will not bee enthrald,
But loues her onely, who at Genoua is cal'd   50

Religion—playne, simple, sullen, yonge,
Contemptuous, yet vnhansom ; as amonge
Leecherous humors, there is one wch judges
Noo wenches holsom but course Cuntry drudges.
Grayus stays still at home heere, and becaus   55
Sum Preachers, vyle ambitious Baudes, and Lawes
Still new, like fashons, bid him thinke that she
Which dwels w^h vs, is onely perfect, hee   with
Embraceth her whome his Godfathers will
Tender to him, beeing tender ; as wardes still   60
Take sutch wives as their Gardens offer, or   guardians
Paye values. Careles Phrygius doth abhorr
All, becaus all cannot be good, as one,
Knowing sum women whores, dares marry none.
Graccus loues all as one, and thinks y^t soe   65
As women doe in diuers countries goe
In diuers habits, yet ar still one kind,
So doth, so is, Religion ; and this blind-
nes too mutch light breedes. But unmoud thou
Of force must one, and forct but one allow,   70
And the right ; Aske thy father wch is she ;
Let him aske his : Though trewth and falshood bee
Nere Twinnes, yet trewth a litell elder is.
Bee busy to seeke her ; beleeue me this,
Hee is not of none, nor worst, wch seek's the best : 75
To adore, or scorne an Image, or protest,
May all be bad : doubt wysely ; In strange waye
To stand enquyering right, is not to straye ;

, To sleepe, or runne wronge, is ; on a huge Hill,   79
Rugged and steepe, Trewth dwells ; and he, that will
Reache her, abought must, and abought it goo,   go
And what the Hill's suddaynes resists, winne soo.   so
Yet stryve so, that before Age, Death's twy light,
Thy mynd rest, for none can worke in y' night.
To will implyes delay, therfore now doe :   85
Hard deedes the bodyes paynes ; hard knowledge to
The mind's endeuors reatch ; And misteryes
Are like the Sunne, dazeling, yet playne to all eyse.
Keepe y⁰ trewth wch thow hast fownd. Men do not stand
In so euell case that God hath w^h his hand   with 90
Sign'd Kinges' blank-Charters, To kill whome they hate,
Nor ar th'y viccars, but Ha[n]gmen to fate.   they
Foole and wretch, wilt thow let thy Sowle be tyed
To man's Lawes, by wch she shall not be tryed
At the last day ; Oh will it then serue thee   95
To saye,—a Phillip or a Gregorye,
A Harry or a Martin, taught the[e] this ?
Is not this excuse for meere contraryes,
Equally strong ? cannot both sydes say soe ?
That thow mayest rightly obey Power, her bounds knowe ;
Those past, her Nature and name is chaunged ; to bee
Then humble to her, is Idolatrye.   102
As streames are, Power is ; Those blest flowers w^ch
        dwell
At the rough streame's calme head, thryne and proue
        well ;

But hauing left ther rootes, and them selues giuen 105
To the streame's tiranous rage, alas, are driuen
T[h]rough Mills, Rocks, and Woods, and at last, almost
Consum'd in going, in the sea ar lost :
Soe perish sowles, which more choose mens vnjust
Power, from God claym'd, then God him selfe to trust.

NOTES AND ILLUSTRATIONS.

Heading : in 1593 MS. 'Sat. 3 :' Stephens' MS. 'Satyra Ter-
tia :' see introductory Note on the Satires on the MS. of this
one.

Line 1, '*choakes :*' 1639 'checks :' 1669 'cheeks :' Stephens'
MS. 'checkes.' As between 'choaks' and 'checks,' pity not
merely ' choaks' it in the throat, but 'checks' it in its origin.
He neither dissembles it nor keeps it down, but 'checks.'

Ib. '*spleen :*' used in several senses in those days. Here,
from the context (line 3), it would seem to mean splenetic
laughter.

Line 3, '*but :*' Stephens' MS. 'and,' and line 4 'May.'

,, 6, '*all :*' this is usually and properly dropped, as it
throws the accents all wrong ; and as in the previous line we
have ' Relig|ion|,' so we must have ' devo|tion|,' not de|votion|.

Line 7, '*Vertu*'= virtus, valour, as shown by 'blinded' and
by ' earth's honour' (line 9). Our MS. reads wrongly ' blind.'

Line 14. Usually ' so easy wayes.' Our MS. ' taught wayes
easy :' usually (as we give) ' so easy wayes :' without the ' so,'
and ' easy wayes' would make the line unscanable, seeing ' near'
cannot be made a dissyllable at the end of a line. ' Neare'=at
hand, therefore not troublesome or laborious.

Line 20, '*daungers :*' so Stephens' MS.: 1633 and usually
' dungeons :' ' dongions' in Lansdowne MS. 740. Badly ' his'
for ' this.' Perhaps ' dungeons' is the preferable word, as the
context seems to show the reference is to mines.

Lines 23-4, '*deuine Children in the Ouen.*' Cf. Daniel iii. 19-
25 = the heats of the tropics and the artillery of Spain, that
claimed those seas and countries.

Line 31, '*Sowldyer:*' so Stephens' MS.: 1633 and usually
'Sentinell.'

Line 33, '*foes.*' 1633 'foe:' but three foes are named. See
lines 37-40.

Line 35, '*ridd:*' usually and in Stephens' MS. '*quitt.*' The
latter apparently used in a sense not attributed to it in dictionaries. To be free of, that is, to be free as a naturalised subject
to go through and enjoy his realm. If Johnson's second meaning were altered to—[make us] set free, it would include this,
and probably be more correct. Donne, however, omits ' of,'
just as his contemporaries used other verbs without a preposition.

Line 45, '*Roome:*' the old pronunciation still occasionally
met with, as by Earl Russell.

Line 49, '*Grants:*' 1633 'Crants,' and usually so. It is
curious that such a name as Crants ('33, '35) or Grants ('69)
should intervene between the classical-sounding names Mirreus, Graius, and Phrygius. Can it be from Gränze or Grenze,
boundary or limit, in allusion to the puritanic limits within
which they withdrew themselves, and placed between themselves and others? Mirreus is probably Myrrheus = perfumed
with myrrh.

Line 51, '*sullen.*' So Shakespeare, 'bright metal on a *sullen*
ground' (1 Henry IV. i. 2). Here=unsocial.

Line 57, '*bid:*' usually but erroneously 'bids.' The nomi-
native is doubly plural, ' Some preachers . . . and lawes.'

Line 61, '*wives:*' in 1593 MS. miswritten 'wayes.'

„   62, '*Paye values.*' A curious law, of which I can find
no record = pay a fine. '*Phrygius:*' 1633 and usually 'Phrygius.' Though our MS. gives 'Prigas,' the word is determined
by the previous 'Graius' to be a Phrygian or Trojan, and therefore 'Phrygius.' The scribe must have blundered over the MS.
he copied. I retain 'Phrygius' accordingly.

Line 64, '*dares:*' Stephens' MS. 'will.'

„   66-69. See introductory Note to the Satires for interlineations here in 1593 MS. I reject 'in diuers *fashons* goe,' for
the usual ' countries.'

Line 70, '*but one.*' Stephens' MS. 'must one.'

„   78, '*straye.*' In 1593 MS. 'staye,' but I accept 'strayc'
from 1633.

Line 79, '*huge:*' Stephens' MS. 'high.'

„   80, '*Ruggued.*' 1633 'Cragg'd,' which is far stronger

and better: and 'stands' for 'dwells,' the latter in Stephens' ms. and preferable.

Line 81. ms. '*it;*' ib. 'her;' the latter adopted by us; and I also accept '*it* goe,' instead of with our ms. deleting it.

Line 84, '*mynd,*' usually 'soul.' As he is speaking of the intelligential power generally, 'soul' is perhaps the better word here, though I follow the ms. of 1593: '*that night:*' so Stephens' ms.

Lines 85-6. Supply 'do,' or as it were reduplicate it—now doe [do] Hard deeds. But 'too' of ms. is a mispelling, or a misleading spelling.

Line 90, '*euell:*' 1633 and usually 'ill.' Cf. note on 'evil' as read '*ill*' in our SOUTHWELL (page 45). But I do not accept 'heere' of the ms. of 1593 before 'that,' being superfluous, and therefore weakening to sense and scansion. So too in line 91, 'charts' of the ms. makes the line defective: rejected.

Line 91, = sign'd blank charters [to] kings, &c.; nor are such kings as kill those who differ from them vicars of Fate or Providence, but her hangmen.

Line 94, 'man's:' so usually; in our ms. 'men's.' 'Men's' might be in opposition to other men's laws; 'man's' laws must be opposed to the laws of something not man: 'man's' adopted by us.

Line 95, '*serue:*' so Stephens' ms.: 1633 'boot.' As between 'boot' and 'serue,' the former is=benefit, and signifies something added, as in booty; and as the plea of the just is the added merits of Christ, 'boot' may be reckoned preferable.

Lines 96-7. Philip [Melancthon], Gregory [the Great, or Gregory of Nazianzen], Harry [the Eighth], Martin [Luther].

Line 97, '*thee:*' 1669 'me'—and perhaps the latter more emphatic, as giving the quotation of the speaker.

Line 101, 'is:' sometimes 'name's,' and sometimes 'are.' As they are distinct things (Nature and name), and cannot be taken as one collective noun, 'are' is certainly more accurate.

Line 102, '*Then.*' 1593 ms. miswrites 'them:' Stephens' ms. 'Then.'

Line 104, '*proue:*' so Stephens' ms.: 1633 'do. G.

SATIRE IV.

WELL; I may now receive, and die.   My sin
Indeed is great, but yet I have been in
A Purgatory, such as fear'd hell is
A recreation, and scant map of this.
My mind, neither with pride's itch, nor yet hath been
Poyson'd with love to see, or to be seen ;   6
I had no suit there, nor new suit to shew,
Yet went to Court.   But as Glare, which did go
To Mass in jest, catch'd, was fain to disburse
The hundred marks, which is the Statute's curse, 10
Before he 'scap't ; So 't pleas'd my destiny
(Guilty of my sin of going) to think me
As prone to all ill, and of good as forget-
'full, as proud, lustful, and as much in debt,
As vain, as witless, and as false as they 15
Which dwel in Court, for once going that way.
Therefore I suffer'd this ; Towards me did run
A thing more strange, than on Nile's slime, the Sun
E'r bred, or all which into Noah's Ark came :
A thing which would have pos'd Adam to name : 20
Stranger than seven Antiquaries' studies,
Than Africk's Monsters, Guianæ's rarities,

Stranger than strangest : One who for a Dane
In the Dane's Massacre had sure been slain,
If he had liv'd then ; and without help dies   25
When next the Prentices 'gainst Strangers rise :
One whom the watch at noon lets scarce go by ;
One, to whom the examining Justice sure would cry,
Sir, by your Priesthood, tell me what you are.
His clothes were strange, though coarse, and black,
        though bare ;   30
Sleeveless his jerkin was, and it had been
Velvet, but 't was now (so much ground was seen)
Become Tufftaffaty ; and our children shall
See it plain Rash a while, then nought at all.
The thing hath travail'd, and, saith [he] speaks all
        tongues,   35
And only knoweth what t' all States belongs.
Made of th' Accents and best phrase of all these,
He speaks one language. If strange meats displease,
Art can deceive, or hunger force my tast ;
But Pedant's motley tongue, souldier's bumbast,   40
Mountebank's drug-tongue, nor the termes of law,
Are strong enough preparatives to draw
Me to hear this, yet I must be content
With his tongue, in his tongue call'd Complement ;
In which he can win widows, and pay scores,   45
Make men speak treason, couzen subtlest whores,
Out-flatter favorites, or outlie either
Jovius or Surius, or both together.

He names me, and comes to me : I whisper, 'God,
How have I sinn'd, that Thy wrath's furious rod,   50
This fellow, chuseth me?' He saith, 'Sir,
I love your judgment ; whom do you prefer,
For the best Linguist?' and I seellily
Said that I thought Calepine's Dictionary.
'Nay, but of men, most sweet Sir?' Beza, then,   55
Some Jesuits, and two reverend men
Of our two Academies I named ; here
He stopt me, and said : 'Nay, your Apostles were
Good pretty Linguists ; so Panurgus was
Yet a poor Gentleman ; all these may pass.   60
But travail?' then, as if he would have sould
His tongue, he praisèd it, and such wonders told,
That I was fain to say, 'If you had liv'd, Sir,
Time enough to have been Interpreter
To Babel's bricklayers, sure the Tower had stood.'   65
He adds, 'If of Court-life you knew the good,
You would leave loneness.' I said, 'Not alone
My loneness is ; but Spartane's fashion,
To teach by painting drunkards, doth not last
Now ; Aretine's pictures have made few chast ;   70
No more can Princes' Courts, though there be few
Better pictures of vice, teach me vertue.'
He, like to a high-stretcht Lute-string, squeakt, 'O Sir,
'Tis sweet to talk of Kings.' 'At Westminster,'
Said I, 'the man that keeps the Abby tombs,   75
And for his price doth, with whoever comes,

Of all our Harrys, and our Edwards talk,
From King to King, and all their kin can walk :
Your eares shall hear nought but Kings ; your eyes meet
Kings only ; The way to it is King's-street.'   80
He smack'd, and cry'd, 'He's base, mechanique, course ;
So are all your English men in their discourse.'   [coarse
' Are not your French men neat ?'   ' Mine ? as you see,
I have but one, Sir ; look, he follows me.
Certes, they are neatly cloath'd.'   ' I, of this mind am,
Your only wearing is your Grogaram.'   86
' Not so, Sir, I have more.'   Under this pitch
He would not fly.   I chaf'd him ; But as itch
Scratch'd into smart, and as blunt Iron grownd   ground
Into an edge, hurts worse ; So I (fool !) found   90
Crossing hurt me.   To fit my sullenness,
He to another key his stile doth dress ;
And asks, what news ?   I tell him of new playes :
He takes my hand, and, as a Still which stayes
A semibrief 'twixt each drop, he niggardly,   95
As loath to inrich me, so tells many a ly,
More than ten Hollensheads, or Halls, or Stows,
Of trivial houshold trash, He knows : he knows
When the queen frownd or smil'd ; and he knows what
A subtile Statesman may gather of that :   100
He knows, who loves whom ; and who by poyson
Hasts to an Office's reversion :
He knows who 'hath sold his land, and now doth beg
A license, old iron, boots, shoos, and egge-

shells to transport; Shortly boyes shall not play   105
At span-counter or blow-point, but shall pay
Toll to some Courtier; and wiser then all us,   than
He knows what Lady is not painted. Thus
He with home-meats cloyes me. I belch, spue, spit,
Look pale and sickly, like a Patient, yet   110
He thrusts on more; And as he had undertook
To say Gallo-Belgicus without book,
Speaks of all States and deeds, that have been since
The Spanyards came to the loss of Amyens.
Like a big wife, at sight of loathèd meat,   115
Ready to travail; so I sigh, and sweat
To hear this Makaron talk; in vain, for yet,
Either my humour, or his own to fit,
He like a priviledg'd spie, whom nothing can
Discredit, libels now 'gainst each great man.   120
He names a price for every office paid;
He saith, our wars thrive ill, because delai'd;
That offices are intailèd, and that there are
Perpetuities of them, lasting as far
As the last day; and that great officers   125
Do with the Pirates share and Dunkirkers.
Who wasts in meat, in cloaths, in horse, he notes;
Who loves Whores, who boyes, and who goats.
I, more amaz'd than Circe's prisoners, when
They felt themselves turn beasts, felt myself then   130
Becoming Traytor, and methought I saw
One of our Giant Statutes ope his jaw

To suck me in; for hearing him, I found
That as burnt venomous Leachers do grow sound
By giving others their soars, I might grow   sores 135
Guilty, and he free : Therefore I did show
All signes of loathing; But since I am in,
I must pay mine and my forefathers' sin
To the last farthing.   Therefore to my power
Toughly and stubbornly I bear this cross ; but the hower
Of mercy now was come : He tries to bring   141
Me to pay a fine to 'scape his torturing,
And sayes, ' Sir, can you spare me ?' I said, ' willingly.'
' Nay, Sir, Can you spare me a crown ?'   Thankfully I
Gave it, as Ransom : but as fidlers still,   145
Though they be paid to be gone, yet needs will
Thrust one more jig upon you ; so did he
With his long complemental thanks vex me.
But he is gone, thanks to his needy want,
And the Prerogative of my Crown : Scant   150
His thanks were ended, when I (which did see
All the Court fill'd with such strange things as he)
Ran from thence with such or more haste than one,
Who fears more actions, doth hast from prison.
At home in wholesom solitariness   155
My piteous soul began the wretchedness
Of suiters at Court to mourn, and a trance
Like his who dream't he saw hell, did advance
Itself o're me : Such men as he saw there,
I saw at Court, and worse, and more.   Low fear 160

Becomes the guilty, not the accuser: Then
Shall I, none['s] slave, of high born or rais'd men,
Fear frowns, and my Mistress, Truth, betray thee
To th' huffing braggart, puft Nobility?
No, no, Thou, which since yesterday hast been   165
Almost about the whole world, hast thou seen,
O Sun, in all thy journey, Vanity
Such as swells the bladder of our Court? I
Think, he which made your waxen garden, and
Transported it from Italy, to stand   170
With us at London, flouts our Courtiers, for
Just such gay painted things, which no sap nor
Tast have in them, ours are; and natural
Some of the stocks are, their fruits bastard all.
'Tis ten a clock and past; all whom the Mues,   Mews
Baloun, Tennis, Diet, or the stews   176
Had all the morning held, now the second
Time made ready, that day in flocks are found
In the Presence, and I, (God pardon me.)
As fresh and sweet their Apparels be, as be   180
The fields they sold to buy them. 'For a King
Those hose are,' cry the flatterer; And bring
Them next week to the Theatre to sell.
Wants reach all states. Meseems they do as well
At stage, as Court; All are players; whoe'r looks 185
(For themselves dare not go) o'r Cheapside Books,
Shall find their wardrobe's Inventory. Now
The Ladies come. As Pirats which do know

That there came weak ships fraught with Cutchanel,
The men board them; and praise (as they think) well
Their beauties; they the mens' wits; both are bought.
Why good wits ne'r wear scarlet gowns, I thought
This cause : These men, mens' wits for speeches buy,
And women buy all reds, which scarlets die.
He call'd her beauty lime-twigs, her hair net;   195
She fears her drugs ill layd, her hair loose set.
Would not Heraclitus laugh to see Macrine
From hat to shoo, himself at door refine,
As if the Presence were a Moschite; and lift
His skirts and hose, and call his clothes to shrift,   200
Making them confess not only mortal
Great stains and holes in them, but venial
Feathers and dust, wherewith they fornicate :
And then by Durer's rules survey the state
Of his each limb, and with strings the odds tries   205
Of his neck to his leg, and waist to thighs.
So in immaculate clothes and Symmetry
Perfect as Circles, with such nicety
As a young Preacher at his first time goes
To preach, he enters; and a Lady, which owes   210
Him not so much as good-will, he arrests,
And unto her protests, protests, protests;
So much as at Rome would serve to have thrown
Ten Cardinals into the Inquisition; .
And whispers by Jesu, so often, that a   215
Pursevant would have ravish'd him away,

For saying of our Ladies' Psalter.   But 'tis fit
That they each other plague, they merit it.
But here comes Glorious, that will plague them both,
Who in the other extreme only doth   220
Call a rough carelessness, good fashion ;
Whose cloak his spurs tear, or whom he spits on,
He cares not, he.   His ill words do no harm
To him, he rushes in, as if arm, arm,
He meant to cry ; And though his face be as ill   225
As theirs, which in old hangings whip Christ, still
He strives to look worse, he keeps all in awe ;
Jests like a licens'd fool, commands like law.
Tyr'd now I leave this place, and but pleas'd so
As men from jails t' execution go,   230
Go through the great chamber (why is it hung
With the seven deadly sins ?) being among
Those Ascaparts, men big enough to throw
Charing-Cross for a bar, men that do know
No token of worth, but Queen's man, and fine   235
Living,—barrels of beef, and flagons of wine,—
I shook like a spied Spie.   Preachers, which are
Seas of Wit and Arts, you can then dare
Drown the sins of this place, for, for me,
Which am but a scant brook, it enough shall be   240
To wash the stains away : Although I yet
(With Machabee's modesty) the known merit
Of my work lessen ; yet some wise men shall,
I hope, esteem my writs Canonical.

NOTES AND ILLUSTRATIONS.

As stated in introductory Note to the Satires, our text of the remainder is that of 1669 (on which see our Preface) ; but in the following Notes and Illustrations, as throughout, various-readings &c. are recorded from MSS. and other editions.

Heading : in 1669 ' Satyro IV. :' Stephens' MS. ' Satyra Quarta.'

Line 1, ' receive'=the Holy Communion.

"   8, ' *Glare:*' 1633 ' Glaze :' Stephens' MS. blank.

"   10, ' *Statute's curse*'=fine or penalty.

"   18, ' *Nile's slime.*' See our note on this in our MARVELL.

Ib. ' *strange,*' used as in the later Ant. and Cleop., so that Donne and Shakespeare probably drew from the same source : perhaps Pliny. Besides the strangeness of their origin, strange tales were told of their affection one for the other, and of their spirit of revenge ; and Pliny, in addition, says, ' Philarchus telleth a strange history of it:' how a tame asp, ' finding that one of its young had bitten the child of the master of the house and killed it, killed its young one in satisfaction, and also forbare the house, and was never knowne to repaire thither againe' (Holland's Pliny). Donne uses ' strange' again in Epistle to Earl of Doncaster :

' Begets *strange* creatures on Nile's durty slime.'

Line 23, ' *strangest.*' I accept this from Stephens' MS., in preference to ' strangers,' as usually.

Line 24, ' *Dane's Massacre.*' Ethelred made peace with and paid tribute to the invading Danes, and ordered a massacre of them on St. Brice's-day, 13th November 1002.

Line 26. The Londoners from jealousies of trade rose against foreigners on what was called afterwards Evil May-day 1517.

Line 33, ' *Tufftaffaty* ... *Rash:*' Nothing more seems to be known of these silk stuffs except that they were cheaper than velvet, and that as appears from this, Tufftaffaty had some fluffiness, while Rash was rasé or smooth.

Line 35, ' he :' I have inserted ' he' from Harleian MS. 4955.

"   40, ' *bumbast*'=bombast. From French. Cf. Thomas Wright's Provincial Dictionary, *s. v.*

Line 43, 'hear:' 1633 'beare.'

,, 48, '*Jovius:*' Paulus Jovius, an Italian who wrote a History of his own timos (1483, 1552).

Ib. '*Surius:*' I know not the reference here.

Line 54, '*Calepine's Dictionary.*' A polyglot dictionary by Ambrogio Calepino, an Italian philologist, who died November 30th, 1511.

Line 56, '*two reverend:*' Stephens' MS. reads 'two other reverend.'

Line 57, '*Academies.*' Query=the Universities (of Oxford and Cambridge)?

Line 59, '*Panurgus,*' of Rabelais' immortality: 1633 'Panirge.'

Line 61, 'But:' usually and wrongly 'By:' so too Stephens' MS.

Ib. 'sould:' a proverbial saying used by Shakespeare (Son. xxi.), 'I will not praise that purpose not to sell;' and again, Troilus and Cress. iv. 1.

Line 62, 'wonders:' 1633 badly, 'words.' .

,, 67, '*loneness:*' 1633 'lonelinesse,' and so in next line.

,, 68, '*Spartane's fashion.*' Lycurgus made prohibitory laws against commerce, and forbad travelling, that the Spartan polity and simplicity might continue unaltered.

Line 69, '*last:*' Stephens' MS. 'do not tast.'

,, 70, '*Now:*' Stephens' MS. 'Nor.'

Ibid. '*Aretine's pictures.*' Aretine's verses would have been more correct. The designs were after paintings by Giulio Romano, for which he was exiled from Rome and lost the Pope's favour. Pietro Aretino, an Italian satirist, a man as profligate in life and writings as those he satirised, wrote verses to accompany the designs.

Line 78, '*walk*'=can walk from, &c.

,, 81, '*smack'd.*' I am not aware of a similar use of this word. It seems to mean, made some interjectional sound of contempt; such is the original of chut, tut, tush, &c.

Line 83, '*neat:*' used variously, as = nice, exact; also = clean, spotless.

Ibid. '*Mine:*' 1633 'Fine:' Lansdowne MS. 740 reads 'Are not yor Frenchmen neat, fine as yo^u see?' with 'mine' in margin. I place (?) after 'Mine,' as in 1639. The following seems the distribution of this dialogue: 'Are not . . . . neat?' The Macaron: 'Mine? . . . cloath'd.' Donne: 'I of . . . Gro-

garam.' The Macaron: 'Not so, sir; I have more, Donne.'
Like Marvell in his ' Flecnoe,' Donne misinterprets every sentence the other speaks.

Line 84. 1633 inserts ' Frenchmen' after ' one ;' so Harleian
MS. 4955.

Line 86, ' *Your Grogaram :*' Stephens' MS. ' this.' ' Grogaram,' Fr. gros-grain=silk of a large or coarse thread.

Line 87 *et seqq.* The distribution of speeches is, as before,
somewhat uncertain; but probably as follows : ' Are ... neat ?'
is Donne—' Mine ? .... cloathed' his persecutor—' I of ....
Grogaram.' Donne's sarcasm on the lackey's dress : ' Not so,
sir ['tis not the only suit I have for him]; I have more,' the
Macaron's reply.

Line 87, ' *pitch*' = the height to which a hawk soars ; and
Donne says under this height to which I soared to swoop, he
my quarry would not rise, but kept himself enmewed, or in
court.

Line 88, ' *chaf'd,*' *not* ' chaff'd,' as there is no example of
the use of ' chaff'd' in those days in our present slang sense.

Line 97, ' Hollensheads' [= Raphael Holinshed]; Halls [=
Edward Hall]; Stows [=John Stowe.]

Line 106, ' *span-counter :*' ' A puerile game, supposed to be
thus played : one throws a counter or piece of money, which
the other wins, if he can throw another so as to hit it or lie
within a span of it.' So Strutt; but I rather think it a game
still played by boys, when they, directly or by rebound, endeavour to play their button or marble into a hole.

Ibid. ' *blow-point :*' supposed to be the same as dust-point.
Weber vaguely surmises that it has to do with blowing dust out
of a hole, and Nares as vaguely that it resembles push-pin; but
nothing is known, except that it was a rustic or schoolboys' or
pages' gambling game. See Nares, *s. v.*

Line 111, ' *on :*' Stephens' MS. ' me :' ' had,' 1633 ' if.'

,, 112. ' *Gallo-Belgicus :*' an annual and then bi-annual
register of news, first published at Cologne in 1598. See
Donne's Epigram on it.

Line 114, ' *loss of Amyens :*' ' since the Spaniards came'
probably means the year of the Armada (1588). They surprised Amiens 11th March 1597 ; and as no mention is made
of its recovery by Henry IV. in September of the same year, it
is not improbable that the Satire was written between those
dates, or at all events in that year. This is the more likely,

as satires were then becoming fashionable. Donne, Hall, and
Marston wrote them. Ben Jonson wrote his 'Comical Satires;'
and as plays must be the reflex of their times, the 'gentle'
Shakespeare gave them some good-natured satire from the
mouth of Jaques in 1598-9, and in the person of the Duke satirises the satirist most severely ('As You like it,' act ii. sc. 6).
Shakespeare's only other satirical play, 'Timon,' is of much
later date; but it is probable that the original drama was a
new play in 1598. In Skialetheia (1598) one epigram speaks
of 'hateman Timon in his cell;' and in Jack Dunn's Entertainment he is again familiarly alluded to. Now it can be proved
that Jack Dunn was partly written by Marston, and formed one
of the series that enraged Jonson, and was quoted by him in
his Poetaster in 1601.

Line 117, '*Makaron.*' Nares states that persons of a certain age remember the word *maccaroni* having been adopted in
the sense of a first-rate coxcomb, or puppy, or the now temporary appellation 'dandy.' He, therefore, and Todd give it
in this passage, and in R. B.'s [query, Richard Brome's?] Elegy
on Donne, the sense of an affected busy-body. But Florio
gives 'Maccarone, a gull, a lubby [looby], a loggar-head that
can doe nothing but eat Maccaroni;' and Vaugon shows that
this sense is still preserved in the saying, 'Piu grosso che
l' acqua de' maccheroni,' spoken, he says, of a man 'scimunito
[foolish or stupid] e di poco intelletto.' 'Makaron' is also used
by Donne in Preface to his Progress of the Soul.

Line 126, '*Dunkirkers*'=the buccaneers of the English seas.

,, 132, 'Giant *statues*' is in Stephens' MS.; but usually
'statutes.' As 'statute' was then one form of 'statue,' a pun
is probably intended, and allusion made to the London Gog
and Magog.

Lines 134-6 left blank in 1633.

,, 135. A belief which still causes crime and disease:
crime because the belief is that the innocent sufferer should,
whether male or female, be a virgin.

Line 141, '*mercy:*' Stephens' MS. 'redemption.'

,, 152, '*as:*' 1633 'then'=than.

,, 158, '*like him who dream't he saw hell*'=DANTE.

,, 164. I accept 'braggarts,' and the punctuation given,
for 'huffing, braggart.' Two classes here correspond to the
other two of l. 162, high-born and raised men.

Line 169, '*your:*' Stephens' MS. 'the;' l. 170, 'transported,'

ib. 'transplanted;' l. 171, 'courtiers,' Haslewood-Kingsborough
MS. 'court here.'

Ibid. '*waxen garden*'=the now common waxwork exhibitions.

Line 170, '*stand.*' In Lansdowne MS. 740 'stand' is cancelled, and rewritten in another hand 'Strand.'

Line 171, '*Courtiers :*' 1683 'Presence.'

„   176, '*Baloun.*' Probably the ancient *follis*, and, except in one respect, the modern football; a game in which a football ball was struck with the arm, armed with a wooden bracer, described, as in Italy, in the form of a shield studded with wooden points.

Line 176, '*Diet :*' the restrictions in diet consequent on visiting the place of resort next mentioned.

Line 178, '*are :*' so Stephens' MS.: usually 'were.'

„   179. Stephens' MS. 'am I?'

„   180, 'be:' Stephens' MS. 'are.'

„   182. Usually 'his flatterers.' I believe the other, 'cries the flatterer,' to be Donne's own later reading; but he overlooked that it did not suit 'bring.'

Line 186. I am not sure whether this means that their apparel was, like stage-apparel, hired; or that, like the latter, it might be found in others' books, because not paid for, and therefore not really their own.

Line 189, '*Cutchanel*'= cochineal.

„   192. I suppose the Lord Mayor and Aldermen of London. Cf. Elegy xv. lines 55-6. Or, is it a hit at the scarlet-gowned doctors of the universities?

Line 196, '*hair loose set :*' Stephens' MS. 'teeth lost set.'

„   199, '*presence :*' Stephens' MS. 'Queen's presence'—another important date-mark. 'Presence' is often thus used, *e. g.* Shakespeare, Taming of Shrew, iv. 3; Richard II. i. 3; 2 Henry IV. iv. 4, *et alibi.* So Massinger:

> 'Some private business of mine own disposed of,
> I'll meet you in the presence.'

The Bashful Lover, i. 1.

and again :

> 'I never saw him
> Since he swoon'd in the *presence.*' Ib. ii. 1.

The word was also used for the presence-chamber, and irrespective of the royal 'presence' there. So Ben Jonson very often.

Ibid. '*Moschite.*' It is to be noted that the preening,

&c. takes place outside, or at the door, before entering the presence, *i. e.* in this case the presence-chamber. Cole's Dictionary (1677), and Du Cange, *s. v.* furnish these explanations of ' Moschite :' the former, 'Mosque,—ea, Mosque, as Moskite, a Turkish church :' the latter, 'Moschite, Moscheda, Moscheta, Muscheta, Meschita, Meschida, Mesquita, Mosquea, templum Mahumetanorum.'

Line 200. Stephens' MS. ' sorts [*sic*] and host.'

,, 204, '*Durer's.*' The great engraver, like Hogarth later, wrote a treatise on the proportions of the human frame.

Line 206. Stephens' MS. 'legg to his neck and wast to his thighs.'

Line 223. Very colloquial and careless construction. His ill words are the ill words of the sufferer.

Line 234, '*bar.*' Throwing the bar was, I suppose, a test of strength prevalent among the royal guards ; for Bp. Corbet in his poem to Lord Mordant, where he satirically describes his going to Court at Windsor, says :

> ' And woe is me, the guard, those men of warre,
> Who but two weapons use, beife and barre,
> Began to gripe me ;'

and again of one of the guard whom he particularises :

> ' This Ironside tooke hold, and sodainly
> Hurled me, by judgment of the standers by,
> Some twelve foot by the square ; takes me againe,
> Outhrowes it halfe a bar.'

The name ' Ironsides,' by the way, as applied to Cromwell's regiments, is here shown not to have been a new one, and it may have even been suggestive of.personal guards.

Line 240, ' *scant :*' 1633 ' scarce :' Stephens' MS. ' Who am a shallow . . .'

Line 242, 'And if *I have done* well, and as is fitting the story, it is that which I have desired : but if slenderly and meanly, it is that which I could attain unto. . . . And here shall be an end' (2 Macc. xv. 38-9). G.

SATIRE V.

Thou shalt not laugh, in this leafe, Muse, nor they
Whom any pity warms. He which did lay
Rules to make Courtiers, he being understood
May make good courtiers, but who courtiers good?
Frees from the sting of jests all who in extreme   5
Are wretched or wicked; of these two a theam
Charity and liberty give me. What is he
Who Officers' rage and Suitors' misery
Can write in jest? If all things be in all,
As I think, since all which were, are, and shall   10
Be, be made of the same elements,
Each thing, each thing implyes or represents;
Then man is a world, in which Officers
Are the vast ravishing seas; and suters
Springs, now full, now shallow, now dry, which to   15
That which drowns them, run: these self reasons do
Prove the world a man, in which officers
Are the devouring stomach, and Suters
The excrements which they void. All men are dust;
How much worse are Suters, who to mens' lust   20
Are made preys? O worse than dust or worms' meat!
For they eat you now, whose selves worms shall eat.

They are the mills which grind you, yet you are
The wind which drives them; and a wastful war
Is fought against you, and you fight it; they   25
Adulterate law, and you prepare the way,
Like wittals; th' issue your own ruin is.
Greatest and fairest Empress, know you this?
Alas, no more than Thames' calm head doth know,
Whose meads her arms drown, or whose corn o'reflow.
You, Sir, whose righteousness she loves, whom I,   31
By having leave to serve, am most richly
For service paid, authoriz'd, now begin
To know and weed out this enormous sin.
O Age of rusty Iron! Some better wit   35
Call it some worse name, if ought equal it.
The iron Age was, when justice was sold; now
Injustice is sold dearer far; allow
All claim'd fees and duties, Gamesters, anon
The money, which you sweat and swear for, is gon 40
Into other hands : So controverted lands
'Scape, like Angelica, the striver's hands.
If Law be in the Judge's heart, and he
Have no heart to resist letter or fee,
Where wilt thou appeal? power of the Courts below 45
Flows from the first main head; and these can throw
Thee, if they suck thee in, to misery,
To fetters, halters. But if th' injury
Steel thee to dare complain, Alas, thou go'st
Against the stream upwards, when thou art most 50

Heavy, and most faint; and in these labors they,
'Gainst whom thou should'st complain, will in thy way
Become great seas, o're which, when thou shalt be
Forc'd to make golden bridges, thou shalt see
That all thy gold was drown'd in them before.   55
All things follow their like; only who have may have
Judges are gods; and He who made them so,   [more.
Meant not men should be forc'd to them to go
By means of Angels. When supplications
Wee send to God, to Dominations,   60
Powers, Cherubins, and all heaven's Courts, if we
Should pay fees, as here, Daily bread would be
Scarce to Kings; so 'tis.   Would it not anger
A Stoick, a Coward, yea a Martyr,
To see a Pursivant come in, and call   65
All his clothes, Copes; Books, Primers; and all
His Plate, Chalices; and mistake them away,
And ask a fee for comming? Oh, ne'r may
Fair Law's white reverend name be strumpeted,
To warrant thefts: she is establishèd   70
Recorder to Destiny on Earth, and she
Speaks Fate's words, and tells who must be
Rich, who poor, who in chairs, and who in jayls:
She is all fair, but yet hath foul long nales,
With which she scratcheth Suiters.   In bodies   75
Of men, so in law, nailes are extremities;
So Officers stretch to more than law can do,
As our nails reach what no else part comes to.

Why barest thou to yon Officer ?   Fool, hath he
Got those goods, for which erst men bar'd to thee ?   80
Fool, twice, thrice, thou hast bought wrong and now
      hungerly
Beg'st right, but that dole comes not till these dy.
Thou had'st much, and law's Urim and Thummim trie
Thou wouldst for more ; and for all hast paper
Enough to cloath all the Great Charrick's Pepper.   85
Sell that, and by that thou much more shalt leese
Then Hammon, when he sold his antiquities.   than
O wretch, that thy fortunes should moralize
Æsop's fables, and make tales, prophesies.
Thou art the swimming dog, whom shadows cozeneth,
Which div'st, near drowning, for what vanisheth.   91

NOTES AND ILLUSTRATIONS.

Heading in 1669 as before, 'Satyre V ;' in Lansdowne MS.
740, 'A Satire 3 ;' Stephens' MS. ' Satyra Quinta.'
    Line 2, 'warms ;' Stephens' MS. ' warne.'
    ,,   2-3. 'He . . . courtiers.' Count Baldassar Castiglione,
an Italian, who wrote a book called Il Corteggiano (The
Courtier), of the import named in the text.   Hence Castilio,
as the author was called in England, became the collective
or representative name of a perfect or affected courtier and
Castilian, or Castilion,—an adjectival form liable to be confounded with Castilian, belonging to a native of Castile.   Cf.
Marston's Satires.
    Line 9, 'jest' [upon or about] — another instance of the
common omission of the preposition.
    Line 12, ' implyes :' 1633 ' employes.'
    ,,   14, ' ravishing :' Stephens' MS. and Harleian MS. 4955
' raveninge.'

Line 16, '*drownes :*' ibid. '*drawes.*'

„ 22, '*do*' is inserted before '*eat ;*' but it makes a syllable too much, and I remove it. As the line is unrhythmical, Donne perhaps put in '*do,*' intending to make some such alteration as '*whom*' for '*whose selves.*'

Line 26, '*the :*' 1633 '*their.*'

„ 31, '*You, Sir,*' &c. Probably Lord Chancellor Ellesmere—a biographic fact.

Line 39, '*claim'd :*' 1633 '*demands.*'

„ 42, '*Angelica*'=St. Angelica.

„ 50, '*when upwards*' = when [thou goest] upwards, as shown by the variant reading '*stream upwards,*' which seems preferable.

Line 57, '*Judges are gods :*' Psalm lxxxii. 1, 2, and 6.

„ 59, '*Angels :*' coins so called = bribes. Angel = as usually stated, *e. g.* by Dyce in his Beaumont and Fletcher frequently, 10*s.*; but Holyoke, in his edition of Ryder's Dictionary (1640), gives it as = 11*s.* (See our Phineas Fletcher for Latin lines to Holyoke, *s. n.*)

Line 61. Names in the angelic hierarchy. Cf. Elegy xii. l. 78, and relative note.

Line 64, '*Stoick :*' Lansdowne MS. 740 '*a stone.*'

„ 65, '*call*' =: call over, and therefore take an inventory of.

„ 67, '*mistake*' = take them wrongly or without right— a sense not given in the dictionaries. The word is probably used in the same sense in Donne's Essays in Divinity, part iii. (p. 77, ed. 1855).

Line 79, '*barest*'=uncoverest.

„ 85, '*Charrick's Pepper*' = carrick or large merchant-ship's cargo of pepper. This word, along with '*Greatest and fairest Empress*' (l. 28), and '*You, Sir,*' &c. (ll. 31 *et seqq.*), helps to the date of this Satire. About 1596 or after, the price of pepper rose from 3*s.* to 8*s.* a pound, owing to the war with Spain and Portugal, and to the unfortunate issues of our mercantile expeditions eastward. On the 31st December 1600 a charter was granted to the Governor and Company of Merchants of London trading to the East Indies, and in the spring of 1601 they sent out four large ships under Captain James Lancaster. He, with his two larger vessels laden with pepper, did not return till September 1603, that is, not till after the accession of James. But ; he had previously sent home the other two with

cargoes composed partly of pepper, cloves, and cinnamon, partly
of calicoes and other Indian manufactures taken out of a *Portuguese carrack* that he had fallen in with and captured' (Pict.
Hist. of England, b. vii. c. 4, ' On the National Industry'). I have
not been able to trace the exact date of the arrival of these two
last-named vessels, so as to make sure that it was in Elizabeth's reign, *i.e.* prior to April 1603; but I take the ' carrack'
to be the great carrack and its pepper mentioned in l. 85 of
this 5th Satire. This is strengthened by the word used; for
though ' carrack' may have been occasionally applied to English
vessels, it was properly and generally applied to any large mer-
chant-vessels of Spanish, Portuguese, or Italian build.

 Line 87, ' *Hammon:*' 1633 ' Haman;' Stephens' MS. has
' all his.' Who he was, I know not.

 Lines 90-1. 1633 reads ' cozenèd . . . vanishèd.'

  ,, 91, ' *div'st:*' Stephens' MS. ' dyved.' G.

SATIRE VI.

TO Sr NICHOLAS SMYTH.

SLEEP, next Society and true friendship,
Man's best contentment, doth securely slip
His passions, and the world's troubles; rock me,
O sleep, wean'd from my dear friend's company,
In a cradle free from dreams or thoughts, there   5
Where poor men ly, for Kings asleep do fear.
Here sleep, and howsed by famous Ariosto,
By silver-tongu'd Ovid, and many moe,
Perhaps by gold-mouth'd Spencer too pardie
(Which builded was two dozen Stories high), storeys 10
I had repair'd, but that it was so rotten,
As sleep awak'd by Ratts from them was gotten:
And I will build no new, for by my Will,
Thy father's house shall be the fairest still
In Excester. Yet, methinks, for all their Wit, Exeter 15
Those wits that say nothing, best describe it.
Without it there is no Sense, only in this
Sleep is unlike a long Parenthesis.
Not to save charges, but would I had slept
The time I spent in London, when I kept   20
Fighting and untrust gallants Company,
In which Natta, the new Knight, seized on me,

And offered me the experience he had bought
With great Expence. I found him throughly taught
In curing Burnes. His thing had had more scars   25
Then T—— himself; like Epps it often wars,
And still is hurt. For his Body and State
The Physick and Councel (which came too late
'Gainst Whores and Dice) he now on me bestows :
Most superficially he speaks of those;   30
I found by him, least sound him who most knows.
He swears well, speakes ill, but best of Clothes,
What fits Summer, what Winter, what the Spring
He had Living, but now these waies comein[ge]
His whole Revenew; Where his Whore now dwells, 35
And hath dwelt since his father's death, he tells.
Yea he tells most cunningly each hid cause
Why Whores forsake their Bawds: To these, some Laws
He knows of the Duel, and touch his Skill
The least Jot in that or these, he quarrel will   40
Though sober, but he 'as never fought. I know
What made his Valour undubd Windmill go
Within a Pint at most! yet for all this
(Which is most strange) Natta thinks no man is
More honest than himself. Thus men may want   45.
Conscience, whilst being brought up ignorant,
They use themselves to vice. And besides those
Illiberal Arts forenam'd, no Vicar knows,
Nor other Captain less then he ; His Schools   than
Are Ordinaries, where civil men seem fools,   50

Or are for being there; His best bookes, Plaies,
Where, meeting godly Scenes, perhaps he praies.
His first set prayer was for his father ill
And sick,—that he might dye : That had, until
The Lands were gone, he troubled God no more :   55
And then ask'd him but his Right, That the whore
Whom he had kept, might now keep him : She, spent,
They left each other on even terms ; she went
To Bridewel, he unto the Wars, where want
Hath made him valiant, and a Lieutenant   60
He is become : Where, as they pass apace,
He steps aside, and for his Captain's place
He praies again : Tells God, he will confess
His sins, swear, drink, dice, and whore thenceforth less,
On this Condition, that his Captain dye   65
And he succeed ; But his Prayer did not ; they
Both cashir'd came home, and he is braver now
Than his captain : all men wonder, few know how :
Can he rob ? No.   Cheat ? No.   Or doth he spend
His own ? No.   Fidus, he is thy dear friend,   70
That keeps him up.   I would thou wert thine own,
Or hadst as good a friend as thou art one.
No present Want nor future hope made me,
Desire (as once I did) thy friend to be :
But he had cruelly possest thee then,   75
And as our Neighbours the Low-Country men,
Being (whilst they were Loyal, with Tyranny
Opprest) broke loose, have since refus'd to be

Subject to good Kings, I found even so,
Wert thou well rid of him, thou't have no moe.   80
Could'st thou but chuse as well as love, to none
Thou should'st be second : Turtle and Damon
Should give thee place in songs, and Lovers sick
Should make thee only Love's Hieroglyphick :
Thy Impress should be the loving Elm and Vine,   85
Where now an ancient Oak with Ivy twine,
Destroy'd, thy Symbole is.   O dire Mischance !
And, O vile verse ! And yet our Abraham Franco
Writes thus, and jests not.   Good Fidus for this
Must pardon me, Satyre's Bite when they kiss.   90
But as for Natta, we have since faln out :
Here on his knees, he pray'd, else we had fought.
And because God would not he should be winner,
Nor yet would have the Death of such a sinner,
At his seeking, our Quarrel is deferr'd,   95
I'l leave him at his Prayers, and as I heard,
His last : and, Fidus, you and I do know,
I was his friend, and durst have been his foe,
And would be either yet ; But he dares be
Neither : Sleep blots him out and takes in thee.   100
' The mind, you know, is like a Table-book,
The old, unwipt, new writing never took.'
Hear how the Huishers,* Checques, Cupbord, and Fire
I pass'd : (by which Degrees young men aspire [*ushers
In Court): And how that idle and she-state   105
(When as my judgment cleer'd) my soul did hate,

How I found there (if that my trifling Pen
Durst take so hard a Task) Kings were but men,
And by their Place more noted, if they erre ;
How they and their Lords unworthy men prefer;   110
And, as unthrifts, had rather give away
Great Summs to flatterers, than small debts pay;
So they their greatness hide, and greatness show
By giving them that which to worth they owe : [grateness
What Treason is, and what did Essex kill,   115
Not true Treason, but Treason handled ill :
And which of them stood for their Countrie's good,
Or what might be the Cause of so much Blood ;
He said she stunck, and men might not have said
That she was old before that she was dead.   120
His Case was hard, to do or suffer; loth
To do, he made it harder, and did both.
Too much preparing lost them all their Lives,
Like some in Plagues kill'd with preservatives.
Friends, like land-souldiers in a storm at Sea,   125
Not knowing what to do, for him did pray.
They told it all the world : where was their wit ?
Cuff's putting on a sword, might have told it.
And Princes must fear Favorites more then Foes,   than
For still beyond Revenge Ambition goes.   130
How since Her death, with Sumpter-horse that Scot
Hath rid, who, at his coming up, had not
A Sumpter-dog.   But till that I can write
Things worth thy Tenth reading (dear Nick) good night.

NOTES AND ILLUSTRATIONS.

Heading in 1669, as before, 'Satyre VI.;' appeared originally in 1669, and has ever since been overlooked by the Editors. It is found in various MSS., e.g. in Stephens', from whence I have taken the inscription 'To Sr Nicholas Smyth' (cf. line 134); and also various-readings from this MS. and from Haslewood-Kingsborough MS. In the latter it is headed 'Satire 9th to Sir Nicho. Smith, 1602.' Its biographic significance in its severity against King James is shown in our Essay, as before. Well was it for Donne that it saw not the light until the king and himself were gone.

Line 2, 'Man's best contentment:' Stephens' MS. 'true contention :' Haslewood-Kingsborough MS. 'best contentment :' and Stephens' MS. 'skypp' for 'slip.' There was probably some known equivoque on 'sleep' and 'slip.' Drunken Sly, wanting to sleep, says, 'Cessa, and let the world slip' (Induction, Taming of Shrew). = [let] slip.

Line 4, 'thy:' Stephens' MS. 'my;' I have accepted the latter.

„ 7. 1669 is nonsense as follows : 'Here sleeps House.' I accept Stephens' MS. Haslewood-Kingsborough MS. reads 'Heere in Sleep's House.'

Line 9, 'gold :' I take this from Stephens' MS.; 1669 'golden.'

Ib. 'pardie'=an old (minced) oath, a substitute for Fr. par Dieu.

Line 10, 'two.' from Stephens' MS., instead of 'some,' as in 1669 and Haslewood-Kingsborough MS.

Line 12, 'them :' from Stephens' MS. for 'thence' of 1669.

„ 13, 'new:' ib. 'more.' The meaning is, 'he would not repair because it was rotten, nor would he build more' (Stephens' MS.) ; but Donne, on revision (as in 1669), saw that 'new' was more correct, and also more distinctive.

Line 15, 'In :' Stephens' MS. 'At.' Here a space equal to three (omitted) lines (lines 15-17). Lines 7-15 seem hopelessly ungrammatical and therefore corrupt.

Lines 17-18. The sentence is liable to be understood in a contrary sense ; but the construction and meaning are—Only in this one thing (that without it there is no sense) is sleep unlike a long parenthesis, i.e. it is like it in every other way.

Line 21, 'untrust'=huffing fellows, who made a point and

boast of not being point device in their attire, but negligent and
with 'untrussed' points.

Line 26, 'T——.' Stephens' ms. 'Things.'

Ibid. 'Epps.' William Epps was a valiant but irascible
Kentish man, killed at the siege of Ostend, 1601-4. He lost an
eye on the walls; afterwards in battle he carried the colours,
'and the Regent that followed his ensigne (by being hardly set
to) giuing ground, and the enemies' ambition thirsting after his
colours, threw at all in hope to winne them. But the destinies
(who fought on their side) mistooke themselves, and in steede
of striking the colours out of his hand, smote him: in so much
that he was twice shot, and twice runne through the body, yet
wold not surrender his hold for al those breaches, but stripping
the prize for which they strove off from the staffe that helde it
vp, and wrapping his dying bodie in it, drewe out his weapon,
with which (before his collours could bee called his winding
sheete) he threwe himselfe into the thickest of danger: where
after he had slaine a horse-man and two others, most valiantlie,
hee came off, halfe dead, halfe aliue, brauely deliuering vp his
spirit in the armes of none but his friendes and fellow souldiers'
(From a much longer panegyric in Dekker's Knight's Conjur-
ing, c. viii. Percy Society edit. pp. 57-9). It is pleasant to be
able thus to reburnish a long-dimmed name of a true hero.

Line 27. Stephens' ms. 'His body and estate.'

„ 32, 'sound:' Stephens' ms. 'soundlie,' and so Haslewood-Kingsborough. The latter 'most' for 'best.'

Line 34, 'comeinge:' Stephens' ms.; 1669 'come in'=he tells
how he had 'living,' i. e. possessions or lands, and how at present, in what, and what ways his revenue comes in. See lines
55, &c.

Line 36, 'father:' Stephens' ms. 'mother dyde.'

„ 37, 'cunningly :' ib. 'p'fectly.'

„ 38. Cf. Shakespeare's As You like it, on this whole
passage.

Line 39, 'duel:' Stephens' ms. 'duello ;' from which I accept
'touch' for 'on.'

Line 41. Stephens' ms. followed, in preference to

'Though sober, but nere fought.'

Line 42. Ibid. reads

'What made his vndaunted valour wynd-myll goe.'

Haslewood-Kingsborough ms. 'undoubted vallore.' This seems

to mean, ' I know to a pint how much liquor this new knight
before he was a knight required to make his mouth-valour go
clack-clack like a mill.'

Line 45. Stephens' MS. ' This man may vaunt.'

„ 46. Ib. ' who being ;' and l. 47, ' except' for ' besides.'

„ 51. Ib. ' book' for ' bookes ;' and l. 52, ' h' bands' for
' scenes.'

Line 53. 1669 has ' father's ill ;' Stephens' MS. our text.

„ 54. Stephens' MS. erroneously fills-in ' liv'd.'

„ 57, ' *spent*'=being spent, worn out and not frequented,
or otherwise done up.

Line 58. Stephens' MS. reads ' On h'selfe ;' but the line
agrees not therewith, but continues nonsensically, ' On h'selfe
each other in [blank], she went.' Haslewood-Kingsborough
MS. ' They left . . . or own.'

Line 59, ' *Bridewel :*' Stephens' MS. ' Brydenæ.'

„ 65. 1669 intercalates ' if.' This was probably our author's variation, and a later one, as—1. It makes the phrase
stronger. 2. I have observed that, in revising at a later date,
Donne did what Shakespeare did in his later writings, allow a
superfluous syllable to end the first half of the line, ' On this |
conditi|on || that if' |

Line 66, ' *succeed :*' Stephens' MS. ' burreed ;' Haslewood-
Kingsborough ' succeed.'

Line 67, ' *braver :*' a pun=better-dressed.

„ 68, ' *few :*' Haslewood-Kingsborough ' none.'

„ 70. 1669 is followed here : the meaning is, ' No [the explanation is], Fidus, he is thy dear friend that [it is that] keeps
him up.' The MS. misreads ' Fidus is the dear friend.'

Line 72. 1669 intercalates [' Thou] hadst,' wrongly.

„ 80, ' *thou't have :*' Stephens' MS. ' hym, thou.'

„ 82. Stephens' MS. ' P'amon.'

„ 83. Our MS. reads

' Should give thee place, in lungs and livers sick,
Should only make thee Love's Hieroglyphic.'

Save that I accept ' thee place' for ' the place,' I follow here
1669, the meaning being ' Then in songs Turtle and Damon
[the stock allusions in songs of love and friendship] should give
place to thee (or give the place [to thee]), and sick lovers should
make thee alone Love's Hieroglyphic.' The change, ' make thee
only,' seems to show that 1669 is the revised text, because ' only
make thee' is ambiguous ; whereas ' make thee only' is accord-

ing to the then use of only make thee alone, and nothing else,
or make thee the only hieroglyphic. Hieroglyphic = emblem.
Haslewood-Kingsborough ms. reads ' sences' for 'livers' above.
Line 85. Stephens' ms. 'they' for ' the ;' and l. 86, ' Where
none can.'
    Line 88, ' our :' Stephens' ms. ' yor.'
    Ibid. ' Abraham France :' i. e. the poet of ' Emanuell,' which
forms one of our Fuller Worthies' Miscellanies, vol. iii.
    Line 97=His last [prayers]—a parenthetic sarcasm. 1669
is here followed : our ms. reads ' His last, Fidus and you and
hee do know.'
    Line 100. 1669 intercalates ' yet' after ' Neither,' wrongly.
    ,,   102. Stephens' ms. ' W^{ch} th' old :' unwipt = being un-
wipt.
    Line 103, ' Hear :' ib. ' Sweare ;' but there seems corrup-
tion here. 1669 reads ' Huishers Checques ;' Haslewood-Kingsborough ' Heer the vsher with clerks.' It is possible that
' Huishers Checques,' while a misreading, really carries in it
our author's alteration, with the intention of reading ' Huishers,
Checques,' &c.   Bp. Corbet, in his poem to Lord Mordant, in
describing his going to a Court ceremony, says, when he begins
to speak of the feast,
            ' And now the favorites of the clarke of th' cheeke
                  .   .   .   .
                These now shall be refresht.'
And again,
        ' By which I learne it is a man's offence
        So neere the clarke of th' check to alter sense.'
                        Edit. Gilchrist, 1807, pp. 74, 77.

Now, as ' clerks' alone is indefinite, I take it that Donne, on
revision, substituted the name of their place, ' Checques' (just
as he uses ' Cupboard'), to make his meaning clearer.   ' The
Check-roll or Checquer-roll contained the names of the king's
or other great persons' menial servants' [rather household].
Coles, s. v.   See also a quotation in Halliwell's edition of Nares.
The clerk of the check (or cheque) was therefore he who had
this roll, and so the regulation of those who were entitled to
' board.'   In our text, accordingly, I read as in 1669, refusing
' Clerkes' for ' Checques.'
    With reference to ' Hear' (l. 103), note that in this Satire-
epistle Donne begins as to sleep, and makes it the exordium to
his satire : ' Would I had slept all the time of my riotous life
in London' (which, by the way, with his reference to James,

shows this Satire to be much later than the others); and having got on Natta, and having done with him, he begins again to his friend, 'Hear also how I in my riotous life pass'd,' &c.

Line 105, '*she-state*'=Elizabeth's later government.

,,   106, '*cleer'd:*' Stephens' MS. 'cleares;' Haslewood-Kingsborough MS. 'cler'd.'

Line 107, '*there:*' Stephens' MS.

,,   109, '*noted:*' so Haslewood-Kingsborough MS.; Stephens' MS. 'notic'd.'

Line 112. Elizabeth's fitful parsimony was notorious.

,,   113. 1669 is here followed; Stephens' MS. reads 'weakness' for the first 'greatness;' which, however, gives the reverse of the sense intended, which is:

'So they their greatness hide, and weakness show;'

hide the true greatness they have, or ought to have. As in margin, I venture to understand the second 'greatness' as = grateness, *i.e.* show their ingrateness or ingratitude.

Line 115, 'Essex kill:' the unhappy favourite of Elizabeth. We have here a glimpse of the current scandals against 'Queen Bess.'

Line 119, '*stunck:*' Stephens' MS. 'stancke.'

Ibid. Query, Is the construction, He said she stunck, and [said] this when men were not allowed to say she was old (*i.e.* Elizabeth)?

Line 120. Stephens' MS.: 'She had bene old before she had bene dead.'

Line 128, '*Cuffe*' = Essex's secretary, 'a man smothered under the habit of a scholar, and slubbered over with a certain rude and clownish fashion that had the semblance of integrity' (Relig. Wottonianæ); recommended the forcible removal of Cecil and others from Court; and Essex prepared to put this plan in execution. Probably Donne means that, instead of his friends telling the design by preparation, and then by praying him off, it would have been better to have told it by Cuff's putting on a sword, *i.e.* by adopting Cuff's recommendation earlier, and so told it to the world at the moment only of action.

Line 133. Stephens' MS.: 'but vntill I can wrighte.'

,,   134. In Stephens' MS. 'Good Night' occupies a separate line as a signature.   G.

SATIRE VII.

MEN write that love and reason disagree,
But I ne'r saw't exprest as 'tis in thee.
Well, I may lead thee, God must make thee see;
But thine eyes blinde too, there's no hope for thee.
Thou say'st she's wise and witty, fair and free; 5
All these are reasons why she should scorn thee.
Thou dost protest thy love, and would'st it show
By matching her, as she would match her foe:
And wouldst perswade her to a worse offence
Than that whereof thou didst accuse her wench. 10
Reason there's none for the[e]; but thou maist vex
Her with example. Say, for fear her sex
Shun her, she needs must change; I do not see
How reason e'r can bring that 'must' to thee.
Thou art a match a Justice to rejoyce, 15
Fit to be his, and not his daughter's choice.
Urg'd with his threats shee'd scarcely stay with thee,
And wouldst th' have this to chuse thee, being free?
Go then and punish some soon gotten stuff;
For her dead husband this hath mourn'd enough, 20
In hating thee. Thou maist one like this meet;
For spight take her, prove kind, make thy breath sweet:

Let her see she 'hath cause, and to bring to thee
Honest children, let her dishonest be.
If she be a widow, I'le warrant her   25
She'l thee before her first husband prefer ;
And will wish thou hadst had her maidenhead,
(She'l love thee so) for then thou hadst been dead,
But thou such strong love, and weak reasons hast,
Thou must thrive there, or ever live disgrac'd.   30
Yet pause a while, and thou maist live to see
A time to come, wherein she may beg thee ;
If thou'lt not pause nor change, she'l beg thee now.
Doe what she can, love for nothing she'll allow ;
Besides, here were too much gain and merchandise,   35
And when thou art rewarded, desert dies.
Now thou hast ods of him she loves ; he may doubt
Her constancy, but none can put the[e] out.
Again, be thy love true, she'l prove divine,
And in the end the good on't will be thine ;   40
For tho' thou must ne'r think of other love,
And so wilt advance her as high above
Virtue as cause above effect can be,
'Tis vertue to be chast, which she'll make thee.

NOTES AND ILLUSTRATIONS.

Heading in 1669, as before, ' Satyre VII.' This is usually
given as ' Satire VI.,' from the singular continued oversight of the
preceding one. In Harl. ms. 4955 it is headed like the other
two, ' To Sr Nicholas Smyth,' who no doubt is the ' dear Nick' of
line 134 of Satire vi. In Steph. ms., while it does not appear,
two leaves are left blank as if intended for it, and therefore

showing knowledge of its existence. Though addressed to Sir
Nicholas Smith, he cannot possibly have been the subject of it,
which is the marriage of an old man otherwise unfit to marry
the young widow he had chosen. As there is no exordium or
poem addressed to Sir Nicholas Smith, perhaps we shall not err
if we judge the heading to him to be a blunder due to the different headings of the Satires, or to the fact that Sir Nicholas, to
whom the previous Satire was addressed, had a copy of this one.
This Satire originally appeared in 1635 edition.

Line 14, '*change*,' *i.e.* change towards thee.

„   17, '*Urg'd*.' I accept this from Haslewood - Kingsborough MS.; usually 'Dry'd,' which is nonsense.

Line 18, '*thus*'=father's threats.

„   29-30. These are words humorously supposed to be
said by the would-be bridegroom. The words 'strong love and
weak reasons' refer to the proverbial saying, that a man cannot
be a lover and wise. Cf. Epithal. Eclogue, line 86.

Line 32, '*beg thee*,' as an idiot or natural.

„   34, '*nothing*.' This seems to be a somewhat equivocal
phrase=she'll.value your love as nothing, and allow nothing in
exchange. Besides, were she to give any love in exchange,
there would be too much gain to you; and, moreover, your desert, being rewarded, would no longer be desert. The conceits
here as elsewhere, and even in Shakespeare, are forced somewhat.

Line 41. Haslewood-Kingsborough MS. reads

'For thou must thinke never on other love.'   G.

II.

THE PROGRESS OF THE SOUL.

NOTE.

The 'Progress of the Soul' appeared originally in the quarto of 1633 (3 pages unnumbered, and pp. 1-27), and has been reprinted in all the after-editions. Our text is Addl. MSS. 18,647, Plut. 201 H, from the Earl of Denbigh's collection (purchased by the British Museum, 10th May 1851). Our collation of 1633 and after-editions satisfied us that this MS. is superior (as a whole) in its readings. In Notes and Illustrations, as before, will be found various-readings, &c., wherein we give reasons for occasionally departing from our adopted MS.

See our Essay for De Quincey's glowing panegyric of the 'Progress:' and yet there are things in it one would wish away —just as one inevitably removes a slug from the rose's heart or lily's chalice—and which perhaps explain, if they do not altogether warrant, Professor Ward's strong censure in his edition of Pope. It may be permitted us to remind the reader, of the heading *Poema Satyricon*, and that the offence is limited to two out of fifty-two stanzas. I point out the relation of the 'Progress' to the still more remarkable 'Anatomie'—hitherto overlooked. See Notes on Epistle immediately following.

The 'Progress of the Soul' takes its place next to the Satires proper, as being called by its Author 'Poema *Satyricon*.' G.

INFINITATI SACRUM,

16 Augusti 1601.

METEMPSYCHOSIS: POEMA SATYRICON.

EPISTLE.

OTHERS at the Porches and entries of their buildings
set their Arms; I my picture; if any coulors can deliver
a minde so plaine and flatt and through-light as mine.
Naturally at a new Author I doubt, and stick, and doe
not quickly saye 'Good.' I censure much and taxe;
And this liberty costs mee more then [than] others,
by how much my own things are worse than others.
Yet I could not be so rebellious against myselfe, as
not to doe it, since I love it [nor so unjust to others,
to do it]; *sine talione.* As long as I give them as good
holde uppon me, they must pardon mee my bytings.
I forbidd no reprehender but him, that like the Trent
Councell, forbidds not books, but Authors, dammninge
whatever such a name hath or shall write. None write
so ill, that he gives not somethinge exemplarie to followe or flie. Now when I beginn this booke, I have
noe purpose [to come] in[to] any man's debt; how
my stock will hould out, I know not; perchaunce
wast, perchaunce increase in use. If I doe borrow
any thinge of Antiquitie, besides that I make account

that I paye it to Posteritie, with as much, and as
good; you shall still finde me to acknowledg it, and
to thanck not him only, that hath digged out treasure
for me, but that hath lighted [me] a candle to the
place. All which I will bid you remember (for I
would have noe such Readers, as I can teach) is, that
the Pithagorian doctrine doth not only carry one soule
from man to man, nor man to beast, but indifferently
to plants alsoe : and therefore you must not grudge to
finde the same soule in an Emperour, in a Post-horse,
and in a Macheron ; since no unreadynes in the soule,
but an indisposition in the Organs worke this. And
therefore, though this soule could not move when it
was a Melon, yet it may remember and now tell mee,
at what lascivious banquett it was serv'd. And though
it could not speake, when it was a Spider, yet it can
remember, and now tell me, who us'd it for poyson to
attaine dignitie. However the bodies have dull'd her
other facultics, her memorie hath [ever] been her owne;
which makes me soe seriously deliver you by her relation all her passages from her first makinge, when she
was that apple which Eve eate, to this tyme when she
is in her, whose life you shall find in the end of this
booke.

NOTES AND ILLUSTRATIONS.

In line 7, the words ' by how much . . . . . . others' are inadvertently dropped in the American edition (1855). A few
words placed in brackets [ ], omitted in our MS., are filled-in
from 1633 and after-editions ; but other superfluous words not

found in our MS. are left out, as noted below. Lines 9-10 read in our MS. 'love it; *sine talione;*' line 17 reads 'noe purpose in any man's doubt, how,' &c.; line 34 'can,' not being in our MS. is omitted, as onward; lines 42-3 are usually misprinted 'when she is she;' the word 'Macheron,' line 31, is explained in relative note on Satire iv. l. 117. Probably the 'Anatomie' was intended to follow, and so the 'life' meant was Mrs. Elizabeth Drury's. This seems tacitly indicated by the title of the 'second Anniversary' of the 'Anatomie,' viz. 'Of the Progress of the Soul.' I am very well aware that the 'Progress of the Soul,' and the 'Anatomie,' and its 'Progress of the Soul,' have fundamental differences, so much so that the later might almost find a place among the 'Divine Poems.' That is to say, it is a Christian poem without allusion to the Pythagorean doctrine, and all its reflections and thoughts are moral and religious. I am also aware that the 'Anatomie,' and its 'Progress of the Soul,' as now extant, belong to a period in advance of the 'Metempsychosis,' which is dated 16th August 1601. The frequent references to the new star prove these references to be after 1604. I am willing to date it even 1610-1, *i.e.* near to the publication of the first part of the 'Anatomie' in 1611 : both parts 1612. But my idea is, that when in 1601, in his Epistle to the 'Metempsychosis,' he named the 'life' to be found ' in the end of the booke,' he had the substance of the 'Anatomie' lying past him; and intended therewith to sing of the 'life' of an ideal Woman, in contrast with the more earthly type of the 'Metempsychosis.' Meanwhile, Mrs. Elizabeth Drury, the child-wife (for she was only fifteen), dying, he fell back on the Verse beside him, and wrought it into a deeper and nobler 'life' than ever he had dreamed of. I do not say Mrs. Drury was the 'great soul' of st. vii. of 'Metempsychosis'—another 'ideal' was then before his imagination—but I feel satisfied that he transferred to her what he intended for that other. This kept in mind, explains the breadth and largeness of the panegyric of the 'Anatomie,' and also those remaining touches of Pythagoreanism, as of Mrs. Drury as the informing soul of the dead World. Our arrangement, made on other and independent grounds, brings the two poems into proximity. See more on all this in our Essay. G.

THE PROGRESS OF THE SOUL.

FIRST SONGE.

I SINGE the progresse of a deathless soule,
Whom Fate—which God made but doth not controule—
Placed in most shapes; all tymes, before the lawe
Yoak'd us, and when, and since, in this I singe;
And the greate world t' his agèd eveninge,   5
From infant morne, through manly noone I drawe;
What the gold Chaldee, or silver Persian sawe.
Greeke brass, or Roman iron, is in this one;
A work to outweare Sethe's pillars, brick and stone,
And (holy writte excepted) made to yeild to none.   10

Thee, eye of Heau'n, this great Soule envies not;
By thy male force is all we have, begott
In the first East thou now beginn'st to shine,
Suck'st early balme, and Iland spices there;
And wilt anone in thy loose-rain'd carrere   15
At Tagus, Po, Sene, Thames, and Danow dine, Seine
And see at night thy Westerne land of Mine; [Danube
Yet hast thou not more Nations seen than shee,
That before thee one day began to be;
And thy fraile light beinge quench'd, shall longe, longe
            outlive thee.   20

Nor holy Janus, in whose soveraigne boate
The Church, and all the Monarchies did floate ;
That swimming College, and free Hospitall
Of all mankinde, that Cage and viuarie
Of foules and beasts, in whose wombe Destinie　25
Us and our latest Nephews did install ;
(From thence are all deriv'd, that fill this All) ;
Didst thou in that greate stewardshipp embarke
So divers shapes into that floatinge parke,
As have beene mou'd, and informed by this heavenly
　　　　sparke.　　　　　　　　　　　　　30

Great Destinie, the Commissarie of God,
That hast mark'd out a path and period
For every thinge ; Who, where wee offspringe tooke,
Our wayes and ends seest at one instant ; Thou
Knott of all causes ; Thou, whose changelesse browe　35
Ne're smiles nor frownes, O vouchsafe thou to looke,
And shew my storie, in Thy eternal booke.
That (if my prayre be fitt) I may understand
So much myselfe, as to know with what hand,
How scant, or liberal, this my life's race is spann'd.　40

To my six lustres, almost now outwore,
Except Thy book owe mee so many more ;
Except my legend bee free from the letts
Of steepe ambition, sleepie povertie,
Spiritt-quenchinge sicknes, dull captivitie,　　　45

Distractinge busines, and from beautie's netts,
And all that calls from this and t' others whetts;
O! let me not launch out, but let me save
The expence of braine and spiritt; that my grave
His right and due, a whole unwasted man maye haue.   50

    But if my dayes be long, and good enough,
In vaine this sea shall enlardge, or enrough
Itselfe; for I will through the wave and fome,
And hold in sad lone wayes, a lively spright,
Make my dark heavie Poem light, and light.   55
For, though through many straights and lands I roame,
I launch at Paradice, and I sayle towards home;
The c[o]urse, I there begann, shall heere be stayd;
Sayls hoysted there, struck heere; and Anchors layde
In Thames, which were at Tygris and Euphrates wayde.

                                             60

    For this great soule, which here amongst us nowe
Doth dwell, and moves that hand, and tongue, and
     browe,
Which, as the Moone the sea, moves us; to heare
Whose story with long patience you will longe;
(For 'tis the crowne and last straine of my songe;)   65
This soul, to whom Luther and Mahomett were
Prisons of flesh; this soule which oft did teare
And men[d] the wracks of th' Empire, and late Rome,
And liu'd where every greate change did come,
Had first in Paradise, a lowe but fatall roome.   70

Yet no lowe roome, nor then the greatest, lesse than
If (as devout and sharpe men fitly guesse)
That Cross, our ioye and greffe (where nayles did tye grief
That All, which always was all, everywhere,
Which could not sinne, and yet all sinns did beare, 75
Which could not dye, yet could not chuse but dye ;)
Stood in the self-same room in Caluarie,
Where first grew the forbidden learnèd tree ;
For on that tree hong in securitie 79
This soule, made by the Maker's will from pullinge free.

Prince of the Orchard, faire as dawninge morne,
Fenc'd with the lawe, and ripe as soone as borne,
That apple grew, which this soule did enlive ;
Till the then-clyming serpent, that now creepes
For that offence, for which all mankinde weeps, 85
Tooke it, and t' her, whom the first man did wiue
(Whom, and her race, only forbiddings drive)
Hee gave it, shee t' her husband ; both did eate :
So perishèd the eaters and the meate ;   [sweate.
And wee (for treason taints the bloud) thence die and

Man all at once was there by woeman slaine ; 91
And one by one we are heare slaine o're againe
By them. The mother poyson'd the well-head,
The daughters here corrupt us, rivolets ;
No smalenes 'scapes, noe greatenes breaks their netts : 95
She thrust us out, and by them wee are led
Astraye, from turninge to whence wee are fledd.

Were prisoners judges, 'twould seeme rigorous;
She sinn'd, we beare; part of our pain is thus [us.
To loue them, whose fault to this paineful loue yoak'd

    So fast in us doth this corruption growe,   101
That now wee dare aske why we should be soe;
Would God (disputes the curious Rebel) make
A lawe, and would not have it kept? Or can
His creature's will cross His? Of every man,   105
For one, will God (and be iust) vengeance take?
Who sinn'd? 'twas not forbidden to the Snake,
Nor her, who was not then made; nor is't writt
That Adame cropt, or knew the Apple; yet   109
The worme, and shee, and hee, and wee endure for it.

    But snatch mee, heavenly Spiritt, from this vayne
Reckoninge their vanitie; less is their gaine
Then hazard, still to meditate on ill,   than
Though with good minde; their reason's like those toyes
Of glassie bubbles, which the gamesome boyes   115
Stretch to so nice a thinnesse through a quill,
That they themselves breake, and do themselves spill.
Arguing is heretiques game; and Exercise,
As wrestlers, perfects them : Not liberties
Of speech, but silence; hands, not tongs, end heresies.

    Just in that instant, when the serpent's gripe   121
Broake the slight veynes, and tender conduit-pipe,
Through which this soul from the tree's roote did drawe

Life and growth to this Apple, fledd awaye
This loose soule, old, one and another daye.   125.
As lightninge, which one scarce dares say he sawe,
'Tis so soone gone, (and better proofe the lawe
Of sense, then faith requires,) swiftlie shee flewe   than
T' a darke and foggy Plott; her, her fates threwe
There through tho' earth's pores, and in a Plant hous'd
       her anewe.   130

The plant, thus abled, to itselfe did force
A place, where no place was; by nature's course
As ayre from water, water fleets awaye
From thicker bodies; by this roote thronged soe
His spongie confines gave him place to growe: 135
Just as in our streetes, when the people staye
To see the Prince, and so fill up the way,
That weesels scarce could pass; when she comes neere,
They throng, and cleave up, and a passage cleare,
As if for that time their round bodies flatned were. 140

His right Arme he thrust out towards the East,
Westward his left; th' ends did themselves digest
Into ten lesser strings, these fingers were:
• And as a slumberer stretchinge on his bedd,
This way hee this, and that waye scatterèd   145
His other legg, which feete with toes up beare;
Grewe on his middle parts, the first day, haire,
To shew, that in love's busines he should still
A dealer bee, and be us'd, well or ill: 149
His apples kindle, his leaves force of conception kill.

A Mouth, but dumbe, he hath; blinde eyes, deafe
And to his shoulders dangle subtile haires;   [eares;
A yonge Colossus there he stands upright :
And, as that ground by him were conquerèd,
A leafie garland weares he on his head   155
Enchas'd with little fruits, so redd and bright,
That for them you would call your love's lipps white;
So of a lone unhaunted place possest,
Did this soule's second Inn, built by the guest,
This livinge buried man, this quiet mandracke, rest. 160

No lustfull woeman came this plant to greive,
But 'twas because there was none yet but Eve;
And she (with other purpose) kill'd it quite :
Her sinne had now brought in infirmities,
And so her cradled child, the moist red eyes   165
Had never shutt, nor slept, since it saw light;
Poppie she knew, shee knew the mandracke's might,
And tore up both, and soe cool'd her child's bloud :
Unvertuous weedes might long unvex'd have stood;
But hee's short-liv'd, that with his death can do most
    good.   170

To an unfetter'd soule's quick nimble hast
Are fallinge stars, and h[e]art's thoughts, but slow-pac'd :
Thinner then burnt aire flies this soule, and shee,   than
Whom foure new cominge and foure parting Sunnes
Had found, and left the mandrack's tennant, runns 175
Thoughtless of change, when her firme destinie
Confin'd, and enjayl'd her, that seem'd so free,

Into a small blew shell; the which a poor
Warme bird o'respread, and satt still evermore,   179
Till her inclos'd child kickt and peck'd itselfe a dore.

Out crept a sparrow, this soul's movinge Inne,
On whose rawe armes stiffe feathers now beginne,
As children's teeth through gummes, to breake with
His flesh is gellie yet, and his bones thredds ; [paine ;
All a new downy mantle ouerspreads.   185
A mouth hee opes, which would as much containe
As his late house, and the first hower speaks plaine,
And chirps alowd for meate.   Meate fit for men
His father steales for him, and soe feeds then   189
One, that within a moneth, will beate him from his hen.

In this world's youth, wise Nature did make hast ;
Things ripned sooner, and did longer last ;
Already this hott cock in bush and tree,
In feild and tent o'reflutters his next hen ;
He askes her not who did so tast, nor when ;   195
Nor if his sister or his neice shee bee,
Nor doth shee pule for his inconstancie,
If in her sights hee change ; nor doth refuse
The next, that calls ; both libertie do use ;
Where store is of both kindes, both kindes may freely
      choose :   200

Men, till they tooke lawes which made freedome
Their daughters and their sisters did ingress ;   [lesse,

Till now, unlawfull, therefore ill 'twas not.
So iollie, that it can move this soule; is
The body so free of his kindnesses,   205
That selfe-preservinge it hath now forgott,
And slackneth so the soule's and bodie's knott,
Which temperance straightens: freely on his shee-freinds
Hee bloud and spiritt, pith and marrow spends,
Ill steward of himselfe, himselfe in three years ends. 210

    Else might he long have liu'd; man did not know
Of gummie blood, which doth in Holly growe,
How to make bird-lyme, nor how to deceive
With faignèd calls, his netts, or enwrapping snare,
The free inhabitants of th' plyant ayre.   215
Man to begett and woman to conceive,
Askd not of rootes, nor of cock-sparrowes leave:
Yet chuseth hee,'though none of these he feares,
Pleasantly three, than straightened twenty yeares straitened
To live; and to increase his race, himselfe outweares. 220

    This coale with over-blowinge quenched and dead,
The soule from her too active organs fledd
To a brooke; a female fishe's sandy Roie   roe
With the male's jelly newly leaven'd was,
For they had intertouch'd as they did passe,   225
And one of those smale bodies, fitted soe,
This soul inform'd, and abled it to roe   row
Itselfe with finny oares, which she did fitt;
Her scales seem'd yet of parchment, and as yet
Perchaunce a fish, but by no name, you could call it.

When goodly, like a shipp in her full trimme, 231
A swann so white, that you may unto him
Compare all whitenes, but himselfe to none,
Glided along, and, as hee glided, watched,
And with his archèd neck this poore fish catch't: 235
It mooved with state, as if to looke upon
Low things it scorn'd; and yet, before that one
Could think hee sought it, he had swallowed cleare
This, and much such; and unblam'd, devour'd there
All, but who too swift, to[o] great, or well arm'd were.

Now swomme a prison in a prison putt, 241
And now this Soule in double walls was shutt;
Till, melted with the Swan's digestive fire,
She left her house the fish, and vapoured forth:
Fate, not affordinge bodies of more worth 245
For her as yet, bids her againe retire
T' another fish, to any new desire
Made a new prey: For he, that can to none
Resistance make, nor complaint, sure is gone;
Weaknes invites, but silence feasts, oppression. 250

Pace with her native stream this fish doth keepe,
And journies with her towards the glassie deepe,
But oft retarded; once with a hidden nett,
Tho' with greate windowes; (for when neede first taught
These tricks to catch foode, then they were not wrought
As now, with curious greediness, to lett 256
None 'scape, but few and fit for use, to gett;)

As in this trapp a ravenous Pike was tane,   50
Who, though himselfe distrest, would faine have slaine
This wretch; So hardly are ill habitts left againe.   260

   Here by her smaleness she two deathes o'repast;
Once, innocence 'scap'd and left the oppresser fast;
The nett through-swome, she keepes the liquid path,
And whether shee leap up sometimes to breath,
And suck in ayre or find it underneath,   265
Or workinge parts like mills, or limbecks hath,
To make the water thinne and ayre-like, faith
Cares not, but safe the Place shee comes unto,
Where fresh with salt waves meete; and what to doe
Shee knowes not, but betweene both makes a boord or
     two.   270

   So farr from hidinge her guests, water is,
That shee showes them in bigger quantities
Than they are.   Thus her, doubtfull of her way,
For game, and not for hunger, a sea-pie
Spide through the traiterous spectacle, from high,   275
The silly fish, where it disputinge laye,
And, t' end her doubts and her, beares her awaye;
Exalted shee is but to the exalter's good,
(As are by great ones, men which lowly stood.)
It rais'd to be the Raiser's instrumente and food.   280

  ·Is any kinde subiect to rape like fish?
Ill unto man they neither doe, nor wish;

Fishers they kill not, nor with noise awake;
They doe not hunt, nor strive to make a prey
Of beasts, nor their young sonnes to beare awaye;   285
Foules they pursue not, nor doe undertake
To spoile the nests industrious birds doe make;
Yet them all these unkinde kindes feed uppon;
To kill them is an occupation,
And lawes make Fasts and Lents for their distruction.

A suddaine stiff land-winde in that selfe hower   291
To seaward forc'd this bird, that did devoure
The fish; he cares not, for with ease he flies,
Fat gluttonie's best orator: at last
So longe he hath flown, and hath flowen so fast,   295
That leagues o'rpast at sea, now tir'd hee lyes,
And with his prey, that till then languisht, dies;
The soules, no longer foes, two wayes did erre.
The fish I follow, and keepe no Calender
Of the other: he lives yet in some great Officer.   300

Into an embrion fish our Soule is throwen,
And in due tyme throwen out againe, and growen
To such vastness as, if unmanacled
·From Greece, Morea were, and that by some
Earthquake unrooted, loose Morea swome;   305
Or seas from Africk's body had severèd
And torne the hopefull Promontorie's head;
This fish would seeme these, and, when all hopes faile,

A great shipp oversett, or without sayle
Hullinge might (when this was a whelpe) be like this
   whale.   310

   At every stroke his brazen finnes do take,
More circles in the broken sea they make,
Then cannons' voices when the ayre they teare :   than
His ribbes are pillars, and his high-arch'd roofe
Of barke, that blunts best steele, is thunder-proofe: 315
Swimm in him swallow'd Dolphins without feare,
And feele no sides, as if his vast wombe were
Some Inland sea ; and ever, as he went,
He spouted rivers up, as if he meant
To join our seas with seas above the firmament.   320

   He hunts not fish, but as an officer
Stays in his Court, at his owne net, and there
All sutors of all sorts themselves enthrall ;
So on his back lies this whale wantoninge,
And in his gulfe-like throate suckes every thinge   325
That passeth neare.   Fish chaseth fish, and all,
Flyer and follower, in this whirlpoole fall ;
O might not states of more equalitie
Consist? and is it of necessity   [die?
That thousand guiltless smales, to make one greate, must
                                                          330
   Now drinks he up seas, and he eats up flocks ;
He jostles Ilands, and he shakes firm rocks :
Now in a roomefull house this soule doth floate,

And, like a Prince, shee sends her faculties
To all her lymbes, distant as Provinces. 335
The Sun hath twenty tymes both Crabb and Goate
Parchèd, since first launch'd forth this livinge boate;
'Tis greatest now, and to destruction
Nearest : There's no pause at perfection ;
Greatnes a period hath, but hath noe station. 340

Two little fishes, whom he never harm'd,
Nor fedd on their kinde, two, not thoroughly arm'd ·
With hope that they could kill him, nor could doe
Good to themselves by his death (they did not eate
His flesh, nor suck those oyls which thence outstreat),
Conspir'd against him ; and it might undoe 346
The plott of all, that the plotters were two,
But that they fishes were, and could not speake.
How shall a Tyrant wise, stronge projects breake, 349
If wretches can on them the common anger wreake ?

The flayle-fin'd Thresher and steel-beak'd Sword-fish
Only attempt to doe, what all do wish :
The Threasher backs him, and to beat beginns ;
The sluggard Whale yealds to oppression,
And, t' hide himselfe from shame and danger, downe
Beginns to sinck ; the sword-fish upward spinns, 356
And goares him with his beake ; his staffe-like finnes
So well the one, his sword the other plies,
That, now a scoff and prey, this tyrant dyes, 359
And (his own dole) feeds with himself all companies.

Who will revenge his death? or who will call
Those to account, that thought and wrought his fall?
Th' heires of slaine kings wee see are often soe
Transported with the joye of what they gett,
That they revenge and obsequies forgett;   365
Nor will against such men the people goe,
Because he's now dead, to whom they should showe
Love in that act; some kings by vice being growne
So needy of subjects' love, that of their owne
They thinck they loose, if love be to the dead Prince
          shown.   lose   370

This Soule now free from prison and passion,
Hath yet a little indignation,
That so small hammers should so soone downe beate
So greate a castle, and havinge for her house
Gott the strait cloyster of a wretched mouse,   375
(As basest men, that have not what to eat,
Nor enioye ought, doe farr more hate the greate
Then they, who good repos'd estates possesse)   than
This Soule, late taught that greate things might by lesse
Bee slaine, to gallant mischiefe doth herself addresse.

Nature's greate master-piece, an Elephant: 381
(The only harmeless great thinge; the gyant
Of beasts; who, thought none had to make him wise,
But to be iust and thankfull, loath to offend),—
Yet Nature hath given him no knees to bend,—   385

Himself he up-props, on himselfe relies,
And, foe to none, suspects noe enemies :
Still sleeping stood, vexed not his fantasie
Black dreames, like an unbent bowe carelesly
His sinewy Proboscis did remisly lie,　　　　　390

 In which, as in a gallery, this mouse
Walk'd, and survey'd the roomes of this vast house ;
And to the brain, the soule's bed-chamber, went,
And gnawed the life-cords there : Like a whole towne
Cleane undermin'd, the slaine beast tumbled downe ;
With him the murtherer dyes, whom envy sent　　396
To kill, not 'scape ; for only he, that went
To dye, did ever kill a man of better roome :
And thus he made his foe his prey and tombe :　　399
Who cares not to turne back, may any-whither come.

 Next hous'd this Soule a Wooluc's yet unborne
  whelpe,
Till the best midwife, Nature, gave it helpe
To issue : it could kill, as soon as goe.
Abel, as white and mild as his sheepe were,
(Who, in that trade, of Church and Kingdome's, there
Was the first type,) was still infested soe　　　406
With this wolfe, that it bredd his loss and woe ;
And yet his bitch, his sentinell, attends
The flock so neare, so well warnes and defends,
That the wolfe (hopelesse else) to corrupt her intends.

He took a course, which since succesfully   411
Great men have often taken, to espie
The counsells, or to break the plotts, of foes ;
To Abell's tent he stealeth in the darke,   414
On whose skirts the bitch slept ; ere she could barke,
Attach'd her with straight gripes, yet he call'd those
Embracements of love ; to love's work he goes,
Where deeds move more then words ; nordothshe showe,
Nor much resist, nor needs he straighten soe   resistance
His preye, for were she loose, shee would not barke
    nor goe.   420

    He hath engag'd her ; his, shee wholly bides :
Who not her owne, none other's secretts hides.
If to the flock he come, and Abell there,
She faignes hoorse barkings, but she biteth not ;   hoarse
Her faith is quite, but not her love, forgott.   425
At last a trapp, of which some everywhere
Abell had placed, ends all his loss and feare,
By the wolve's death ; and now iust time it was,
That a quick soule should give life to that mass
Of bloud in Abel's bitch, and thither this did passe.
    430
    Some have their wiues, their sisters some begott ;
But in the lives of Emperours you shall not
Read of a lust, the which may equall this :
This wolfe begott himselfe, and finishèd,
What hee begann alive, when hee was dead.   435

Sonne to himselfe, and father too; hee is
A ridling lust, for which Schoolmen would misse
A proper name.   The whelpe of both those laye
In Abell's tent, and with soft Moaba,
His sister, beinge yonge, it us'd to sport and playe.   440

He soone for her too harsh and churlish grew,
And Abell (the dam dead) would use this new
For the feild; beinge of twoe kinds thus made,
Hee as his dam, from sheepe drove wolues awaye,
And, as his Sire, he made them his owne prey.   445
Five years he liv'd, and couzoned with his trade,
Then, hopeless that his faultes were hid, betrayd
Himselfe by flight, and by all followèd,
From doggs a wolfe, from wolues a dogge, he fledd;
And, like a spie to both sides false, he perishèd.   450

It quickned next a toyfull Ape, and soe·
Gamesome it was, that it might freely goe
From tent to tent, and with the children playe;
His organs now so like theirs he doth finde,
That, why he cannot laugh and speake his minde,   455
He wonders.   Much with all, most he doth staye
With Adam's fift daughter, Siphateria:
Doth gaze on her, and, where she passeth, passe,
Gathers her fruits, and tumbles on the grasse;
And, wisest of that kind, the first true lover was.   460

He was the first, that more desired to have
One than another; first, that ere did crave

Loue by mute signes, and had no power to speake ;
First, that could make loue-faces, or could doe
The vaulter's sombersalts, or us'd to woe   woo   465
With hoyting gamboles, his own bones to breake,
To make his Mistress merry ; or to wreake
Her anger on himselfe.   Sinns against kinde
They easily doe, that can lett feede their mind
With outward beauty ; beauty they in boyes and beasts
    do finde.   470

By this misled, too lowe things men have proov'd,
And too high ; beasts and Angells have been lou'd :
This Ape, though els through-vayne, in this was wise ;
Hee reach'd at things too high, but open waye
There was, and hee knew not she would say naye. 475
His toyes prevayle not, likelier meanes he tryes,
He gazeth in her face with teare-shott eyes,
And up-lifts subtly with his russett pawe
Her kid-skin apron without feare or awe   479
Of Nature ; Nature hath no jayle, though shee hath lawe.

First she was silly, and knew not what he meant :
That vertue, by his touches chaf'd and spent,
Succeeds an itchye warmth, that melts her quite
She knew not first, then cares not what he doth,   484
And willinge halfe and more, more then half wroth   than
Shee neither pulls nor pushes, but outright
Now cryes, and now repents ; when Thelemite,
Her brother, entred, and a greate stone threwe

After the Ape, who thus prevented flew. 489
This house was battred down, the soule possest a new.

And whether by this change shee loose or winne, lose
She comes out next, where th' Ape would have gone in.
Adam and Eve had mingled blouds, and nowe
Like Chymique's equall fires, her temperate wombe
Had stew'd and form'd it : and part did become 495
A spungie liver, that did ritchly allowe,
Like a free conduit on a high hil's browe,
Life-keepinge moysture unto every part ;
Part hardened itselfe to a thicker h[e]art,
Whose busie furnaces life's spiritts doe impart. 500

Another part became the Well of sence,
The tender well-arm'd feelinge braine, from whence
Those sinewy strings, which do our bodies tye,
Are raueled out ; and, fast there by one end,
Did this Soule limbes, these limbes a soule attend ; 505
And now they ioyn'd, keeping some qualitie
Of every past shape ; she knew treachery,
Rapine, deceipt, and lust, and ils enough
To be a woeman : Themech she is nowe, 509
Sister and wife to Cayne, Caine, that first did plowe.

Whoere thou bee that reade this sullen Writt,
Which just so much courts thee, as thou do'st it,
Let me arrest thy thoughts ; wonder with mee
Why plowing, building, rulinge and the rest,

And most of those arts, whence our lives are blest, 515
By cursèd Cain's race invented bee,
And blest Seath vext us with Astronomy.
There's nothing simply good nor ill alone,
Of every qualitie comparison
The only measure is, and judge, Opinion.   520

NOTES AND ILLUSTRATIONS.

Line 6, '*through :*' our MS. reads 'to;' but the Poet says
he sings all times, and draws the great world *from* infant morn
to his aged evening, (therefore) '*through*' manly noon.   Hence
'through,' not ' to,' is correct, the three clauses corresponding
to ' before,' ' when,' and ' since,' of ll. 3-4.

Line 9, ' Sethe's pillars :' mythical antediluvian memorials.

   ,,   11-12, 'thee,' ' thy :' our MS. mistakenly reads 'the'
and ' this ;' and so elsewhere, to the disjointing of the contextual
phraseology.

Line 17, ' *Mine :*' query = gold (mines) ?

   ,,   21, ' *holy :*' our MS. again misreads ' any' for ' holy.'
There was but one Janus in ancient mythology, and Donne
could hardly fail to remember this.   Janus too, in the Latin
mythology, was a particularly 'holy' god, and named before
Jupiter as the beginner of all things, and the oldest of the gods
in Italy.   Then Donne clearly adopts the belief that Janus was
Noah.   He was led to use Janus, first, because his theme of
Metempsychosis is a pagan one; and secondly, because the mention of the sun led up to it, Janus being the sun-divinity under
another name.

Line 26, ' *Nephews*' = descendants.   See Thomas Wright's
Prov. Dict. *s.v.* for examples.

Line 31, ' *Commissarie.*' Donne probably was thinking of
those commissaries of the army who had the mustering of the
men, and to all and everything being properly accoutred; for
at the date it is less likely that he would choose an ecclesiastical metaphor, viz. the Bishop's commissary, 'who exercises

ecclesiastical jurisdiction in those parts of the diocese so far remote from the see, that the chancellor cannot call the subjects thereof to the bishop's principal consistory without too much trouble' (Dyche's Dict. *s.v.*). The same thought occurs again in Funeral Elegy on Mrs. Drury, 1. 95.

Line 36, '*vouchsafe :*' our MS. inadvertently reads 'O vouch thou safe.'

Line 54, '*hold . . . lone :*' our MS. reads 'shall' for 'hold,' and 'love' for 'lone;' but the text seems preferable, agreeably to 1635, 1639, and others.

Line 63, '*the sea :*' our MS. misreads 'and,' no doubt from the confounding of 'yᵗ' and '&.'

Line 66, '*soul :*' our MS. miswrites 'songe,' caught from preceding line; and in 1. 74 drops 'always,' while in 1. 83 'enlive' is left blank, and 1. 94 'rivolets.'

Line 84, '*Till :*' our MS. 'Then.' Looking to the description of its state, 'fair and fenc'd that apple grew,' I think 'Till' makes the determinate change (cf. 1. 124) better than 'then,' which merely indicates a succession or sequence.

Line 90, '*taints :*' a legal reference or simile; for 'the descendants of one attainted of treason cannot be heirs to him, and if he be male, his posterity is thereby degraded; nor can this corruption of blood be taken away but by act of Parliament or writ of error' (Dyche, *s.v.* Attainted).

Line 99, '*pain :*' our MS. misreads 'sinn.' I say misreads, for it is not correct, and does not express the Poet's meaning to read 'sinn.' By 1. 98 he is speaking of the sentence pronounced; the sentence would seem rigorous, viz. this one, that for her sin we bear punishment; and then says part, not of our 'sin,' but of the result of the sin—part of the 'pain,' *pœna*, or punishment inflicted on us—is to love, &c.

Line 108, '*Nor :*' our MS. miswrites 'Not.'

  ,, 110, '*worme*' = the Serpent. So Shakespeare uses 'worm:' 'Hast thou the pretty *worm* of Nilus?' (Antony and Cleopatra, v. 2) and frequently.

Line 123, '*this :*' our MS. 'the,' which makes it too general, while it is '*this*' particular soul that is the subject of the poem.

Line 130, '*pores :*' cf. our note on '*Abyss*' in SOUTHWELL, p. 47. Our MS. misspells 'powers.' The thought is: As the water of a spring runs into the ocean, and thence filters back through the secret ways or veins of the earth to reappear as

another spring, so this returned soul, infused into the seed,
came up with the plant through the earth's 'pores.'

Line 131, ' *The plant.*' By the description, this was a mandrake. Occasionally the roots do, I believe, present a very
grotesque resemblance to the human figure; but of much of
Donne's description may be said, with Parkinson, in Theat.
Botan. (1640), 'and therefore those idle formes of the man-
drakes and womandrakes, as they are foolishly so called, which
have been exposed to publick view, both in ours and other
lands and countries, are utterly deceitfull, being the work of
cunning knaves, onely to get mony by their forgery.' It would
seem by his 'Paradisus' that Parkinson tried to get the city
magistrates to forbid the exhibition of these indecent forgeries,
and with about the same success as in the later cases of 'Ana-
tomical Museums;' and he is reasonably wrathful on the subject.

The most established virtue of the mandrake was as a nar-
cotic, and it is said to have been used as a 'pain-killer,' as
chloroform is now, in surgical operations. It was also said to
be cooling, and locally an absorbent, and a remedy for inflamed
eyes (ll. 165-8). Legends link to it the love-charms of Circe,
and it comes up in St. Augustine and other Fathers and mediæval Preachers to 'point a moral,' if not 'adorn a tale.' Donne
works all manner of odd folk-lore into his descriptions, fresh
probably from Holland's 'Pliny,' and the like.

Line 134. The construction is, The spungy confines [being]
thronged so or thrust about by this root.

Line 137, '*fill :*' our MS. misreads ' fill'd.'

  ,,   144, 'As' dropped in our MS. inadvertently.

  ,,   150, ' *kindle :*' our MS. 'kinde,' and so too 1633. ' Kindle' was doubtless the author's word=his apples ' kindle' force
of conception, or are aphrodisiac; his leaves [having the oppos-
ing effect] kill force of conception, or are anaphrodisiac.

Lines 156-7. Whether Donne drew from some of the knave-
ries spoken of by Parkinson, we cannot tell; but the fruit is
described by the latter in his first book of the ' Paradisus' as
pale red, and in his Theat. Botan. as 'yellow as gold, and the
bignesse of a reasonable pippin.' Bartholomew also calls it
yellow.

Line 168, ' *child's :*' MS. ' cheek's :' a mistake.

  ,,   171. See this idea expanded in 2d Anniversary, l. 185
et seqq.

Line 178, '*a :*' MS. '*was.*'

,,   180, '*inclos'd :*' ib. '*encloth'd.*

Ibid. '*peck'd :*' usually '*picked*' and '*pic'd :*' reminds of the slang phrase, '*Does your mother know you're out ?*'

Line 200. This thought is freely used in the Elegies, as noted in the places.

Line 202, '*ingress*'=engross or take possession of: here= marry, a verb and sense probably peculiar to Donne.

Line 203 ='*Till now* [till they have taken laws] '*twas not unlawful, therefore* ['twas not] ill or evil.' All this is parenthetical or digressional. Then Donne returns from his digression to his '*sparrow,*' and says, '*So jolly is this body that it can move this soul* (or bear it along to sympathise with its lust); *so free* [is it] *of kindness* ['his' being used as ='its,' and '*kindness*' in a punning sense of acts of kind] that, &c.

Line 204, '*iollie.*' See Satire i. 1. 7. The two senses in which this word is used seem to have arisen from a fusing into one of two similar-sounding words—one the French *joli*, the other from the root *joy*, or from a using of the more foreign *joli* as a quasi *joy-ly.*

Line 210. Pliny records a belief that the cock-sparrow only lived a year, the hen longer. Bartholomew states, contrary to Donne, that '*the cock is very jealous of his wife, and fighteth oft for her, as Aristotle saith.*'

Line 212, '*gummie blood.*' It would seem that bird-lime was formerly extracted from holly.

Line 217. The sparrow, when eaten, was supposed from its nature to be provocative, like the roots of the mandrake, cringoes, and potatoes. Its gall was alleged to have the same effect, and its dung powdered in wine, and specially its brains and eggs.

Line 227, '*inform'd*'=gave it form.

,,   258, '*As.*' I place='*so*' in margin=in that manner, also, a usage not uncommon. Otherwise we have an intolerably long ellipse.

Line 265. Our MS. misreads '*and*' for '*or,*' and '*her*' for '*like;*' and l. 267, '*weather*' for '*water;*' and l. 279, '*And are*' for '*As are.*'

Line 266, '*limbeck*' = alembic: said to mean properly the head fitted on to a flask or other distilling vessel. Gesner's Jewell of Health, translated by Baker, fol. 23; but used by the same author and others to mean the distilling vessel generally.

Line 251. Usually 'the' for 'her,' badly; and line 275, 'the' for 'his,' badly.

Line 290. In Elizabeth's reign fish-days were enacted, not as religious fast-days, but to encourage the fish-trade and our breed of seamen.

Line 298, 'erre'=go, wander away.

„ 310, 'hullinge'=making a vessel like a (mere) hull, by taking in all or almost all sail. This is done either in calms or when a ship is lying-to in a storm.

Line 315, 'barke'=skin. Cf. sere-bark, Elegy ii., and related note.

Line 345, 'out-streat:' our ms. misreads 'ore-streat.' For the sake of the rhyme straight or straught, the past forms of stretch, is brought down to 'streat.' Therefore from the verb used, and from the verb suck, the preposition must be 'out,' not 'ore.' The sense is—nor suck those oils which [were] thence outstretched or out-drawn, or (if we take the verb not in a passive sense, but as neuter-reflective) which thence stretched [themselves] out, or exuded, or poured out. I accept 'outstreat' of the printed text.

Line 360, 'dole:' share, portion : from the verb to 'deal.' So Hall (Satires, b. iv. s. ii.), 'more than is some hungry gallant's dole.'

Line 376, 'have not:' our ms. reads 'not havinge,' but does not correct itself grammatically, as it leaves 'not enjoy,' and requires 'not enjoying.'

Line 383. Our ms. reads 'though noe had gone,' which is somewhat bewildering. The usual printed text which we have accepted is poorly expressed yet intelligible=the elephant did not seek to be intellectually or cunningly wise after the world's wisdom, and like a tyrant, great one, or statesman, but sought to be morally wise and good.

Line 385. I do not know the originator of this belief, for Pliny, and Bartholomew following him, make him able to kneel.

Line 395. 'Of all other living creatures, they [elephants] cannot abide a mouse or rat, and if they perceiue that their provender lying in the manger tast or scent never so little of them, they refuse it and will not touch it' (Holland's Pliny, book viii. c. 11). The death by a mouse comes up often elsewhere.

Line 398, 'roome'=station or state.

„ 400, 'any-whither:' our ms. misreads 'any-where.'

„ 403. I do not know where Donne got this idea. Bartholomew says, 'the wolfe whelpeth blind whelpes.'

Line 410, 'else.' American edit. misprints 'self,' and in line 437 'riding.'

Line 429, 'quick'=living. See Mr. W. Aldis Wright's Bible Word-Book, s.v.

Line 462, 'another:' our ms. reads 'the other.' The ms. at first sight seems better; but it is seen, on consideration, to limit him to two, as though he were Isaac, whereas he is speaking of such community as exists among the sparrows.

Line 465. From other writings it appears that the lovers of Elizabeth's days used to woo their mistresses with, and vaunt their feats of activity on, the vaulting horse. Sombersalts means any such feats of leaping, not summersets merely as now understood. Cf. Cotgrave. Mercury [describing Hedon, a court gallant] '... He courts ladies'with how many great horse he hath rid that morning, or how oft he hath done the whole or half the pommado [vaulting the wooden horse] in a seven-night before: and sometimes ventures so far upon the virtue of his pomander, that he dares tell 'em how many shirts he has sweat at tennis that week' (Cynthia's Revels, act ii. sc. 1).

Line 466, 'hoyting:' Richardson says, to 'hoit' is to raise, leap up or about; and, to prove it, gives the remarkable proof that under Hausser, to hoise, Cotgrave explains=that would set him on the hoight. From the two senses in which Hoydon and Hoyden are used=lumpish, clownish, and full of frolic, and from the similar significations given to Hoit in Halliwell's Arch. Dict., it may be that two words have become confounded; and this is rendered likely by Jonson's phrase (T. of a Tub, ii. 1), as compared with Heywood's and Cotgrave's. But I am inclined to deduce one sense, if not both, from hoi, the term used by swineherds. A hoydon would then be a stupid lumpish fellow, like a swineherd; and hoit might be riotous, like one who cries hoi. To be riotous suits the passage from B. and Fletcher, and suits Donne here better than 'leaping,' and agrees better with the phrase 'hoity-toity.'

Line 481, 'silly' = innocent, as shown by the succeeding words, 'that virtue.'

Line 482. There is here the common and reprehensible omission of a preposition; reprehensible, because it is required to show that the construction is inverted=an itchy warmth succeeds [to] that virtue of innocence.

Line 484, 'then :' usually ' nor.'

,, 511, '*sullen*'=unsociable. See Satire iii. line 51.

,, 515, ' And :' usually ' or.' G.

97

III.

ELEGIES.

NOTE.

'Elegy,' in its primary and restricted sense, was a song of mourning, like the nightingale's; and as such is popularly associated with deaths and funerals. There has always been a wider sense in which it has been applied to poems 'intermeddling' with any intellectual, moral, or spiritual subject, composed in the elegiac metre or distich, and sometimes irrespective of the metrical form. We have a magnificent example of such Elegy in the *Nosce teipsum* of Sir John Davies. Donne probably calls his 'Elegies' after the *Amores* of Ovid, touching as they all do, directly or inferentially, on the lights and shadows of Love.

I place these Elegies next to the Satires, because throughout they partake of their characteristics alike in subject and treatment; so much so, that I have found them in various contemporary MSS. headed Satires, with the numbers running on continuously from the usual six, and in others some of the six intermingled with them. So too are the Epistles found. On these MSS. and related topics, see our Preface (vol. i.), and Essay (vol. ii.).

I remove the 'Anatomie' from the 'Funeral Elegies' to this division, because (a) it is the avowed continuation of the earlier 'Progress of the Soul,' as pointed out in the relative note at close of its Epistle. (b) It was not really a 'funeral' elegy, but an indulgence of the 'Pleasures of Imagination' on an ideal woman, not without sarcastic and satiric castigation of the sex and the times, as in the Satires. (See extracts from one of Dr. Donne's Letters bearing on this in our Essay.) (c) It claims an early place in the volume as having been the only considerable poem published by the author himself. On the other hand, I have assigned to the 'Funeral Elegies' one usually included in the Elegies simple (explained in its place), viz. that which begins, 'Language, thou art too narrow,' &c.

An endeavour has been made to rearrange these 'Elegies,' so as to give more homogeneity to them. I put in the place of honour the finest of them all—and it is supremely fine—that magnanimous and pathetic celebration of his farewell to his young wife when refusing her passionate appeal to be allowed to accompany him in the guise of a page; a poem that has justly won the high praise of all capable critics from the time of its publication to Coleridge and Dean Milman.

One of these Elegies I should willingly have left unprinted. It is sensual and abominable; but on consulting with literary friends, I found the judgment unanimous that an expurgated edition of Donne would be of no value to students of our Literature and Manners; and I have, though reluctantly, acquiesced, keeping in mind that my limited number of copies and non-publication secures that the book will find its way only to those who turn to it for literary ends. The remark applies to others and occasional lines—on all which, and above critical opinions, I speak farther in my already-named Essay.

Full information on the source of each Elegy will be found in the Notes and Illustrations appended in their successive places. One that has been claimed for Ben Jonson ('The Expostulation') I show in related note to belong to Donne, notwithstanding its appearance in that most uncritical *posthumous* collection of the 'Underwoods.' G.

FUNERAL ELEGIES.

I.

1. AN ANATOMIE OF THE WORLD:
2. OF THE PROGRESSE OF THE SOVLE:

In Commemoration of Mrs. Elizadeth Drury.

NOTE.

The earliest known edition of the 'Anatomie' bears the date of 1611, and it consists of only 'The First Anniversary.' Two copies have come down, one preserved in the Bridgewater Library, and another in the peerless Library of the Rev. Thomas Corser, M.A., Stand Rectory, Manchester. I give a description of it (*penes me*) from Dr. Kingsley of Bridgewater House : 'An Anatomy of the World. Wherein by occasion of the untimely death of Mistris Elizabeth Drury, the frailty and the Decay of this whole world is represented. London: Printed for Samuel Macham, and are to be solde at his shop in Paules Churchyard, at the Signe of the Bulhead, An. Dom. 1611.' 8vo, 16 leaves.

In 1612 both parts were issued with separate title-pages, as follows :

The First Anniuersarie.

AN) ·

ANATOMIE
of the World.

Wherein,
By Occasion Of
the vntimely death of Mistris
ELIZABETH DRVRY,
the frailtie and the decay of
this whole World is
represented.

[Printer's device]

LONDON,
Printed by *M. Bradwood* for *S. Macham*, and are
to be sold at his shop in Pauls Church-yard at the
signe of the Bull-head. 1612.

[Collation: Title-page (as above), To the praise of the dead, &c. pp. 6 [unpaged] and pp. 54; 'A Fvnerall Elegie,' occupying pp. 45-54, and two blank pages with head and margin lines.]

The Second Anniuersarie.

OF

THE PROGRES

of the Soule.

Wherein:

By Occasion Of The
Religious Death of Mistris

ELIZABETH DRVRY,

the incommodities of the Soule
in this life and her exaltation in
the next are Contemp-
plated.

LONDON,

Printed by *M. Bradwood* for *S. Macham*, and are
to be sould at his shop in Pauls Church-yard at
the signe of the Bull-head.

1612.

[Collation: Title-page (as above), The Harbinger to the Progress, pp. 5 (reverse blank; unpaged) and pp. 49, with three pages blank, and head and margin lines.]

Another edition of the complete Poem was published in 1621 with separate title-pages (as before) identical with the former, but 'Printed by *A. Mathewes* for *Tho. Dewe*, and are to be sold at his shop in Saint Dunstons Church-yard in Fleetestreete, 1621:' same number of pages in each. The last recorded separate edition appeared in 1625, again identical with the preceding; but 'Printed by *W. Stansby* for *Tho. Dewe*, and are to be sold in S. Dunstanes Church-yard, 1625.' These are all neat, quaint little volumes (18mo), and are excessively rare.

Our text is that of 1625, as being the last issued during the Author's lifetime; but the result of an anxious collation of all the printed editions and mss. shows variations to be mostly mere differences in orthography; but see our Notes and Illustrations at close.

It will be noticed that the name of Donne nowhere appears in the four editions enumerated; but it immediately became known that he was the author of the 'Anatomie.' A hitherto overlooked evidence of this I have discovered in John Davies of Hereford's 'The Muse's Sacrifice,' published in 1612, that is in the same year with the first edition of the completed poem. In 'A Funeral Elegie on the death of the most virtuous and no lesse louely Mrs. Elizabeth Dutton, eldest daughter of the worthy and generally beloued Sir Thomas Egerton, . . . 1611,' we read as follows :

> ' I must confesse a priest of Phebus, late
> Vpon like text so well did meditate,
> That with a sinlesse enuy I doe runne
> In his Soule's Progresse, till it all be DONNE.
> But, he hath got the start in setting forth
> Before me, in the trauell of that worth :
> And me out-gone in knowledge eu'ry way
> Of the Soule's Progresse to her finall stay.—
> But his sweet Saint did vsher mine therein ;—
> Most blest in that—so, he must needs beginne ;
> And read vpon the rude Anatomy
> Of this dead World ; that now, doth putrifie.
> Yet greater will to this great enterprize—
> Which in great matters nobly doth suffice—
> He cannot bring than I ; nor can—much lesse—
> Renowne more worth than is a Worthinesse !
> Such were they both ; for such a worthy Paire—
> Of louely vertuous maides, as good as faire—
> Selfe-Worthiness can scarse produce, sith they ;
> Liu'd like celestiall spirits, immur'd in clay !
> And if all-powerfull Loue can all performe,
> That in it hath rare matter, or like forme,
> Then should my lines haue both so accomplishèd,
> As from the graue to Heau'n shudd draw the dead ;
> Or, will her taper-pointed-beaming name,
> Naile her to Heau'n, and in Heau'n clench the same.'
> (pp. 117-118.)

These lines, rough and obscure in parts, are yet of rare interest in relation to our Worthy as ' a priest of Phebus.' I am not aware that they have ever been noticed before.

Of ' Mrs. Elizabeth Drury' and these poems, see more in our Essay prefixed to vol. ii.   G.

ANATOMIE OF THE WORLD.

TO THE PRAISE OF THE DEAD, AND THE ANATOMY.

WELL dy'de the World, that we might liue to see
This world of wit, in his Anatomie :
No euill wants his good ; so wilder heyres
Bedew their fathers' toombs with forcèd teares,
Whose state requites their losse: whiles thus we gaine, 5
Well may we walke in blacks, but not complaine.
Yet how can I consent the world is dead,
While this Muse liues? which in his spirit's stead
Seemes to informe a World, and bids it bee,
In spight of losse, or fraile mortalitee?   10
And thou the subiect of this wel-borne thought,
Thrise-noble maid, could'st not haue found nor sought
A fitter time to yeeld to thy sad fate,
Then whiles this spirit liues ; that can relate   than
Thy worth so well to our last nephews' eyne,   15
That they shall wonder both at his, and thine :
Admirèd match ! whore striues in mutuall grace
The cunning pencill and the comely face !
A taske, which thy faire goodnesse made too much
For the bold pride of vulgar pens to tuch :   20

Enough is us to praise them that praise thee,
And say that but enough those praises bee,
Which, had'st thou liu'd, had hid their fearefull head
From the 'angry checkings of thy modest red :
Death bars reward and shame ; when enuy's gone   25
And gaine ; 'tis safe to giue the dead their owne.
As then the wise Egyptians wont to lay
More on their tombes then houses ;—these of clay,   than
But those of brasse or marble were ;—so wee
Giue more unto thy ghost then unto thee.   than   30
Yet what wee giue to thee, thou gauest to us,
And maie'st but thanke thyselfe for being thus :
Yet what thou gau'st and wert, O, happy maid,
Thy grace profest all due, where 'tis repayd.
So these high songs, that to thee suited bine,   35
Serve but to sound thy Maker's praise in thine ;
Which thy deare soule as sweetly sings to Him
Amid the quire of saints and seraphim,
As any angel's tongue can sing of thee ;
The subjects differ, tho the skill agree :   40
For as by infant yeares men iudge of age,
Thy early loue, thy vertues did presage
What hie part thou bear'st in those best of songs,
Whereto no burden, nor no end belongs.
Sing on, thou virgin soule, whose lossefull gaine   45
Thy loue-sicke parents haue bewail'd in vaine ;
Ne'er may thy name be in our songs forgot,
Till we shall sing thy ditty and thy note.

AN ANATOMIE OF THE WORLD.

THE FIRST ANNIVERSARIE.

WHEN that rich soule which to her heauen is gone
Whom all doe celebrate, who know they 'haue one,—
For who is sure he hath a soule, vnlesse
It see, and iudge, and follow worthinesse,
And by deedes praise it; hee who doth not this,   5
May lodge an inmate soule, but 'tis not his,—
When that queene ended here her progresse-time,
And, as t' her standing-house, to heauen did clymbe,
Where, loath to make the saints attend her long,
Shee's now a part both of the quire and song.   10
This world, in that great earthquake languishèd;
For in a common bath of teares it bled,
Which drew the strongest vitall spirits out,
But succour'd them with a perplexèd doubt,
Whether the world did loose, or gaine in this;—   15
Because since now no other way there is
But goodnesse, to see her, whom all would see,
All must endenour to bee good as shee.—
This great consumption to a feuer turnd,
And so the world had fits; it ioy'd, it mournd;   20
And, as men thinke, that agues physicke are,
And th' ague being spent, giue ouer care,

The entric into the worke.

So thou, sicke World, mistak'st thy selfe to bee
Well, when alas, thou 'art in a letargee.   lethargy
Her death did wound and tame thee than, and than then
Thou mightst haue better spar'd the sunne or man; 26
That wound was deepe, but 'tis more misery,
That thou hast lost thy sense and memory :
'Twas heauy then to heare thy voice of mone,
But this is worse, that thou art speechlesse growne. 30
Thou hast forgot thy name thou hadst ; thou wast
Nothing but she, and her thou hast o'repast.
For as a child kept from the fount, vntill
A prince, expected long, come to fulfill
The ceremonies, thou vnnam'd hadst laid,   35
Had not her comming, thee her palace made :
Her name defin'd thee, gaue thee forme and frame,
And thou forgetst to celebrate thy name.
Some moneths shee hath bene dead—but being dead,
Measures of times are all determinèd—   40
But long shee 'ath beene away, long, long : yet none
Offers to teil vs, who it is that's gone ;
But as in states doubtfull of future heyres,
When sicknesse without remedy empayres
The present prince, they're loth it should be said, 45
The prince doth languish, or the prince is dead,
So mankind, feeling now a generall thaw,
A strong example gone, equall to law,
The cyment, which did faithfully compact
And glue all vertues, now resolu'd and slack'd,   50

Thought it some blasphemy to say sh' was dead,
Or that our weaknesse was discouerèd
In that confession; therefore spoke no more
Then tongues, the soule being gone, the losse deplore.
But, though it be too late to succour thee,   55
Sicke World, yea, dead, yea, putrified, since shee,
Thy 'ntrinsicque balme and thy preseruatiue,
Can neuer be renew'd, thou neuer liue;
I—since no man can make thee liue—will trie
What we may gaine by thy Anatomy.   60

    Her death hath taught vs dearely, that thou art
Corrupt and mortall in thy purest part.
Let no man say, the World it selfe being dead,
'Tis labour lost to haue discouerèd
The World's infirmities, since there is none   65
Aliue to study this dissectione:
For there's a kind of world remaining still.   What life
                                                                              the world
Though shee which did inanimate and fill   hath still.
The world, be gone, yet in this last long night
Her ghost doth walke; that is, a glimmering light, 70
A faint weake loue of vertue, and of good
Reflects from her on them which vnderstood
Her worth; and though she haue shut in all day,
The twilight of her memory doth stay,
Which from the carcasse of the old world, free,   75
Creates a new world; and new creatures bee

Produc'd : the matter and the stuffe of this,
Her vertue,—and the forme, our practise is.
And though to be thus clemented, arme
These creatures, from hom-borne intrinsique harme—
For all assum'd vnto this dignitee,   81
So many weedlesse paradises bee,
Which of themselues produce no venemous sinne,
Except some forraine serpent bring it in—
Yet, because outward stormes the strongest breake, 85
And strength it selfe by confidence growes weake,
This new world may be safer, being told

The sick- The dangers and diseases of the old;
nes of the
World. For with due temper men doe then forgoe
Or couet things, when they their true worth know. 90

Impossi- There is no health ; physitians say that wee
bilitie of
health. At best enioy but a neutralitee ;
And can there be worse sicknes then to know, than
That we are neuer well, nor can be so?
Wee are borne ruinous : poore mothers cry,   95
That children come not right, nor orderly,
Except they headlong come, and fall vpon
An ominous precipitation.
How witty's ruine ! how importunate
Vpon mankinde ! it labour'd to frustrate   100
Euen God's purpose, and made woman, sent
For man's reliefe, cause of his languishment ;
They were to good ends, and they are so still,
But accessorie, and principall in ill ;

For that first marriage was our funerall ;   105
One woman at one blow then kild vs all ;
And singly, one by one they kill vs now.
Wee doe delightfully ourselues allow
To that consumption ; and profusely blinde,
We kill ourselues to propogate our kinde.   110
And yet we doe not that ; we are not men :
There is not now that mankinde, which was then,
Whenas the sun, and man, did seeme to striue—   Shortnesse of life.
Joynt-tenants of the world—who should suruive ;
When stag and rauen, and the long-liu'd tree,   115
Compar'd with man, dy'de in minoritee ;
When, if a slow-pac'd starre had stolne away
From the obseruer's marking, he might stay
Two or three hundred yeeres to see't againe,
And then make vp his obseruation plaine ;   120
When, as the age was long, the sise was great ;
Man's grouth confess'd and recompenced the meat,
So spacious and large, that euery soule
Did a faire kingdome and large realme controule ;
And when the very stature thus erect   125
Did that soule a good way towards heauen direct ;
Where is this mankind now ? who liues to age,
Fit to be made Methusalem, his page ?
Alas ! we scarse liue long enough to trie
Whether a true-made clocke run right, or lie.   130
Old gransires talke of yesterday with sorrow,
And for our children we reserue to-morrow.

So short is life, that euery peasant striues,
In a torne house, or field, to haue three liues.
And, as in lasting, so in length, is man   135
Contracted to an inch, who was a span ;

Smalnesse
of stature.

For had a man at first in forrests stray'd
Or shipwrack'd in the Sea, one would haue laid
A wager, that an elephant or whale.
That met him, would not hastily assaile   140
A thing so equall to him ; now alasse !
The fayries and the pigmies well may passe
As credible ; mankinde decayes so soone,
We're scarse our fathers' shadowes cast at noone :
Onely death ads t' our length ; nor are we growne adds
In stature to be men, till wee are none.   146
But this were light, did our lesse volume hold
All the old text ; or had we chang'd to gold
Their siluer, or dispos'd into lesse glas
Spirits of vertue, which then scattred was :   150
But 'tis not so : we're not retir'd but dampte !
And, as our bodies, so our mindes are crampte :
'Tis shrinking, not close weaving, that hath thus
In minde and bodie both bedwarfèd vs.
We seeme ambitious God's whole worke t' vndoe ; 155
Of nothing He made vs, and wee striue too,
To bring ourselues to nothing backe ; and we
Do what we can to do't so soone as He :
With new diseases on ourselues we warre,
And with new physicke, a worse engin farre.   160

Thus Man, this world's vice-emperour, in whom
All faculties, all graces are at home,—
And if in other creatures they appeare,
They're but man's ministers and legats there,
To worke on their rebellions, and reduce 165
Them to ciuility and to man's vse ;—
This man, whom God did woo, and loth t' attend
Till man came vp, did downe to man descend ;
This man, so great, that all that is, is his,
Oh what a trifle, and poore thing he is ! 170
If man were any thing, he's nothing now ;
Helpe, or at least some time to wast, allow
T' his other wants, yet when he did depart,
With her whom we lament, hee lost his heart.
She, of whom th' Ancients seem'd to prophesie, 175
When they call'd vertues by the name of Shee ;
She, in whom vertue was so much refin'd,
That for allay vnto so pure a minde alloy
Shee took the weaker sex ; shee, that could driue
The poysonous tincture and the stayne of Eue 180
Out of her thoughts and deedes, and purifie
All, by a true religious alchimy ;
Shee, shee is dead, shee's dead : when thou knowest this,
Thou knowest how poore a trifling thing man is,
And learn'st thus much by our Anatomee, 185
The heart being perish'd, no part can be free,
And that except thou feede—not banquet—on
The supernaturall foode, Religion,

Thy better growth growes whithèrèd and scant ;
Bee more than man, or thou'rt lesse than an ant.   190

Then, as mankinde, so is the world's whole frame
Quite out of ioynt, almost created lame :
For, before God had made vp all the rest,
Corruption entred and deprau'd the best ;
It seis'd the angels, and then first of all   195
The world did in her cradle take a fall,
And turn'd her brains, and tooke a generall maime,
Wronging each joynt of th' vniversall frame.

Decay of
nature in
other
parts. The noblest part, man, felt it first ; and than   then
Both beasts and plants, curst in the curse of man ; 200
So did the world from the first houre decay,
That euening was beginning of the day ;
And now the Springs and Sommers which we see,
Like sonnes of women after fiftie bee.
And new philosophy calls all in doubt,   205
The element of fire is quite put out ;
The sunne is lost, and th' Earth ; and no man's wit
Can well direct him where to looke for it.
And freely men confesse that this world's spent,
When in the planets and the firmament   210
They seeke so many new ; they see that this
Is crumbled out againe to his atomis.
'Tis all in pieces, all cohærence gone,
All iust supply, and all relation :

Prince, subject, father, sonne, are things forgot,   215
For euery man alone thinkes he hath got
To be a phœnix, and that there can be
None of that kinde, of which he is, but he.
This is the world's condition now, and now
She, that should all parts to reunion bow ;   220
She, that had all magnetique force alone
To draw and fasten sundred parts in one ;
She, whom wise nature had inuented. then,
When she obseru'd that euery sort of men
Did in their voyage in this world's Sea stray,   225
And needed a new compasse for their way ;
Shee that was best and first originall
Of all faire copies, and the generall
Steward to Fate ; she, whose rich eyes and brest
Guilt the West-Indies, and perfum'd the East ;   230
Whose hauing breath'd in this world, did bestow
Spice on those Iles, and bade them still smell so ;
And that rich Indie which doth gold interre,
Is but as single money coyn'd from her ;
She, to whom this world must it self refer,   235
As suburbs, or the microcosme of her ;
Shee, shee is dead, shee's dead : when thou knowest this,
Thou knowest how lame a cripple this world is,
And learn'st thus much by our Anatomy,
That this world's generall sicknesse doth not lie   240
In any humour, or one certaine part,
But as thou sawest it rotten at the heart,

Thou seest a hectique feuer hath got hold
Of the whole substance, not to be contrould ;
And that thou hast but one way not t' admit   245
The world's infection,—to be none of it.

For the world's subtilst immateriall parts
Feele this consuming wound, and Age's darts.
For the world's beauty is decay'd or gone,
Beauty, that's colour and proportion.   250
We thinke the heauens enioy their sphericall,
Their round proportion embracing all,
But yet their various and perplexèd course,
Obseru'd in diuerse ages, doth enforce
Men to finde out so many eccentrique parts,   255
Such diuers downe-right lines, such ouerthwarts,
As disproportion that pure forme ; it teares
The firmament in eight-and-forty sheeres,
And in these constillations then arise   constellations
New starres, and olde do vanish from our eyes ;   260
As though heau'n suffered earthquakes, peace or war,
When new towers rise, and old demolish't are.
They haue impayld within a Zodiake
The free-borne sun, and keep twelue signes awake
To watch his steppes ; the Goat and Crabbe controule
And fright him backe, who els to either pole—   266
Did not these Tropiques fetter him—might runne ;
For his course is not round ; nor can the sunne

Disforui-
ity of
parts.

Perfit a circle, or maintaine his way   perfect
·One inche direct; but where he rose to day   270
He comes no more, but with a cousening line,
Steales by that point, and so is serpentine,
And seeming wearie with his reeling thus,
He meanes to sleepe, being now falne nearer vs.
So, of the starres, which boast that they doe runne   275
In circle still, none ends where he begunne :
All their proportion's lame, it sinckes, it swels ;
For of meridians and parallels,
Man hath weaued out a net, and this net throwne
Vpon the Heauens ; and now they are his owne.   280
Loth to goe vp the hill, or labour thus
To goe to heauen, we make heauen come to vs ;
We spur, we raigne the starres, and in their race   rein
They're diuersly content t' obey our peace.   pace
But keepes the Earth her round proportion still?   285
Doth not a Tenarif, or higher hill
Rise so high like a rocke, that one might thinke
The floating moone would shipwracke there, and sinke
Seas are so deepe, that whales being strooke to-day,
Perchance to-morrow scarse at middle way   290
Of their wish'd iourney's ende, the bottom, dye :
And men, to sound depths, so much line vntie,
As one might iustly thinke that there would rise
At end thereof one of th' Antipodies :
If vnder all, a vault infernall bee—   295
Which sure is spacious, except that we

Inuent another torment, that there must
Millions into a strait hot roome be thrust—
Then solidnesse and roundnesse haue no place :
Are these but warts and pockholes in the face   300
Of th' earth? Thinke so ; but yet confesse, in this
The world's proportion disfigured is ;
That those two legges whereon it doth rely,
Reward and punishment, are bent awry :
And, oh ! it can no more be questionèd,   305
That beautie's best proportion, is dead,
Since euen Griefe it selfe, which now alone
Is left vs, is without proportion.
She, by whose lines proportion should beè
Examin'd, measure of all symmetree,   310
Whom had that Ancient seene, who thought soules made
Of harmony, hee would at next haue said
That harmony was shee, and thence infer
That soules were but resultances from her,
And did from her into our bodies goe,   315
As to our eyes the formes from obiects flow ;
Shee, who, if those great doctors truely said
That the arke to man's proportion was made.
Had been a type for that, as that might be
A type of her in this, that contrary   320
Both elements and passions liu'd at peace
In her, who caus'd all ciuill war to cease ;
Shee, after whom what forme soe're we see,
Is discord and rude incongruitee ;

Disorder
in the
world.

Shee, shee is dead, shee's dead; when thou knowest this,
Thou knowest how vgly a monster this world is; 326
And learnst thus much by our Anatomee,
That here is nothing to enamour thee ;
And that not onely faults in inward parts,
Corruptions in our braines, or in our hearts, 330
Poysoning the fountaines, whence our actions spring,
Endanger vs ; but that if euery thing
Be not done fitly 'nd in proportion,
To satisfie wise and good lookers on—
Since most men be such as most thinke they bee—
They're lothsome too, by this deformitee. 336
For good and well must in our actions meete ;
Wicked is.not much worse then indiscreet.   than

But beautie's other second element,
Colour, and lustre now, is as neere spent ; 340
And had the world his iust proportion,
Were it a ring still, yet the stone is gone ;
As a compassionate turcuoyse which doth tell,
By looking pale, the wearer is not well,
As gold falls sicke, being stung with mercury, 345
All the world's parts of such complexion bee.
When nature was most busie, the first weeke,
Swadling the new-borne Earth, God seemd to like
That she should sport her selfe sometimes, and play,
To mingle and vary colours euery day ; 350

And then, as though shee could not make inow,
Himselfe His various rainbow did allow.
Sight is the noblest sense of any one,
Yet sight hath onely colour to feede on,
And colour is decayd; Summer's robe growes   . 355
Duskie, and like an oft-dyed garment showes.
Our blushing redde, which vs'd in cheekes to spred,
Is inward sunke, and onely our soules are red.
Perchance the world might haue recouerèd,
If shee, whom we lament, had not beene dead ;   360
But shee, in whom all white, and red, and blew— blue
Beautie's ingredients—voluntary grew,
As in an vnuext Paradise ; from whom
Did all things' verdure and their lustre come ;
Whose composition was miraculous,   365
Being all colour, all diaphanous—
For ayre and fire but thicke grosse bodies were,
And liueliest stones but drowsie and pale to her—
Shee, shee is dead, shee's dead: when thou knowst this,
Thou knowest how wan a ghost this our world is ; 370
And learnst thus much by our Anatomee,
That it should more affright then pleasure thee ; than
And that, since all faire colour then did sinke,
'Tis now·but wicked vanitie to thinke
To colour vitious deeds with good pretence,   375
Or with bought colors to illude men's sense.

Nor in ought more this world's decay appeares,   Weaknesse
Then that her influence the heau'n forbeares,   than   want of
Or that the elements doe not feele this.   dence of
The father or the mother barren is :   380 and earth.
The cloudes conceive not raine, or doe not powre,
In the due birth-time, downe the balmy showre ;
Th' ayre doth not motherly sit on the Earth,
To hatch her seasons, and giue all things birth ;
Spring-times were common cradles, but are toombes ;
And false conceptions fill the generall wombes ;   386
Th' ayre showes such meteors, as none can see
Not onely what they meane, but what they bee :
Earth such new wormes, as would haue troubled much
Th' Egyptian Mages to haue made more such.   Magi
What artist now dares boast that he can bring   391
Heauen hither, or constellate any thing,
So as the influence of those starres may bee
Imprisoned in an hearbe, or charme, or tree,
And doe by touch all which those starres could doe ?
The art is lost, and correspondence too ;   396
For heauen giues little, and the Earth takes lesse,
And man least knowes their trade and purposes.
If this commerce 'twixt heauen and Earth were not
Embarr'd, and all this traffique quite forgot,   400
Shee, for whose losse wee haue lamented thus,
Would worke more fully and pow'rfully on vs ;
Since herbs, and roots by dying, lose not all,
But they, yea ashes too, are medicinall,

Death could not quench her vertue so, but that   405
It would be—if not follow'd—wondred at,
And all the world would bee one dying swan,
To sing her funerall praise, and vanish than.   *then*
But as some serpents' poison hurteth not,
Except it be from the liue serpent shot,   410
So doth her vertue need her here, to fit
That unto vs ; she working more then it.   *than*
But she, in whom to such maturity
Vertue was grown past grouth, that it must die ;
She, from whose influence all impression came,   415
But by recciuer's impotencies, lame ;
Who, though she could not transubstantiate
All states to gold, yet guilded euery state,
So that some princes haue, some temperance,
Some counsellors some purpose to aduauce   420
The common profite ; and some people haue
Some stay, no more then kings should giue, to craue;   *than*
Some women haue some taciturnity,
Some nunneries, some graines of chastity,—
She, that did thus much, and much more could do,   425
But that our age was iron, and rusty too ;
Shee, shee is dead, shee's dead; when thou knowest this,
Thou knowest how drie a cinder this world is,
And learnst thus much by our Anatomic,
That 'tis in vaine to dew or mollifie   ·   430
It with thy teares, or sweat, or blood : no thing
Is worth our trauaile, griefe, or perishing,

But those rich ioyes, which did possesse her heart,
Of which shee's now partaker, and a part.

But, as in cutting vp a man that's dead, 435 Conclu-
The body will not last out, to haue read   sion.
On euery part, and therefore men direct
Their speech to parts, that are of most effect;
So the world's carkasse would not last, if I
Were punctuall in this Anatomy; 440
Nor smels it well to hearers, if one tell
Them their disease, who faine would thinke they're well.
Here therefore be the end; and, blessed maid,
Of whom is meant what euer hath beene said,
Or shall be spoken well by any tongue, 445
Whose name refines course lines, and makes prose song;
Accept this tribute, and his first yeeres rent, [coarse
Who, till his darke short taper's end be spent,
As oft as thy feast sees this widowed earth,
Will yeerely celebrate thy second birth, 450
That is, thy death; for though the soule of man
Be got when man is made, 'tis borne but than, then
When man doth die. Our bodi's as the wombe,
And, as a midwife, Death directs it home;
And you her creatures, whom she workes vpon, 455
And haue your last and best concoction
From her example and her vertue, if you
In reuerence to her doe thinke it due,

That no one should her prayses thus rehearse,
As matter fit for Chronicle, not verse;   460
Vouchsafe to call to minde that God did make
A last, and lastingst piece, a song.   He spake
To Moses to deliuer vnto all
That song; because He knew they would let fall
The Law, the Prophets, and the Historie,   465
But keepe the song still in their memory :
Such an opinion—in due measure—made
Me this great office boldly to inuade ;
Nor could incomprehensiblenesse deterre
Me from thus trying to emprison her ;   470
Which when I saw that a strict graue could doe,
I saw not why verse might not doe so too.
Verse hath a middle nature ; heauen keepes soules,
The graue keeps bodies, verse the fame enroules.

A FVNERALL ELEGIE.

'Tis lost, to trust a toombe with such a ghest,
Or to confine her in a marble chest ;
Alas, what's marble, jeat, or porphirie,
Priz'd with the chrysolite of either eye,
Or with those pearles and rubies which shee was !   5
Ioyne the two Indies in one tombe, 'tis glas—
And so is all—to her materials,
Though euery inche were ten Escurials ;

Yet shee's demolished; can we keepe her then
In workes of hands, or of the wits of men?   10
Can these memorials, ragges of paper, giue
Life to that name, by which name they must liue?
Sickly, alas, short-liu'd, aborted bee
Those carkas verses, whose soule is not shee;
And can shee, who no longer would bee shee,   15
Being such a tabernacle, stoope to bee
In paper wrapt; or, when shee would not lie
In such an house, dwell in an elegie?
But 'tis no matter; we may well allow
Verse to liue so long as the world will now,   20
For her death wounded it. The world containes
Princes for armes, and counseilers for braines,
Lawyers for tongues, diuines for hearts—and more,
The rich for stomachs, and for backes the poore;
The officers for hands, merchants for feet,   25
By which remote and distant countries meet;
But those fine spirits, which doe tune and set
This organ, are those peeces which beget
Wonder and loue; and these were she; and she
Being spent, the world must needs decrepit bee: 30 *Smalnesse of stature.*
For since death will proceed to triumph still,
He can finde nothing, after her, to kill,
Except the world it selfe, so great as shee.
Thus braue and confident may Nature bee;
Death cannot giue her such another blow,   35
Because shee cannot such another show.

But must we say shee's dead? may't not be said,
That as a sundred clocke is peecemeale laid,
Not to bee lost, but by the maker's hand
Repolish'd without errour then to stand,   40
Or, as the Affrique Niger streame enwombs
It selfe into the earth, and after comes—
Hauing first made a naturall bridge, to passe
For many leagues—farre greater then it was,   than
May't not be said, that her graue shall restore   45
Her greater, purer, firmer then before?   than
Heauen may say this, and ioy in't; but can wee,
Who liue, and lacke her, here this 'vantage see?
What is't to vs, alas, if there haue been
An Angell made a Throne or Cherubin?   50
We lose by't; and, as agèd men are glad,
Being tasteless growne, to ioy in ioyes they had,
So now the sicke-staru'd world must feed vpon
This ioy, that we had her, who now is gone.
Reioyce then, Nature and this world, that you—   55
Fearing the last fires hastning to subdue
Your force and vigor—ere it were neere gone,
Wisely bestow'd and laid it all on one;
One, whose cleare body was so pure and thin,
Because it need disguise no thought within,   60
'Twas but a through-light scarfe, her mind t' enroule,
Or exhalation breath'd out from her soule;
One, whom all men, who durst no more, admir'd,
And whom, whoere had worth enough, desir'd;   whoe'er

As, when a temple's built, saints emulate   65
To which of them it shall be consecrate.
But as when heauen lookes on vs with new eyes,
Those new starres euery artist exercise ;
What place they should assigne to them, they doubt,
Argue, and agree not, till those starres go out ;   70
So the world studied whose this peece should be,
Till she can be no bodie's else, nor shee :
But like a lampe of balsamum, desir'd
Rather t' adorne then last, shee soone expird,   than
Cloth'd in her virgin-white integritie ;   75
For marriage, though it doe not stain, doth dye.
To 'scape th' infirmities which waite vpon
Woman, shee went away before sh' was one ;
And the world's busie noise to ouercome,
Tooke so much death as seru'd for opium ;   80
For though she could not, nor could chuse to die,
Shee 'ath yeelded to too long an exstasie.
He which, not knowing her said history,   sad
Should come to reade the booke of destinie,
How faire and chast, humble and high shee 'ad been, 85
Much promis'd, much perform'd, at not fifteene,
And measuring future things by things before,
Should turne the leafe to read, and read no more,
Would thinke that either Destinie mistooke,
Or that some leaues were torne out of the Booke ;   90
But 'tis not so : Fate did but vsher her
To yeares of reason's vse, and then infer

Her destinie to her selfe ; which libertie
Shee tooke, but for thus much, thus much to die ;
Her modestie not suffering her to bee   95
Fellow-commissioner with Destinee,
She did no more but die : if after her
Any shall liue, which dare true good prefer,
Euery such person is her deligate,
T' accomplish that which should haue beene her fate. 100
They shall make vp that Booke, and shall haue thankes
Of Fate and her, for filling vp their blankes.
For future vertuous deeds are legacies,
Which from the gift of her example rise ;
And 'tis in heau'n part of spirituall mirth,   105
To see how well the good play her, on earth.

FINIS.

OF THE PROGRESS OF THE SOUL.

THE HARBINGER TO THE PROGRESSE.

Two soules moue here, and mine—a third—must moue
Paces of admiration, and of loue.
Thy soule, deare virgin, whose this tribute is,
Mou'd from this mortall sphere to liuely blisse ;
And yet moues still, and still aspires to see   5
The world's last day, thy glorie's full degree ;
Like as those starrs, which thou orelookest farre,
Are in their place, and yet still mouèd are :
No soule—whiles with the luggage of this clay
It cloggèd is—can follow thee halfe way,   10
Or see thy flight, which doth our thoughts outgoe
So fast, as now the lightning moues but slow.
But now thou art as high in heauen flowne,
As heaun's from vs ; what soule besides thine owne
Can tell thy ioyes, or say, he can relate   15
Thy glorious iournals in that blessed state ?
I enuie thee, rich soule, I enuy thee,
Although I cannot yet thy glorie see :
And thou, Great spirit, which her's follow'd hast
So fast, as none can follow thine so fast,   20

So far, as none can follow thine so farre—
And if this flesh did not the passage barre,
Hadst caught her—let me wonder at thy flight,
Which long agone had'st lost the vulgar sight,
And now mak'st proud the better eyes, that thay   they
Can see thee less'ned in thine aery way.   26
So while thou makst her soule by progresse knowne,
Thou makst a noble progresse of thine owne;
From this world's carkasse hauing mounted hie
To that pure life of immortalitie ;   30
Since, thine aspiring thoughts themselues so raise,
That more may not beseeme a creature's praise ;
Yet still thou vow'st her more, and euery yeare
Mak'st a new progresse, while thou wandrest here.
Still vpward mount ; and let thy Maker's praise   ·35
Honor thy Laura, and adorne thy laies :
And since thy Muse her head in heauen shrouds,
Oh, let her neuer stoope below the clouds !
And if those glorious sainted soules may know
Or what we doe, or what wee sing below,   40
Those acts, those songs shall still content them best,
Which praise those awfull Powers, that make them
        blest.

THE SECOND ANNIVERSARIE.

NOTHING could make me sooner to confesse,
That this world had an euerlastingnesse,   *The en-
trance.*
Then to consider that a yeare is runne,   *than*
Since both this lower world's and the sunne's sunne,
The lustre and the vigor of this All,   5
Did set; 'twere blasphemic to say, did fall.
But, as a ship which hath strooke sailes, doth runne
By force of that force which before, it wonne;
Or as sometimes in a beheaded man,
Though at those two Red Seas, which freely runne, 10
One from the trunke, another from the head,
His soule be saild to her eternall bed,
His eyes will twincke, and his tongue will roll, *twinkle*
As though he beckned and cal'd backe his soule,
He graspes his hands, and he puls vp his feet, 15
And seemes to reach, and to step forth to meet
His soule; when all these motions which we saw,
Are but as ice, which crackles at a thaw;
Or as a lute, which in moist weather, rings
Her knell alone, by cracking of her strings; 20
So struggles this dead world, now shee is gone:
For there is motion in corruption.
As some daies are, at the creation nam'd,
Before the sunne, the which fram'd daies, was fram'd,

So after this sunne's set some show appeares,   25
And orderly vicisitude of yeares.
Yet a new deluge, and of Lethe flood,
Hath drown'd vs all; all haue forgot all good,
Forgetting her, the maine reserue of all;
Yet in this deluge, grosse and generall,   30
Thou seest me striue for life; my life shall bee
To bee hereafter prais'd for praysing thee,
Immortall mayd, who though thou would'st refuse
The name of mother, be vnto my Muse
A father, since her chast ambition is   35
Yearely to bring forth such a child as this.
These hymes may worke on future wits, and so
May great grand-children of thy prayses grow,
And so, though not reuiue, embalme and spice
The world, which else would putrefie with vice.   40
For thus, man may extend thy progeny,
Vntill man doe but vanish, and not die:
These hymns thy issue may encrease so long
As till God's great 'Venite' change the song.

A just esti-
mation of
this world. Thirst for that time, O my insatiate soule,   45
And serue thy thirst with God's safe-sealing bowle.
Bee thirsty still, and drinke still, till thou goe
To th' onely health; to be hydroptique so,
Forget this rotten world, and vnto thee
Let thine owne times as an olde storie be;   50
Be not concern'd, studie not why, nor whan,   when
Doe not so much as not beleeve a man;

For though to erre be worst, to try truths forth
Is far more busines then this world is worth.   than

The world is but a carkasse ; thou art fed   55
By it, but as a worme that carkasse bred ;
And why should'st thou, poore worme, consider more
When this world will grow better then before,   than
Then those thy fellow-wormes doe thinke vpone
That carkasse's last resurrectione ?   60
Forget this world and scarse thinke of it so
As of old cloaths cast off a yeere agoe.
To be thus stupid is alacritie ;
Men thus lethargique haue best memory.
Looke vpward, that's towards her, whose happy state   65
We now lament not, but congratulate.
Shee, to whom all this world, twas but a stage
Where all sat harkning how her youthfull age
Should be emploid, because in all shee did
Some figure of the golden times was hid ;   70
Who could not lacke whatere this world could giue,
Because shee was the forme that made it liue ;
Nor could complaine that this world was vnfit
To bee staid in, then, when shee was in it ;
Shee, that first tried indifferent desires   75
By vertue, and vertue by religious fires ;
Shee, to whose person paradise adhear'd,
As Courts to princes ; shee, whose eyes enspheard
Star-light inough, t' haue made the South controll—
Had shee beene there—the starfull Northern pole ;   80

Shee, shee is gone, shee is gone: when thou knowest this,
What fragmentary rubbidge this world is
Thou knowest, and that it is not worth a thought;
He honours it too much, that thinkes it nought.   84

Contem-
plation of
our state
on our
deathbed.
        Thinke then, my soule, that death is but a groome,
Which brings a taper to the outward roome,
Whence thou spiest first a little glimmering light,
And after brings it nearer to thy sight;
For such approches doth heauen make in death:
Thinke thy selfe labouring now with broken breath,   90
And thinke those broken and soft notes to bee
Diuision, and thy happiest harmonee;
Thinke thee laid on thy death-bed, loose and slacke;
And thinke that but vnbinding of a packe,
To take one precious thing, thy soule, from thence;   95
Thinke thy selfe pach'd with feuer's violence;
Anger thine ague more, by calling it
Thy physicke; chide the slacknes of the fit.
Thinke that thou hear'st thy knell, and thinke no more,
But that, as bels cal'd thee to Church before,   100
So this to the triumphant Church calls thee;
Thinke Satan's sergeants round about thee bee,
And thinke that but for legacies they thrust;
Giue one thy pride, to another giue thy lust;
Giue them those sins, which they gaue thee before,   105
And trust th' immaculate blood to wash thy score;
Thinke thy friends weeping round, and thinke that thay
Weepe but because they goe not yet thy way;

Thinke that they close thine eyes, and thinke in this,
They that confesse much in the world, amisse,   110
Who dare not trust a dead man's eye with that,
Which they from God and angels couer not;
Thinke that they shroud thee vp, and thinke from thence,
They re-inuest thee in white innocence;
Thinke that thy body rots, and (if so lowe—   115
Thy soule exalted so—thy thoughts can goe)
Thinke thee a prince, who of themselues create
Wormes which insensibly devour their state;
Thinke that they bury thee, and thinke that right   rite
Laies thee to sleepe but a saint Lucie's night;   120
Thinke these things cheerfully, and if thou bee
Drowsie or slacke, remember then that shee;
She, whose complexion was so euen made,
That which of her ingredients should inuade
The other three, no feare, no Art could guesse: 125
So farre were all remou'd from more or lesse;
But as in mithridate, or iust perfumes,
Where all good things being met, no one presumes
To gouerne, or to triumph on the rest,
Onely because all were, no part was, best;   130
And as, though all doe know, that quantities
Are made of lines, and lines from points arise,
None can these lines or quantities vnioynt,
And say, this is a line, or this a point;
So, though the elements and humors were   135
In her, one could not say, this gouernes there;

Whose-euen constitution might have wonne
Any disease to venter on the sunne,
Rather then her; and make a spirit feare,   than
That he to disuniting subicct were;   140
To whose proportions if we could compare
Cubes, th' are vnstable; circles, angulare;
Shee, who was such a chaine as Fate emploies
To bring mankind all fortunes it enioyes,
So fast, so euen wrought, as one would thinke   145
No accident could threaten any linke;
Shee, shee embrac'd a sicknesse, gaue it meat,
The purest blood and breath that ere it eat;
And hath taught vs, that though a good man hath
Title to heauen, and plead it by his faith,   150
And though he may pretend a conquest, since
Heauen was content to suffer violence;
Yea, though he plead a long possession, too—   [do—
For they're in heauen on Earth, who heauen's workes
Though he had right, and power, and place before, 155
Yet death must vsher and vnlocke the doore.

Incommo-   Thinke further on thy selfe, my soule, and thinke
dities of
the Soule How thou at first wast made but in a sinke;
in the
Body.   Thinke, that it argued some infirmitee,
That those two soules, which then thou found'st in mee,
Thou fedst vpon, and drewst into thee, both   161
My second soule of sence, and first of growth;
Thinke but how poore thou wast, how obnoxious,
When a small lumpe of flesh could poyson thus:

This curded milke, this poore vnlittered whelpe,　165
My body, could, beyond escape or helpe,
Infect thee with originall sinne, and thou
Couldst neither then refuse, nor leaue it now ;
Thinke, that no stubborne sullen anchorit,
Which fixt to a pillar, or a graue, doth sit　170
Bedded, and bath'd in all his ordures, dwels
So fowly as our soules in their first-built cels :
Thinke in how poore a prison thou didst lie
After, enabled but to sucke and crie ;
Thinke, when 'twas growne to most, 'twas a poore inne,
A prouince pack'd vp in two yards of skinne ;　176
And that vsurped, or threatned with the rage
Of sicknesses, or their true mother, Age ;
But thinke that Death has now enfranchis'd thee,　Her liberty by death.
Thou hast thy expansion now, and libertee ;　180
Thinke, that a rusty peece discharg'd is flowen
In peeces, and the bullet is his owne,
And freely flies ; this to thy soule allow ;　[now ;
Thinke thy sheell broke, thinke thy soule hatch'd but
And thinke this slow-pac'd soule, which late did cleaue
To a body, and went but by the bodie's leaue,　186
Twentie perchance or thirtie mile a day,
Despatches in a minute all the way
'Twixt heauen and earth ; shee staies not in the ayre,
To look what meteors there themselues prepare ;　190
Shee carries no desire to know, nor sense,
Whether th' ayr's middle region be intense ;

For th' element of fire, shee doth not know :
Whether she past by such a place or no ;
Shee baits not at the moone, nor cares to trie   195
Whether in that new world men liue and die ;
Venus retards her not, to enquire how shee
Can—being one star—Hesper and Vesper bee ;
Hee, that charm'd Argus' eyes, sweete Mercury,
Workes not on her, who now is growen all ey ;   200
Who, if shee meet the bodie of the sunne,
Goes through, not staying till his course be runne ;
Who findes in Mars his campe no corps of guard,
Nor is by Ioue, nor by his father, bar'd,
But ere she can consider how she went,   205
At once is at and through the firmament.
And, as these starres were but so many beades
Strunge on one string, speed vndistinguish'd leades
Her through those spheares, as through the beades a string,
Whose quicke succession makes it still one thing : 210
As doth the pith, which, least our bodies slack,
Strings fast the little bones of necke and backe ;
So by the soule doth death string heauen and Earth ;
For when our soule enioyes this her third birth—
Creation gaue her one, a second, Grace—   215
Heauen is as neare and present to her face,
As colours are and obiects in a roome,
Where darkenesse was before, when tapers come.
This must, my soule, thy long-short Progresse bee :
To aduance these thoughts ; remember then, that shee,

Shee, whose faire body no such prison was,   221
But that a soule might well be pleasd to passe
An age in her; she, whose rich beauty lent
Mintage to others' beauties, for they went
But for so much as they were like to her;   225
She, in whose body—if wee dare prefer
This low world to so high a marke, as shee—
The Western treasure, Easterne spiceree,
Europe and Afrique, and the vnknowne rest
Were easily found, or what in them was best;—   230
And when w' have made this large discoueree
Of all, in her some one part then will bee
Twenty such parts, whose plenty and riches is
Enough to make twentie such worlds as this;—
Shee, whom had they knowne, who did first betroth 235
The tutelar angels, and assigned one, both
To nations, cities, and to companies,
To functions, offices, and dignities,
And to each seuerall man, to him, and him,
They would haue giuen her one for euery limme;   240
Shee, of whose soule if we may say, 'twas gold,
Her body was th' electrum, and did hold
Many degrees of that; wee vnderstood
Her by her sight; her pure and eloquent blood
Spoke in her cheekes, and so distinctly wrought, 245
That one might almost say her body thought;
Shee, shee thus richly and largely hous'd, is gone,
And chides vs, slow-pac'd snailes, who crawl vpon

Our prison's prison, earth, nor thinke vs well,
Longer then whil'st wee beare our brittle shell. than 250

IIer igno-
rance in
this life
and know-
ledge in
the next.

But 'twere but little to haue chang'd our roome,
If, as we were in this our liuing tombe
Oppress'd with ignorance, we still were so.
Poore soule, in this thy flesh what do'st thou know?
Thou knowst thy selfe so little, as thou knowst not 255
How thou didst die, nor how thou wast begot;
Thou neither knowst, how thou at first camest in,
Now how thou took'st the poyson of man's sin;
Nor dost thou—though thou knowst that thou art so—
By what way thou art made immortall, know.   260
Thou art too narrow, wretch, to comprehend
Euen thy selfe, yea, though thou would'st but bend
To know thy body.   Haue not all soules thought
For many ages, that our body is wrought
Of ayre and fire, and other elements?   265
And now they thinke of new ingredients;
And one soule thinks one, and another way
Another thinkes, and 'tis an euen lay.
Knowst thou but how the stone doth enter in
The bladder's caue, and neuer brake the skin?   270
Knowst thou how blood, which to the heart doth flow,
Doth from one ventricle to th' other goe?
And for the putrid stuffe, which thou dost spit,
Know'st thou how thy lungs haue attracted it?
There are no passages; so that there is—   275
For ought thou knowst—piercing of substances.

And of those many opinions, which men raise
Of nayles and haires, dost thou know which to praise?
What hope haue we to know ourselues, when wo
Know not the least things which for our vse be? 280
We see in authors, too stiffe to recant,
A hundred controuersies of an ant;
And yet one watches, starues, freeses, and sweats,
To know but catechismes and alphabets
Of vnconcerning things, matters of fact, 285
How others on our stage their parts did act,
What Cæsar did, yea, and what Cicero said:
Why grasse is greene, or why our bloud is red,
Are mysteries which none haue reach'd vnto;
In this low forme, poore soule, what wilt thou doe? 290
When wilt thou shake off this pedantery,
Of being taught by sense and fantasy?
Thou look'st through spectacles; small things seeme great
Below; but vp vnto the watch-towre get,
And see all things despoyld of fallacies; 295
Thou shalt not peepe through lattices of eies,
Nor heare through laberinths of cares, nor learne
By circuit or collections to discerne;
In heauen thou straight know'st all concerning it,
And what concerns it not, shall straight forget. 300
There thou—but in no other school—maist bee
Perchance as learnèd and as full as shee;
Shee, who all libraries had throughly red   read
At home in her owne thoughts, and practisèd

So much good, as would make as many morc ;   305
Shee, whose example they must all implore,
Who would or doe or thinke well, and confesse
That all the vertuous actions they expresse,
Are but a new and worse edition
Of her some one thought, or one action ;   310
Shee who in th' art of knowing Heauen was growen
Here vpon Earth to such perfection,
That shee hath, euer since to heauen shee came—
In a far fairer print—but read the same ;
Shee—shee not satisfied withall this waite— weight 315
(For so much knowledge as would overfraite
Another, did but ballast her) is gone
As well t' enioy, as get, perfectionc.
And cals vs after her, in that shee tooke—
Taking her selfe—our best and worthiest bookc.   320

Of our
company
in this life
and in the
next.   Returne not, my soule, from this ecstasee,
And meditation of what thou shalt bee,
To earthly thoughts, till it to thee appeare
With whom thy conuersation must be there.
With whom wilt thou conuerse ? what station   325
Canst thou choose out free from infection,
That will not giue thee theirs, nor drinke in thine ?
Shalt thou not finde a spungy slacke diuine
Drinke and sucke in the instructions of great men,
And for the Word of God, vent them agen ?   330
Are there not some Courts—and then, no things bee
So like as Courts—which, in this let vs see,

That wits and tongues of libellars are weake,
Because they doe more ill, then these can speake? than
The poyson is gone through all; poysons affect   335
Chiefly the chiefest parts; but some effect
In nailes, and haires, yea excrements, will show;
So lies the poyson of sin in the most low.
Vp, vp, my drowsie soule, where thy new care
Shall in the angels' songs no discord heare;   340
Where thou shalt see the blessed mother-maid
Ioy in not being that, which men haue said;
Where shee is exalted more for being good,
Then for her interest of motherhood :   than
Vp to those Patriarckes, which did longer sit   345
Expecting Christ, then they 'haue enjoy'd Him yet; than
Vp to those Prophets, which now gladly see
Their prophesies growen to bee historee;
Vp to th' Apostles, who did brauely runne,
All the sun's course, with more light then the sunne; than
Vp to those Martyrs, who did calmely bleed   351
Oyle to th' Apostles' lamps, dew to their seed;
Vp to those Virgins, who thought that almost
They made ioynte tenants with the Holy Ghost,
If they to any should His temple giue;   355
Vp, vp, for in that squadron there doth liue
Shee, who hath carried thither new degrees—
As to their number—to their dignitees;
Shee, who beeing to her selfe a state, enioyd
All royalties, which any state emploid;   360

For shee made wars, and triumph'd ; reason still
Did not ouerthrow, but rectifie her will ;
And shee made peace ; for no peace is like this,
That beauty and chastity together kisse ;
She did high iustice ; for she crucified   365
Euery first motion of rebellious pride ;
And she gaue pardons, and was liberall,
For, onely her selfe except, shee pardond all ;
Shee coynd ; in this, that her impressions gaue
To all our actions all the worth they haue ;   370
She gave protections ; the thoughts of her breast
Satan's rude officers could nere arrest.
As these prerogatiues being met in one,
Made her a soueraigne state, Religion
Made her a Church ; and these two made her all. 375
Shee, who was all this all, and could not fall
To worse, by company ;—for she was still
More antidote, then all the world was ill—   than
Shee, shee doth leaue it, and by death surviue
All this in heauen ; whether who doth not striue whither
The more because shee's there, he doth not know 381
That accidentall ioyes in heauen do grow.

Of essen-
tial ioy in
this life
and in the
next.

But pause, my soule, and study, ere thou fall
On accidentall ioyes, th' essentiall ;
Still before accessories doe abide   385
A triall, must the principall bee tride ;
And what essentiall ioy canst thou expect
Here vpon earth ? what permanent effect

Of transitory causes? Dost thou loue
Beauty?—and beauty worthy'st is to moue;—   390
Poore cousened cos'cnor, that she, and that thou,
Which did begin to loue, are neither now;
You are both fluid, chang'd since yesterday;
Next day repaires—but ill—last daye's decay;
Nor are—although the riuer keepe the name—   395
Yesterdaye's waters and to-daie's the same:
So flowes her face, and thine eies; neither now,
That saint nor pilgrime, which your louing vow
Concernd, remaines; but whilst you thinke you bee
Constant, you are hourely in inconstancee.   400
Honour may haue pretence vnto our loue,
Because that God did liue so long aboue
Without this honour, and then lou'd it so,
That He at last made creatures to bestow
Honour on Him; not that He needed it,   405
But that to His hands man might grow more fit.
But since all honours from inferiours flow—
For they do giue it; princes doe but show
Whom they would haue so honord—and that this
On such opinions and capacities   410
Is built, as rise and fall, to more and lesse,
Alas, 'tis but a casuall happinesse.
Hath euer any man to himselfe assigned
This or that happinesse to arrest his mind,
But that another man, which takes a worse,   415
Thinke him a foole for hauing tane that course?

They who did labour Babel's tower to erect,
Might haue consider'd, that for that effect
All this whole solid earth could not allow,
Nor furnish forth materials enow,   420
And that his center, to raise such a place,
Was farre too little to haue been the base;
No more affoords this worlde foundatione
To erect true ioye, were all the meanes in one.
But as the heathen made them seuerall gods   425
Of all God's benefits, and all His rods—
For as the wine and corne and onions are
Gods vnto them, so agues bee, and warre—
And as by changing that whole precious gold
To such small copper coynes, they lost the old,   430
And lost their onely God, who euer must
Be sought alone, and not in such a thrust;
So much mankinde true happinesse mistakes;
No ioye enioyes that man, that many makes.
Then, soule, to thy first pitch worke vp againe;   435
Know that all lines which circles doe contain,
For once that they the center touch, doe touch
Twice the circumference; and be thou such;
Double on heauen thy thoughts; on earth emploid,
All will not serue; onely who haue enioyd   440
The sight of God in fulnesse, can thinke it;
For it is both the obiect and the wit;
This is essentiall ioye, where neither hee
Can suffer diminution, nor wee;

'Tis such a full and such a filling good,   445
Had th' angels once look'd on Him, they had stood.

To fill the place of one of them, or more,
Shee, whom we celebrate, is gone before;
Shee, who had here so much essentiall ioy,
As no chance could distract, much lesse destroy; 450
Who with God's presence was acquainted so—
Hearing, and speaking to Him—as to know
His face is any naturall stone or tree,
Better then when in images they bee ;   than
Who kept, by diligent deuotion,   455
God's image in such reparation
Within her heart, that what decay was growne,
Was her first parent's fault, and not her owne ;
Who, being solicited to any act,
Still heard God pleading His safe precontract ; 460
Who by a faithfull confidence was here
Betrothed to God, and now is married there ;
Whose twilights were more cleare than our mid-day ;
Who dreamt devoutlier then most vse to pray; than
Who being here fild with grace, yet stroue to be 465 .
Both where more grace, and more capacitee
At once is giuen ; she to heauen is gone,
Who made this world in some proportion
A heauen, and here became vnto vs all,
Ioye—as our ioyes admit—essentiall.   470 Of acci-
But could this low world ioyes essentiall touch, dentall
 ioyes in
Heauen's accidentall ioyes would passe them much. both
 places.

How poore and lame must then our casuall bee ?
If thy prince will his subiects to call thee
My Lord, and this doe swell thee, thou art than   then
By being greater, growen to be lesse man.   476
When no physician of redress can speake,
A ioyfull casuall violence may breake
A dangerous apostem in thy brest ;
And whilst thou ioyest in this, the dangerous rest, 480
The bag may rise vp, and so strangle thee.
Whateie was casuall, may euer bee :   aye
What should the nature change? or make the same
Certaine, which was but casuall when it came?
All casuall ioye doth loud and plainely say,   485
Onely by comming, that it can away.
Onely in heauen ioye's strength is neuer spent,
And accidentall things are permanent.
Ioy of a soule's arriuall neere decaies—
For that soule euer ioyes, and euer stayes ;—   490
Ioy, that their last great consummation
Approches in the resurrection,
When earthly bodies more celestiall
Shall be, then angels were—for they could fall—   than
This kind of ioy doth euery day admit   495
Degrees of growth, but none of loosing it.
In this fresh ioy, 'tis no small part, that shee,
Shee, in whose goodnesse he that names degree
Doth iniure her ;—'tis losse to be cald best,
There where the stuffe is not such as the rest ;—   500

Shee, who left such a bodie, as even shee
Onely in heauen could learne, how it can bee
Made better; for shee rather was two soules,
Or like to full-on-both-sides-written rols,
Where eies might read vpon the outward skin   505
As strong records for God, as mindes within;
Shee, who, by making full perfection grow,
Peeces a circle, and still keepes it so,
Long'd for, and longing for it, to heauen is gone,
Where shee receiues and giues addition.   510

Conclu-
sion.

Here, in a place, where misdeuotion frames
A thousand praiers to saints, whose uery names
The ancient Church knew not, heauen knowes not yet,
And where what lawes of poetry admit,
Lawes of religion haue at least the same,   515
Immortall Maide, I might invoque thy name.
Could any saint prouoke that appetite,
Thou here should'st make mee a French conuertite,
But thou wouldst not; nor wouldst thou be content
To take this, for my second yeere's true rent,   520
Did this coine beare any other stampe then His   than
That gaue thee power to doe, me to say this:
Since His will is that to posteritee
Thou shouldest for life and death a patterne bee,
And that the world should notice haue of this,   525
The purpose and th' authoritie is His;
Thou art the proclamation; and I ame
The trumpet, at whose voyce the people came.

NOTES AND ILLUSTRATIONS.

Divisions of the 'Anatomie' and 'Progress.'

I have arranged these Poems in paragraphs, denoted by spaces at the several, somewhat distant, places. In the 'Anatomie' proper there is an evident close of each section of thought in the repeated phrases,

'And learn'st thus much by our Anatomie,'

and the like. Our arrangement is as follows : The Proem, or exposition of the World's illness and dead body, ends at line 60. Then the first lesson ends at line 190, the second at line 246, the third at line 338, the fourth at line 376, the fifth at line 434, and the Close is from this to the end.

Of the 'Progress,' the Proem ends at line 54, the first stage at line 84, the second at line 156 (see the thought that is expanded therein at line 85), the third at line 250, the fourth at line 320, the fifth at line 382, the sixth at line 446, and then the Close.

With reference to the second title, 'Progress of the Soul,' the word 'Progress' had in those days a special sense=the state progress of a Monarch through some part of his or her dominions ; and as in the opening of the 'First Anniversary' he spoke (line 7) of 'When that queene ended here her progresse-time,' so now he speaks of the Progress of her royal soul. Every one knows the splendid as erudite volumes of Nichols on the 'Progresses' of Elizabeth and James.

Commendatory Verses.

It is of the 'Curiosities of Literature' that the critics have not observed that the present and correspondent poem in the '2d Anniversarie' were 'commendatory,' and so not by Donne but for Donne. It is also singular that men of mark (e.g. David Laing, Esq. LL.D., Dr. Hannah, and others), while recording and annotating or quoting this entry in the celebrated Conversations of Drummond and Ben Jonson, 'Joseph Hall, the harbenger of the Anatomie,' have utterly failed to observe that this carries in it the specially interesting fact that the author of the present 'commendatory' poem, and doubtless of its companion piece in the '2d Anniversary,' was the (afterwards) renowned Bishop Joseph Hall, a trenchant Satirist and vigorous Poet, as well as a most suggestive sermon-writer and meditator. In our Essay we show the significance of this in relation to the Satires, and Hall's claim to be the 'first' (English) Satirist—also hitherto overlooked.

I. To THE PRAISE OF THE DEAD, AND THE ANATOMY.

Lines 8-9, ' *His*' = its—which, instead of the spirit of the world, now seems to give form, and therefore 'being,' to its remains.

Line 12, ' *Thrise*' = thrice.

,, 15, ' *nephews*'=descendants generally, as before.

,, 18, in 1612 misprinted ' ceomly :' corrected in 1621.

,, 21, ' *is us.*' so in 1612, 1621, and 1625 ; a various-reading is ' it is'—not an error.

Line 27, ' *wont.*' Donne, differing from at least most of his contemporaries, uses this without the substantive verb (see like remark in Elegies). This Writer does the same.

Line 34, ' where :' in 1612, 1621, and 1625 misprinted ' were.'

,, 35, ' *bine*'= [have] been.

,, 36, ' in thine :' usually misprinted ' *and* thine.'

,, 39, ' *tongue :*' 1669 has ' tongues.'

,, 41, ' as by infant yeares men iudge of age.' We have here an early form of Wordsworth's ' boy is father to the man.'

Line 43, ' What hie . . .' In 1612 ' *an* hie :' corrected in 1621.

Line 47. 1669 reads ' Never may thy name be in songs forgot.'

II. AN ANATOMIE OF THE WORLD : THE FIRST ANNIVERSARIE.

Margin-notes : these are restored throughout, having been hitherto wrongly omitted, from 1669 onward.

Line 2, ' all doe :' in 1612 ' all they :' corrected in 1621.

,, 40, ' *determinèd*'=ended, a legal term then in common use. Cf. Shakespeare, Son. xiii. ll. 5-6, &c.

Line 47, ' *thaw :*' used quaintly (probably in stress of rhyme) for dissolution.

Line 73, ' *shut in*'—by descent to the tomb. Our phrase is ' shut out.' It is not unlikely that the variation is due to shutters having been then outdoor- and inward-closing, as still to be seen in old Elizabethan and even Jacobean villages in England.

Line 79, ' though :' misprinted ' thought,' 1621 and 1625. I accept ' though' from 1612.

Line 95, '*ruinous*'=full of ruin ; or, as explained in the following lines, '*falling*.' The natural mode of birth is head foremost, and according to the then custom, the woman was seated, as in the time of Moses (Exodus i. 16), or kneeling.

Line 99, '*witty's*'=wise.

  ,, 110, '*kill ourselues to propogate our kinde.*' The allusion, I presume, is to the belief that crept into theology that the Fall was sexual intercourse—one interwoven by Milton into his account, and made much of by the late Dr. Donaldson in his nasty '*Jasher*,' but which is contrary to revelation (Genesis i. 28) and the analogy of nature. Or the allusion may be to the belief entertained by some that propagation of the species shortened life, and this for reasons founded on the (erroneous) philosophy of the day, and because it was believed that eunuchs, whether naturally so or made, and castrated animals, lived longer ; while the lives of partridges, cocks, and sparrows were shortened by their excess in venery. See Sir Thomas Browne, as above, V. E. ; and Progress of the Soul, st. xxi.-ii.

Line 115, '*stag and rauen.*' These were supposed to much exceed the age of man. The tree is probably the platane or plane. Cf. Elegy ix. line 29. See our Phineas Fletcher, *s.v.* Cf. also Sir Thomas Browne, Vulgar Errors, book iii. c. 9 ; and for raven, Pliny, N. H. b. viii. c. 82.

Line 117, '*starre:*' see note on line 259.

  ,, 120. I am somewhat doubtful whether, as in two examples in the Elegies (xviii. line 16), and elsewhere, there is here an unusual form of ellipse, where the middle words are supposed to be repeated—'Man's growth confessed,' &c. . . . . and 'Man's growth [was] so spacious ;' or whether line 122 is parenthetical, and the size great (. . . .) so spacious and large that, &c.; or whether the phrase is equal to Man's growth recompensed the meat so spaciously and largely. Either this or the second seems less harsh, and this, if adopted, requires meat (,); and thus I punctuate.

Line 121. Ed. 1612 misprints 'the the sise :' corrected in 1621.

Line 134, 'a *torn* house :' the poet speaks of an ordinary form of lease for the term of three lives, and 'torn' is a characteristically strange quibble on a house or field '*rented*' from the owners.

Line 135. A Talmudical belief.

  ,, 138, '*shipwrack'd :*' an extreme instance of an irregular but then common ellipse, where the passive part, auxiliaries have to be supplied from the active, [had been] shipwracked out of 'had straid.'

Line 144, 'scarse :' misprinted 'searse' in 1612 and 1621.

„ 145, 'death ads t' our length.' Not only were nails and hair supposed to grow after death, but it was popularly believed, and is now perhaps by some, that the body does so. We measure longer in the morning after repose, than in the evening after a day of the erect posture ; but the difference is too slight to explain the ' Vulgar Error.' The thinning of the body in illness, and the rigid straightness of a 'streaked' corpse, may have helped the belief ; but it probably arose from the more than usual growth occasionally noticeable in children during a fatal, and it may be short, illness. Every one remembers the exclamation of his enemy over the coffined Henry IV., that he was ' taller' and more majestical dead than alive.

Line 150, ' Which [vertue] then scattered was.' Led to it by the previous words, the allusion is chemical or alchemical, —'had we concentrated or essentialised into a spirit by distillation into a smaller vessel.'

Line 151. Here, as in the next line, we have the metaphor elucidated. We are not altered like a snail or worm, that continues of the same bulk though it retire itself into apparently smaller compass; but we are shrunk like a damped woollen cloth, not close-wove, but our threads twisted up and cramped.

Line 153, ' close weaving :' misprinted ' wearing' in 1612, 1621, and 1625 : cf. line 279.

Line 161, ' Thus :' 1669 ' this.' Probably the alteration into ' this' from ' thus' of all the author's own editions was to bring line 161 into (imagined) agreement with lines 167, 169. But ' thus' is the general fact, and the after ' this is' the particulars, beginning with the ' this' of line 161, ' Thus Man, this . . .'

We have in this striking passage a remembrance and adaptation of Hamlet's—

' What a piece of work is a man ! how noble in reason ! how *infinite in faculty !* in form and moving [suggestive of ' grace'] how express and admirable ! . . . the beauty· of the world! [whom God did woo] . . . And yet to me what is this quintessence of dust !' (act ii. sc. 2.)

Line 164, ' legats :' so in 1612 and 1621 : in 1625 ' legate ;' the former accepted.

Lines 172-3, ' *Help* . . . *wants :*' obscure. Probably in accordance with his former conceit that the world is dead, yet with some seeming of life: he means, allow if you will help to his other wants, or allow time for him to waste, as not altogether dead; yet he hath lost his heart, and is therefore mortally struck, and must die.

Line 173, ' *depart:*' not, leave with her, but=part with, that is, part with her (*de*) from himself. This use of it was common. Cf.

> ' John, to stop Arthur's title in the whole,
>   Hath willingly *departed* with a part '
>   K. John ii. 2 ; and Love's Labour Lost, ii. 1.

There would seem from this passage, and from lines 377-402, to have been some such interchange of seasons and unseasonable sickly weather as Shakespeare feigned in Athens (Timon of Athens, act ii. sc. 1), and as occurred in England about 1594, previous to the writing of King John and Midsummer's Night Dream, as may be seen by Strype and Bishop King's Lenten Sermons on Jonah (see our edition in Nichol's ' Puritan Commentaries'). Taking this view, that the poem refers to and is founded on contemporary and exceptional phenomena, one can better understand, and in a greater degree pardon, the otherwise extravagant conceits.

Line 202. A beautiful adaptation of the Hebrew phrase, ' And the evening and the morning were the first day.'

Line 204, ' *sonnes*'—*i. e.* none at all, fifty being held to be woman's limit in child-bearing.

Line 205, ' *new philosophy*.' I do not know what this ' new philosophy' was, for the present chemical views as to the elements are of much later date. There is another reference to the same in Second Anniversary, lines 263-6.

Line 217, ' *there:*' 1669 and usually ' that,' wrongly ; 1612, 1621, and 1625 misprint ' then.'

Line 232, ' *Spice*'=the Moluccas or Spice Isles.

„ 233, ' *interre:*' a strong personification, implying the country to be so rich that, like a miser, it buries its hoards of treasure.

Line 234, ' *single money*'=smaller coin. Thus, in opposition to the single crown, ducat, pistolet, and sovereign, were the double crown, ducat, and pistole, and great double and great triple sovereign, as well as the doblon (doubloon).

Line 260, ' *New stars*.' In 1604 a star of the first magnitude appeared in the right foot of Ophiuchus, and in a few

months disappeared. It was written of by Kepler, and brought
to mind the star brighter than Venus and visible at noonday that
showed itself for a time in Cassiopeia in 1572, and that was
written of by Tycho Brahe. The same phenomenon is referred
to by Donne in the 'Funeral Elegy' (lines 67-70), and Verse-
Epistle to Countess of Huntingdon (lines 6-8); and the con-
siderations thus arising, and the attention called to the heavens
generally, are seen in lines 210 and 117.

Line 273, ' with :' usually misprinted ' of.'

Line 286, ' Tenarif :' 1669 *Tenarus*. The latter is not a
misprint, for, except here, Donne always calls Teneriffe by that
name. It will be remembered that Marvell and Milton have
associated their names with the ' great mountain.'

Line 289, ' *strooke*'=struck, as in 1669.

,, 298, ' *strait*'=straight.

,, 311, ' *that Ancient*' = Pythagoras. Here is another
linking-on of the ' Anatomie' with the other ' Progress of the
Soul.'

Line 314, ' *resultances* :' query, a Donne coinage?

,, 317, ' doctors :' 1612 spelled oddly ' douctors.'

,, 343, ' *turcuoyse*'=turquoise; a precious stone supersti-
tiously regarded long ago, in common with all precious stones.
With a rare want of credulity, Bartholomew says (b. xvi. c. 98),
' The Indians know none other vertue but this fayreness [of
colour].'

Line 345, ' *falls sicke* :' the alchemical phrase.

,, 349, ' *and* play :' usually misprinted ' *in* play.'

,, 363-64, ' Paradise . . . things' verdure'=from whom
did come the verdure of all things and their lustre.

Line 392, ' *constellate* :' explained by next two lines as
making a thing one in influence with a star or stars, or giving
it an influence drawn from them. Sir John Davies and contemporaries have ' stellify.'

Line 410, ' *serpent* :' no record of this belief in Pliny, Bartholomew, or Browne.

Line 422, ' *stay*'=restraint.

,, 432, ' *perishing* :' not in sense of dying, as now, but
as is still preserved in the phrase, ' *perishing* with cold ;' that
is, in the sense of shrinking, pining, and wasting away, in
which the poets used *pereo* in reference to love.

Line 440, ' *punctuall*'=treating it point by point.

,, 474, ' fame :' in a copy of the 1612 edition now before

me, Donne (I think) has himself written 'fame,' lest the long s, so like an f, should be mistaken.

III. A FVNERALL ELEGIE.

In the Stephens' MS., now in possession of F. W. Cosens, Esq., and with which he kindly intrusted me, there is a copy of this portion of the 'Anatomie.' It is headed 'The Funerall Elegie vppon yᵉ death of Mᵣˢ Elizabeth Drury.' No variations noticeable.

Line 1, 'ghest;' I accept this spelling of 1612, in preference to 'guhest' of 1621 and 1625.

Line 4, '*priz'd*'=put a price or valuation on it; appraise.

  ,,   8, ' Escurials :' in 1612 and 1621 printed with small ' c.'

  ,,   13, '*aborted :*' 1669 ' abortive.'

  ,,   33, ' as :' usually misprinted ' was.'

  ,,   41. A peculiarity generally given to the Nile ; and here perhaps not spoken of our Niger, but of the Nile before it is so called, when, according to Pliny, after having twice been underground, and the second time for twenty days' journey, it issues at the spring Nigris (Pliny, N. H. b. v. c. 9). As I write this note, tidings reach England from the long-lost Livingstone. May he be spared to return, with this world-old secret of the Nile in his hand, to a well-earned evening-time of rest !

Line 50. See note on Elegy.

  ,,   57. As force and vigour represent one thing, or phases of one quality, he says ere 'it' according to the grammar of the thought, and not of the expression.

Line 61, ' *through-light*'=diaphanous. Used by Donne elsewhere, as in Epistle before Progress of the Soul, where 1669 edition omits the hyphen.

Line 67. See note on ' Anatomie,' line 260, &c.

  ,,   83, ' *said :*' so in 1612, 1621, and 1625.

  ,,   86, [had] promis'd, &c., from the ' had' of ' she had been,' a now irregular but then common form of ellipse.

Line 92, ' *infer*'=bring into one, in sense of offer or furnish, as in the quotation given by Johnson (where, however, ' produce' is an imperfect gloss) :

> ' Full well hath Clifford play'd the orator,
> *Inferring* arguments of mighty force.'

Line 96, ' *fellow-commissioner*'—*i. e.* as joint-delegate of the Deity. See Progress of the Soul, st. iv. l. 1, and Second Ep. to Sir Henry Wotton, l. 11.

Line 105. Metre and rhythm irregular, that 'spiritual' might be emphasised and used at full length.

IV. THE HARBINGER TO THE PROGRESSE.

Line 16, '*iournals :*' used by the author [Bp. Hall] of these commendatory verses as=days' doings, or=the glorious news or diary of thy days' doings.

' Line 23, 'caught:' 1612 reads 'raught'=reached.

„ 27, 'soule:' 1612 misprints 'soules:' corrected in 1621.

„ 36, '*thy Laura :*' likening Donne's praise of Mrs. Drury to Petrarch's praise of Laura.

V. THE PROGRESS OF THE SOULE: THE SECOND ANNIVERSARIE.

Line 10, 'Though:' in 1612, 1621, and 1625, misprinted 'Through.' In the copy, already noted, of 1612, Donne (I think) has himself again corrected by writing opposite 'Though' for 'Through.'

Line 22, '*motion.*' Motion was considered the characteristic of life, and hence stood for life or a living body; and thence, by a curious return, it came to signify both a puppet (that moved as with life) and a puppet-show. But of corruption also, according to the old belief, arose life, as worms in dead bodies, bees from the carcass of an ox, &c.; and such motion or life, says Donne, is that that is now found in the world dead, and now after a year corrupt.

Line 43, 'thy:' 1621 and 1625 misprint 'they:' 1612 is correctly 'thy.'

Line 46, 'safe-sealing:' it looks like 'fealing' in 1621 and 1625, as well as 1612.

Line 48, '*hydroptique :*' note on Elegy.

„ 54, '*busines,*' rather = over-business, business being taken in its stronger and worse sense.

Line 56, '*that :*' an example, of which several are noted in our SOUTHWELL, of 'that' used as=that that.

Line 67, ''twas:' 1669 'was.'

„ 72, '*forme.*' According to mediæval philosophy, 'forma,' which was more than mere shape, was that which, when added to the 'substantia,' made the visible existing thing, whatever that thing might be. Thus in transubstantiation the 'form' of the bread or wine is said to remain; and hence, too, 'form' was sometimes used in the old Writers in a similar sense to that in the now-common sporting phrase of being 'in form,' the full significance of which is to be derived from the mediæval scholastic term.

Line 75, '*indifferent*'=neither good nor bad.

,,   80, '*starfull Northern pole.*' There are more visible stars in the Southern hemisphere than in the Northern, but fewer near the South Pole.

Line 82. Mrs. Gamp and the Cockneys have in this not corrupted the vernacular.

Line 94, '*packe.*' Said a good old man on his death-bed, when asked how he felt, 'My *pack* is ready, and I'm just waiting.'

Line 103, '*legacies.*' There have been several examples of such bequests.

Line 104. Cf. Funeral Elegy, lines 103-4.

,,   113, 'shroud:' so in 1612, misprinted 'shourd' in 1621 and 1625.

Line 117, '*prince . . . themselves.*' The plural is here used as in Shakespeare, there being a reference to acts of royalty, in which the Prince speaks or writes of himself as 'we.'

Line 120, '*Saint Lucie's night*'=the shortest night.

,,   127, '*mithridate :*' properly a composite antidote against poison, supposed to have been used by King Mithridates. It was also applied generically to such compositions as were either vaunted as the true and genuine article, or were better than it. Donne elsewhere (First Ep. to C. of Bedford) uses it in a metaphorical sense.

Line 129, 'on :' 1612 misprints ' no :' corrected in 1621 and 1625.   •

Line 130. Ellipse, only because all were [best], &c.

,,.   135, 'elements and humors :' another Shakespearean reminiscence.

Line 137, 'wonne :' usually misprinted ' won.'

,,   143, '*chaine :*' an allusion to the Homeric chain of gold, on which see our SIBBES, *s. v.* with after-examples.

Line 160, ' *two soules :*' making therefore three in each body. See 5th Verse-Epistle to Countess of Bedford (lines 37-9), and to Countess of Salisbury (lines 51-6). The soul of growth, or Anima Vegetalis, because it is that that is in plants, died with the body. So also died the soul of sense, or Anima Sensibilis, which is [superadded] in beasts. The Anima Rationalis was alone immortal, and lived either with or without a body. See Bartholomew, book iii. c. 7-13. It would seem also, from him, that there was some diversity, not to say jumble, of opinions as to whether there were three souls or a threefold working of one soul; or whether the two souls were in beasts and the three in man; or whether the Anima Sensibilis gave life and growth as well as feeling to the Anima Rationalis, life, feeling, and reason.

Line 163, '*obnoxious:*' not so much in the original latinate sense of liable to punishment, as readily liable to ill.

Line 172, '*first-built cels*'=womb or the enclosing membrane.

  ,, 177, 'the:' usually misprinted 'a.'

  ,, 182, '*his owne*'=its own, free; not obedient only to impulses from that which it is with or that which confines it.

Line 203, '*corps of guard:*' used both for the guard itself and the guard-house or station, whither all strangers would be brought and questioned.

Line 213. Herbert uses this passage. See our Essay.

  ,, 224, 'others' beauties:' 1669 'other.' The former perhaps agrees better with 'whose beauty;' but 'other beauties' agrees best with 'they went,' and 'they were like.'

Line 226, '*prefer*'=advance, exalt, raise, as in preferring one to any western treasure=riches of America and Western Indies.

Line 228. This form of the ever-recurring microcosm thought is given in its comic side by Shakespeare in the Comedy of Errors (iii. 2).

Line 242, '*electrum:*' an adaptation of the fact that amber or electrum enclosed various extraneous substances, one which seems to have been constantly present to the older poets, through the much-used epigram of Martial, *De apide electro*, &c.

Line 242-43, 'did hold many degrees of that:' apparently= did surpass by many degrees. See note on line 358, its (the amber's) purity, &c.

Line 245, 'distinctly:' spelled 'distinckly' in 1612 and 1621.

  ,, 268, '*lay*'=wager.

  ,, 278. See Batman on Bartholomew for various of these opinions.

Line 292, 'taught:' 1612 and 1621 misprint 'thought.'

  ,, 297, '*laberinth:*' part of the inner ear so called.

  ,, 308, 'are:' *sic* in all the three editions, usually 'all.'

  ,, 314, '*far fairer print.*' See our Essay for after-use of this onward to Benjamin Franklin.

Line 314, 'print:' in all the three editions misprinted 'point.'

Lines 331-2. The parenthesis seems to have the following construction and meaning: Are there not some Courts (and than [Courts] no things are so like as Courts, [therefore all Courts as well as some]) ?

Line 352, '*seed :*' a variant of the saying, 'the blood of the martyrs the seed of the church.'

Line 353, 'thought:' in the three editions, as before, misprinted 'thoughts.'

Line 354, '*ioynte tenants ;*' *i. e.* made others joint tenants.

  ,, 358. As the phrase 'carry new degrees to their dignities' might at that time be taken to mean 'raise these dignities higher,' or place them on higher steps of honour, Donne adds —as to their number—to show his meaning, viz. that she, as different from patriarchs, apostles, and martyrs, and as different also from the virgins he speaks of, would add a new order among these dignities.

Line 382=That as well as the essential joy of heaven, there are joys which are not of the essence of heaven, but as it were its accidentals, such as joy over sinners saved, the remembrance of friends and former intercourse, and of their good deeds, &c.

Line 421, ' his :' 1612 'this.'

  ,, 432, ' thrust' = crowd. For verbal use of same, see line 103.

Line 435, ' vp:' 1612 and 1621 misprint 'vpon.'

  ,, 441=can conceive the fulness of the Godhead, for it is both the object of our thought and that which gives it power to conceive it. It is the light which makes us see the Light, and only the in-poured Spirit which enables us to comprehend the fulness of God. Donne, with all his play, has great reaches and depths of solemn thought.

Line 477, ' redress :' in all three editions misprinted 'reders.'

  ,, 477-81. This shows that the variously-told tale of a suffocating quinsy-abscess breaking through sudden laughter, was known in Donne's time; but I know not whether the after-result (lines 480-1) be or be not an addition by him.

Line 482, ' ere'=aye, as before : 1612 and 1621 so : usually ' e'er.'

Line 486, ' *onely by comming ;*' *i. e.* if only by its coming.

  ,, 504, ' *on-both-sides-written :*' this is as much a composite hyphened word as that comic one (Elegy v. line 31).   G.

I.

REFUSAL TO ALLOW HIS YOUNG WIFE

TO ACCOMPANY HIM ABROAD AS A PAGE.

By our first straunge and fatall interview,
By all desyres which thereof did ensue,
By our longe starvinge hopes, by that remorse,
Which my words' masculyne-persuasive force
Begott in thee, and by the memory   5
Of hurts, which spies and rivals threatned mee,
I calmlie begg; but by thy parents' wrath,
By all payns which want and divorsement hath,
I coniure thee;—and all those oaths, which I
And thou haue sworne to seale ioynt constancy,   10
Here I unswear and oversweare them thus;
Thou shalt not loue by wayes so dangerous;—
Temper, O fayr loue, Loue's impetuous rage,
Be my true mistris still, not my fayn'd Page.
I'le goe, and, by thy kinde leaue, leave behynd   15
Thee, only worthy to nurse in my mynd
Thirst to come back; Oh, if thou dye before,
From other lands my sowle towards thee shall soare.
Thy els almightie bowty cannot move
Rage from the seas, nor thy loue teach them loue,   20
Nor tame wilde Boreas' harshnes: Thou hast read
How roughly hee in pieces shyverèd

Faire Orethea, whom he swore he lov'd.
Fall ill or good, 'tis madness to haue prov'd
Daungers unurg'd ; feed on this flatterie,   25
That absent lovers one in th' other bee,
Dissemble nothing, not a boyc, nor change
Thy bodye's habytt, nor mynde's ; be not strange
To thy selfe only.   All will spie in thy face
A blushinge, womanly, discov'ringe grace.   30
Richlie cloth'd apes, are call'd apes ; and as soonc
Eclipst as bright, wee call the moone the moone ;
Men of Fraunce, changable camelions,
Spittles of diseases, shopps of fashyons,
Love's fuelers, and the rightest company   35
Of Players, which uppon the world's stage bee,
Will too too quickly knowe thee ; and alas !
The indifferent Italyan, as wee pass
His warme Land, well content to thinke thee a Page,
Will haunt thee with such lust, and hydeous rage,   40
As Lott's faire guests were vext ; but none of these,
Nor spungie hidroptique Dutch, shall thee displease,
If thou stay heare.   Oh stay here ; for, for thee
England is only a worthy gallery,
To walke in expectation, till from thence   45
Our great King call thee unto His presence.
When I am gone dreame me some happines,
Nor let thy lookes our longe-hid loue confesse ;
Nor praise, nor dispraise mee ; nor bless nor curse
Openly Love's force ; nor in bed fright thy nurse   50

With mydnight startinges, crying out, ' Oh ! oh !
Nurse, oh ! my love is slayne; I saw him goe
O'er the white Alpes alone ; I sawe him, I,
Assail'd, taken, fight, stabb'd, bleed, fall, and dye !'
Augure me better chaunce, except dread Jove   55
Think it enough for mee t' haue had thy love.

NOTES AND ILLUSTRATIONS.

Our text in the present Elegy and throughout—with the few
slight verbal exceptions recorded in their places—is from the
Stephens' MS., where it is headed ' Elegia Quinta :' but various-
readings from the printed editions and other MSS. are given in
the successive Notes and Illustrations.

This Elegy originally appeared in the edition of 1635 (pp.
255-6), oddly enough, among the Funeral Elegies or Epicedes ;
and so it has been continued in 1639 (pp. 269-70), 1649 (pp.
257-8), and in all the after-editions.   See our Essay for Dean
Milman's remarks on this Elegy.

Line 3, ' starvinge :' so '35 : ' striving' '69 : ' starvelinge'
Addl. MSS. 18647.

Line 7, ' parents' :' ibid. ' father's :' ' parents'' is an addi-
tional biographic fact.

Line 9, ' those :' ibid. ' the :' so '69.

„ 12, ' wayes :' 1669 and Addl. MSS. 18647 ' meanes.'

„ 14, ' still :' so '35, '39, '49 : '69 drops it, and perhaps
Donne struck it out as superfluous, intending a stress to be
laid on ' feignèd,' in opposition to ' true mistris.'

Line 18. 1635, '39, '49, and '69 read

' My soul from other lands to thee shall soare.'

' Towards' seems to express a fine humility in the reunion.

Line 23, ' Orethea :' '69 ' The faire O.'

„ 28, ' mynde's :' I have accepted this from Addl. MSS.
18647 : usually ' minde.'

Line 31, ' apes.' It will serve to explain the thought, if it be
remembered that ' pages' were frequently called ' apes.'

Line 34, ' Spittles' = hospitals.   ' The Spittle' was long the
name.

Line 36, '*stage.*' This saying, which Shakespeare puts into the mouth of Jacques, is by Ben Jonson, in his Every Man out of his Humour, attributed to a philosopher. It has also been assigned to Pythagoras.

Line 37. I accept this line from 1669 in preference to '35, '39, '49:

> ' Will quickly knowe thee; and no lesse, alas!'

Our MS. reads confusedly

> ' Will quickly knowe thee; and knowe thee, alas :'

18647 even worse,

> ' Will quickly know thee, and knowe thee, and alas.'

Line 40, ' haunt :' usually ' hunt.'

„ 41, '*vext.*' Modern English would require ' with,' which Donne I suppose considered sufficiently expressed in the ' with' of the previous line.

Line 46, ' great :' usually ' greatest.'

„ 50, ' *Love's force*' = [probably] the forcing of or violence done to love : 18647 reads badly ' lovers.'

Line 51, ' Oh :' in 18647 ' oh ô :' usually ' midnight's.'

„ 53, ' *alone :*' our MS. misreads ' alas :' our text '35 to '69.

„ 55, ' dread :' our MS. has ' greate ;' but ' dread' of '35 to '69 is better. G.

II.

JEALOUSIE.

FOND woman, which wold'st haue thy husband dye,
And yet complayn'st of his great jealousie :
If swolne with poison he lay in his last bedd,
His body with a sere-barke coverèd,
Drawinge his breath as thick and short, as can   5
The nimblest crotchetinge musitian,
Ready with loathsome vomitinge to spewe
His sowle out of one helle into a newe,

Made deafe with his pore kyndred's howling cries,
Begginge with few fayn'd tears, great legacies ;   10
Thou wold'st not weepe, but jolly and frolicque be,
As a slave, which to-morrow shold be free ;
Yet weep'st thou, when thou seest him hungerlie
Swallow his owne death, hart's-bane, JEALOUSY.
O give him many thanks, he's curtious,   15
That in suspectinge, kyndly warneth vs ;
We must not—as we usde—floute openly
In scoffinge ryddles, his deformity ;
Nor, at his board together being sate,
With words, nor touch, scarse lookes, adulterate :   20
Nor, when he, swolne and pamper'd with great fare, ·
Sits downe and snorts, cag'd in his basket-chayre,
Must we usurpe his owne bedd any more,
Nor kisse and play in his howse as before.
Now I see many daungers ; for that is   25
His realme, his castle, and his dyocesse.
But if—as envyous men, which wold revyle
Their prince, or coyne his gold, themselues exile
Into another contry and do yt there— ·
We play in another's howse, what shold we feare ?   30
There we will scorne his household polycies,
His sillye plotts and pentionary spyes :   silly
As the inhabitants of Thames' right side
Do London's Maior, or Germans the Pope's pryde.

NOTES AND ILLUSTRATIONS.

Our text is from Stephens' MS., with various-readings, &c. below, as before. This Elegy originally appeared in the 4to of 1633, where it is headed simply ' Elegie I.' (pp. 44-5). It has been reprinted in all the after-editions, and is found in all the MSS. Stephens' heads it ' Elegia Prima.' It was first entitled Jealousie in 1635 edition, and so in 1639 and 1649. I have marked the source of each title by printing the word or words in small capitals.

Line 4, ' *sere-barke :*' so in all the printed editions, except 1669, which reads ' sere-cloth.' It was a then belief that some poisons produced a tetter over the skin; and having spoken of poison and a swoln body, the poet alters the idea of ' sere-clothed' body (as in 1669) to one so covered or barked with a tetter that it is enclosed as in a sere-cloth. A curious example of the belief occurs in the last scene of Middleton's Women beware Women, where, as is clear from Bianca's words, her face shows as ' tettered,' from kissing the lips of the poisoned Duke. The sight of a person covered with the drying-up and black emphor of confluent small-pox best explains Donne's idea; and his form of words is interpreted by the Ghost's

> ' And a most instant tetter bark'd about
> Most lazar-like with vile and loathsome crust
> All my smooth body.'   Hamlet, i. 5.

Cf. also bark=skin, in Progress of the Soul, st. xxxii. line 5. On account therefore of these instances, we must suppose the person satirised was a great glutton rather than a high feeder (line 21); such a one as Marvell describes Clarendon and others.

Line 10, ' *few:*' MS. 18647 reads ' some few.'

 ,, 11, ' *jolly.*' See note on this word in Satire i. line 7.

 ,, 20. The construction may be—Nor adulterate our scarce looks with words nor touch—or, Nor adulterate as we sit together with words or with touch, and scarcely even with looks.

 Line 23. Stephens' MS. unrhythmically, ' We must not usurp his our bed any more.' I accept 1669 and usual text here.

Line 25, ' *many.*' 1669 reads ' Now do I see my dangers.' G.

III.

THE ANAGRAM.

MARRY, and love thy Flavia, for shee
Hath all things, wherby others beawtious bee;
For, though her eyes be small, her mouth is great;
Though theirs be ivory, yet her teeth are jet;
Though they be dymme, yet she is light enough,　　5
And though her harsh haire fall, her skin is tough;
What thoughe her cheeks be yellow, her hayre's redd,
Give her thyne, and she hath a maydenhead.
These things are bewty's elaments; where these　elements
Meet in one, that one must, as perfect, please.　　10
If redd and whyte, and each good quallitye
Be in thy wench, ne're ask where it doth lye.
In buyinge things perfumde, we ask if there
Be muske and amber in yt, but not where.
Thoughe all her parts be not in the usual place,　　15
Yet she hath the ANAGRAM of a good face.
If we might put the letters but one way,
In that lean dearth of words, what cold we say?
When by the gamcutt some musitians make
A perfect songe, others will undertake　　20
By the same gamut chaunged to æquall it.
Things symply good can neuer be vnfytt;
Shee's faire as any, if all be like her,
And if none be, then she is singular.

All love is wonder; if we justly doe   25
Account her wonderfull, why not louely too?
Loue built on bewtie, soone as bewty, dyes:
Chuse this face, chang'd by no deformityes.
Woomen are all like angels; the fayre bee
Like those that fell to worse; but such as shee,   30
Like to good angels, nothing can impaire:
'Tis les greif to be fowle then to 'have bene fayre.   than
For one night's revels, silk and gold we chuse,
But in long jorneys cloth and leather use.
Bewty is barren oft; best husbands say   35
There is best land where is ye fowlest way.
Oh! what a soveraigne plaister will she bee,
If thy past synns haue taught thee jealosye!
Heere needs no spyes nor eunuches, her commyt
Safe to thy foes, yea, to a marmosit.   40
When Belgia's cittyes the fowll country drowns,
That durty fowlness guards and armes the towns;   dirty
Soe doth her face guard her, and soe for thee
Which forct by busines absent oft must bee:
She, whose face, like the clowds, turnes day to night, 45
Who (mightier than the sea) makes Mores seem white; ·
Whom, thoughe seven years she in the stews had layd
A nunnerie durst receive, and thinke a mayd;
And though in chyld-birth's labour she did lye,
Midwives wold swear 'twere but a tympanie,   50
Whom, if she 'accuse her self, I credytt lesse
Then witches, which impossibles confesse.

Whom dildoes, bed-staves, and her veluet glasse
Wold be as loath to touch as Joseph was.
Ono like none, and lik'd of none, fittest were ;   55
For things in fashion euery man will ware.   wear

NOTES AND ILLUSTRATIONS.

Our text is from Stephens' MS., with various-readings, &c.
below, as before. It is there headed ' Elegia Decima Septima.'
It appeared originally in the 4to of 1633 (pp. 45-47), where it
is ' Elegie II. ;' and has been reprinted in all the after-editions.
It was first headed ' The Anagram' in 1635 edition.

Line 4, ' theirs.' I accept this from 1669 ; usually and in
our MS. ' they.'

Ib. ' are:' usually ' be.'

Line 5, ' she is,' as usually, I prefer to ' is she' of Stephens' MS.

„ 6, ' fall :' sometimes in MSS. ' fonle,' wrongly.

Ib. ' tough,' as in 1639: Stephens' MS. ' rough.' It is diffi-
cult to choose a reading, and I fancy it puzzled Donne here ;
but there is some anagrammatising in ' hairs fall' and ' skin'
being to make up for it ' tough :' none in ' rough.' The former
therefore is accepted.

Line 7, ' yellow:' 1669 spells ' yallow,' and MS. 18647 ' yal-
lowe.'

Line 12, ' wench:' our MS. reads badly ' mouth :' from 1633
onward ' wench.'

Line 14, ' amber:' see note in our MARVELL.

„ 16, ' the :' usually ' an,' but ' the' in 1635 also : in 1669
' anagrams.'

Line 18, ' that:' our MS. ' the' not so good.

„ 21, ' gamut chaunged :' our MS. ' gamut - change' — a
blunder. The first song is . . . notes in gamut order and a
gamut-change cannot be the ' same ;' while a second song we
can understand to bring notes of the gamut anagrammatised, or
the same gamut changed or read according to some other order-
ing.

Line 25, ' wonder:' our MS. misreads ' wonderfull,' probably
caught from next line.

Line 30, ' that,' usually ' which.'

„ 33, ' night's revels:' our MS. misreads ' night-revels.'

Line 35, ' *husbands*' = husbandmen.

,,   36, ' *is y^e :*' usually ' there is.'

,,   40, ' marmosit :' a term apparently for rakish gallants, taken from that species of licentious monkey-tribe which were the pets of the ladies.

Line 41. 1635 to 1649 read ' When Belgiae's cities the round countreis drowne :' 1669 ' Like Belgia's cities when the Country is drown'd.'

Line 46, ' *sea :*' ' sun' sometimes found in MSS. (*e.g.* Chetham MS.), wrongly. There is a reference to the proverbial saying as to the impossibility of washing a blackamoor white.

Line 49, ' *chyld-birth's :*' in 1633 ' child-bed's.' The former is preferable, because a child-bed labour may result in a tympany or mooncalf, whereas Donne says in accord with the context, were it a veritable child-birth labour no midwife would believe it to be such. See Cotgrave as quoted in our MARVELL, pp. 42-3, and also our SOUTHWELL, p. 92 : ' tympanie,' a false conception, mola, or mooncalf. The word was also used in its present acceptation by medical writers and others. See Boord's Brev. of Health, b. i. c. 345 ; and Holyoke, *s.v.*

Lines 53-4. First printed in 1669 edition : dildoes, see before : ' velvet glass,' see Marston in his Satires and Scourge of Villany (*bis*).   G.

IV.

CHANGE.

ALTHOUGH thy hand and faith and good works too
Haue seal'd thy love, which nothinge shold undoe ;
Yea, though thou fall back, that apostacye
Confirmes thy loue ; yet much, much I fear thee.
Women are like the Arts, forct vnto none;   5
'Open to all searchers, vnpriz'd if vnknowne.
If I have caught a bird, and let hym fly,
Another fouler, using these means as I,

May catch the same bird; and, as these things bee,
Women are made for man, not him, nor mee. 10
Foxes and goats—all beasts—change when they please,
Shall women, more hott, wilie, wyld, then these, than
Be bownd to one man? and did Nature then
Idly make them apter to endure then men? than
They are our cloggs, not their own; if a man be 15
Chayn'd to a gally, yet the gallie's free.
Who hath a plow-land, casts all his seed-corn there,
And yet allowes his grownd more corne should beare;
Though Danuby into the sea must flowe,
The sea receives the Rhine, Volga and Po: 20
By nature, which gave it, this liberty
Thou lov'st, but oh! can'st thou love it and me?
Likenes glews love; and then if so she doe,
To make vs like and love, MUST I CHANGE TOO?
More then thy hate, I hate it; rather let mee than 25
Allowe her CHANGE, then change as oft as shee; than
And soe not teach, but force my opyn'on,
To love not any one, but every one.
To live in one land is captivitye,
To run all countryes a wild roguery; 30
Waters stink soone, if in one place they 'byde,
And in the vast sea are worse putrifyde.
But when they keepe one banck, and leaving this
Never looke back, but the next bank do kisse,
Then are they purest; Change is the nursery 35
Of musique, joye, life, and eternitie.

NOTES AND ILLUSTRATIONS.

Our text is from Stephens' MS. with various-readings, &c.
below, as before. It is there numbered ' Elegia Duodecimo.'
It appeared originally in 1633 edition, and has been reprinted
in all since.   It was first headed ' Change' in 1635 : usually
simply ' Elegie III.'
    Line 2, ' shold :' MS. 18647 ' could.'
    ,, 3. This is extremely elliptical. This woman is change-
able, and he conceits upon it thus—As one who apostatises
[and then by returning to his old faith] confirms his belief
more than if he had continued in it through mere habit and
prejudice, so, though thou fell away from me [and by returning
to my love] hast confirmed thy previous protestations, yet still
I fear thee. This agrees with the general argument of the
poem in favour of occasional change like his, but not of immoderate like hers.
    Line 10, ' man :' usually and in our MS. ' men :' I accept
' man' from MS. 18647.
    Line 11. Our MS. and usually ' Foxes, goats, and all beasts,'
wrongly : our text 1635.
    Line 15, ' not :' our MS. reads ' and :' ' not' 1635 and usually.
    ,, 17, ' plow-land' = as much as one plough will culti-
vate : MSS. badly ' plough'd.'
    Line 23. Our MS. ' then if so she,' wrongly : MS. 18647 ' then
. . . thou.'
    Line 28. I accept ' nor' as usually printed, rather than ' but'
of our MS., inasmuch as he humorously praises change, but
exclaims against immoderate, his opinion that he would enforce
being ' neither to love any one alone nor yet every one.' Then,
' to live in one land,' he goes on to say, is ' captivity,' to run all
countries a wild vagabondage, and so lines 31-2; after which he
returns to his vow by the simile of waters in a river. See note
on line 3.
    Line 30, ' roguery :' not in the derivative sense of cheatery,
but in the original of vagabondism.
    Line 32, ' worse :' usually ' more :' 1669 reads ' purif'd.'   I
don't understand the philosophy here.
    Line 33, ' keepe :' usually ' kisse.'   G.

V.

THE PERFUME.

ONCE, and but once fownd in thy companie,
All thy supposdo escapes are layd on mee;
And as a theife at bar is question'd there
By all the men that haue been rob'd that yeare,
So am I (by this traiterous means surprisedc)   5
By thy hydroptique father catechized.
Though he had wont to search with glazod eyes,
As though he came to kill a cokatrice;
Though he hath oft sworne that he will removo
Thy beauty's bewty, and food of our love,   10
Hope of his goods, if I with thee were seene;
Yet close and secret, as our sowles, we have bene.
Though thy immortall mother, which doth lye
Still buryed in her bedd, yet will not dye,
Takes that advantage to sleep out daylight,   15
And watch thy entryes and retornes all night;
And when she takes thy hands, and would seem kynd,
Doth search what rings and armlots she can finde;
And kissinge notes the color of thy face,
And, fearing least thou art swolne, doth thee embrace; 20
And to try if thou long, doth name strango meats,
And notes thy palencss, blushinghs, sighs, and sweats,
And politiquely will to thee confesso
The sins of her owne youth's rancke wantones;

Yet loue these sorceryes did remove, and move   25
Thee to gull thine owne mother for my loue.
Thy little brethren, which like feary sprightes   fairy
Oft skipt into our chamber those sweet nightes ;
And kyst and ingled on thy father's knee,
Were bryb'd next day, to tell what they did see :   30
The grym eight-foote-highe iron-bownd serving-man,
That oft names God in oathes, and only than,   then
He that to barr the first gate doth as wyde
As the great Rhodian colossus stryde,
Which, if in hell no other paines there were,   35
Makes me feare hell, because he must be there :
Though by thy father he were hyrde to this,
Could never wytnes any touch or kisse.
But, oh ! too common ill, I brought with mee
That, which betraid me to myne enemye,—   40
A lowd PERFUME, which at my entrance cryde
Even at thy father's nose,—so we were spyde ;
When, like a tyran-king, that in his bedd
Smelt gunpowder, the pale wretch shyverèd ;
Had it bene some badd smell, he would have thought
That his own feet or breath the smell had wrought; 46
But as we in our isle imprisonèd,
Where cattell only and dyvers doggs are bredd,
The precious unicorne, straunge monstrous call ;
So thought he good strange, that had none at all.   50
I taught my sylks their whistlings to forbeare,
Even my opprest shoes dumbe and speachles were :

Onely, thou bytter-sweet, whom I had layd
Next mee, mee traytorously hast betrayde,
And, unsuspected, hast invisablie   55
Att once fledd unto him, and stayd with mee.
Base excrement of earth, which dost confound
Sense from distinguishing the sick from sound;
By thee the sillie Amorous sucks his death,
By drawing in a leprous harlott's breath;   60
By thee the greatest staine to man's estate
Falls on us,—to be call'd effeminate;
Though you be much lov'd in the Prince's hall,
There things, that seeme, exceed substantiall.
Gods, when yee fum'd on alters, were pleas'd well, 65
Because you were burnt, not that they lik'd your smell:
You are loathsome all, being taken simply alone,
Shall wee love ill things ioyn'd, and hate each one?
If you were good, your good doth soone decaye;
And you are rare,—that takes the good away.   70
All my perfumes, I give most willingly
T' enbalm thy father's coorse. What! will he dy?

NOTES AND ILLUSTRATIONS.

Our text is Stephens' MS., with various-readings, &c. below,
as before, but it ends at line 58; from line 58 to end our text is
from Addl. MSS. 18647. It appeared originally in 4to of 1633,
where it is 'Elegie IV.' It was first headed 'The Perfume' in
1635, and so onward.

Line 2, ' *escapes*'=escapades.

,, 5, ' this:' our MS., catching it from next line, misreads
' thy.'

Line 6, '*hydroptique :*' the constant spelling in Donne, and not peculiar to him, for hydropic or dropsical.

Line 7, '*wont.*' Donne always uses this verb without the substantive verb, thereby differing from the generality at least of his contemporaries.

Line 8. It was a belief that the cocatrice or basilisk 'slayeth all things that hath lyfe [except the weasel] with breathe and with sight;' and it was also a belief controverted by Sir Thomas Browne in his Pseudodoxia Ep. that it killed 'by priority of vision,' and therefore that it was necessary to safety to see it first. Hence the simile well describes her father's intent and suspicious searchings.

Line 10, 'Thy beauty's bewty :' our MS. 'Thy bewtious bewty,' which seems tautological. The idea 'The beauty of thy various beauties' (face, arm, shape, &c.) seems better otherwise: accepted, and so usually.

Line 16, '*retornes :*' our MS. badly 'retorne :' and also badly 'the' for 'all' of 1633, &c.

Line 21, 'And :' our MS. 'To try if thou dost long :' but I accept the usual text, the more so that to commence several lines with the same word was a conceit of the day.

Line 22, '*blushinghs :*' 1669 'blushes.'

,,　24, '*wantones :*' usually 'lustiness.'

,,　29, 'kist'= [being kist].

Ib. '*ingled :*' 1669 'dandled.' Ingled=petted, and probably cosied as in an ingle.

Line 43, '*tyran :*' invariably so spelled by the purist Ben Jonson.

Line 45, 'smell :' see former note on Satire i. line 90.　　.

,,　50, 'good :' 1669 'sweet :' the antithesis is between 'bad' (line 45) and '*good*' here.

Line 53, 'bytter-sweet'=the poisonous *Solanum dulcamara.*

,,　60, '*breath :*' alluding to the use of perfumed comfits and sweets such as are still used by men who smoke, and by women, and also to the then fixed belief that the constitutional results of the morbus gallicus were contagious.

Line 63, 'you :' and so usually: our MS. 'thou.' I prefer beginning the change to the plural 'you' here, instead of at line 65, chiefly on account of the verb 'loved.' There was a great distinction made between 'thou' and 'you' in matter of affection, the 'thou' being, like the second singular in French and German, a sign of endearment and great affection. The 'thou' and 'thee' and 'thine' of Shakespeare's Sonnets become 'you,' &c. in those occasional passages where any real or feigned estrangement is spoken of. G.

VI.

THE POET'S PICTURE.

HERE TAKE MY PICTURE, though I bidd farewell;
(Thine, in my hart where my sowle dwels shall dwell;)
'Tis like me now, but I dead, 'twil be more   [heart
When we ar shadowes both, then 'twas before. than
When weather-beaten I come back, my hand   5
Perhaps with rude oares torn, or sunbeames tan'd ;
My face and brest of hayrecloath, and my head
With Care's harsh suddaine hoariness o'respread ;
My body a sack of bones, broaken within,
And powder's blew staines scatterd on my skyn :   10
If rivall fooles tax thee to have lov'd a man
So fowle and course, as, oh ! I may seeme than, then
This shall say what I was : and thou shalt say,
Do his hurts reach me ? doth my worth decay ?
Or do they reach his judginge mynd, that hee   15
Should now loue less, what he did loue to see ?
That which in him was faire and delicate,
Was but the milk, which in Loue's childish state
Did nurse it : who now is growne strong enough
To feed on that, which to weak tastes seems tough. 20

Our text is from Stephens' MS. as before, where it is numbered 'Elegia Secunda.' It appeared originally in 4to of 1633
(pp. 51-2), and in all after-editions. It is headed 'His Picture'
in 1635. We have made the heading more definite.   ' ' '

Line 8. 1633, 'With care's rash sodaine stormes, being
o'rspread.'

Line 16, 'now loue less ;' so usually : our MS. ' lyke and louo
less.' The former I accept. Loving involves liking, and the
only excuse for the two would be the repetition of both in the
second half of the clause and line. 'Love less' also seems to require 'now,' or some mark of time ; and the rhythm of the MS.
reading is harsh, and puts the pause at 'love,' while the scansion is irregular.

Line 19, '*nurse*.' I accept 'nurse' of 1633 and usually
rather than 'nourish' of our MS. 'Nurse' better keeps up the
suggestion of the infantile state than 'nourish,' which is ap-
plicable to the strong food of a man. To 'nurse' is a form of
'nourish ;' but as Richardson says, 'to *nurse* is more especially
applied when that which is nursed is young or sickly.' I accept
also the usual 'weak,' rather than 'disus'd,' of our MS. 'Disus'd' gives bad scansion, and 'weak' agrees better with the context, 'childish state,' and is in opposition to '*strong*' stomach
of manhood. Then the love of his rivals may be, as he says,
'weak,' but it was not 'disus'd.' It was his and hers that was
disus'd by absence, though in fact it is not supposed to be disus'd or in abeyance.

Line 20, '*disus'd*,' 1633 ; our MS. 'disyre's ;' usually 'weak.'
G.

VII.

FAVORITE IN ORDINARY.

OH ! let me not serve soe, as those men serue,
Whom Honor's smoaks at once fatten and sterve,
Poorly enriched with great men's words or lookes ;
Nor so write my name in thy loving bookes,

As those idolatrous flatterers, which still   5
Their Prince's style with many realms fulfill,
Whence they no tribute haue, and where no sway.
Such services I offer as shall pay
Themselues; I hate dead names : oh then let me
FAVORITE IN ORDINARY, or no favorite bee.   10
Whenas my sowle was in her bodie sheath'd,
Nor yet by oathes betrothed, nor kisses breath'd
Into my purgatorie, faithles thee ;
Thy hart seem'd wax, and steele thy constancy : heart
So careles flowers, strode on the water's face, strewed 15
The curled whirlpoles smack, suck, and embrace,
Yet drownes them ; soe the taper's beamy eye,
Amorously twinckling, beckons the giddie fly,
Yet burnes his wings; and such the Devill is,
Scarse visitinge them who are entyrely his.   20
When I behold a streame, which from the spring
Doth with doubtfull melodious murmiringe,
Or in a speechles slumber calmly ride
Her wedded channel's bosome, and there chyde
And bend her browes, and swell, if any bovgh   25
Doe but stoope downe to kisse her utmost browe ;
Yet if her often-gnawinge kisses wynn
The trayterous bancks to gape and let her in,
She rusheth vyolently, and doth divorce
Her from her native and her long-kept course,   30
And roares and braves it, and in gallant scorne,
In flattering eddies promising returne,

She flowtes her channell, which thenceforth is dry;
Then say I, that is she, and this am I.
Yet let not thy deepe bitternes begett　　　　35
Carelesse dispair in me, for that will whett
My mynd to scorne; and, oh! Love dul'd with paine,
Was ne're so wise, nor well arm'd with disdain.
Then with new eyes I shall survay thee, and spie
Death in thy cheekes, and darknes in thyne eye :　40
Though hope breed faith and loue, thus taught, I shall,
As nations doe from Rome, from thy loue fall;
My hate shall outgrow thyne, and utterly
I will renownce thy dallyance : and when I
Am the Recusant, in that resolute state　　　　45
What hurts it me to be excommunycate?

NOTES AND ILLUSTRATIONS.

Our text is from Stephens' ms. as before, where this Elegy
is numbered ' Elegia Octava.' It appeared originally in 4to of
1633 (pp. 53-5), and in all after-editions. I have headed it
' Favorite in Ordinary.'

　　Line 4, '*my* . . . *thy*,' and so usually; our ms. ' thy . . . my.'
I accept the former. The subsequent simile is at its best bad;
but the ms. changes here, though at first sight they seem to im-
prove it, make it worse. If Donne put her name in his books,
he certainly would not insert her lovers, his rivals. Therefore
he cannot be said to ' fulfil his Prince's style.' Again, what he
is referring to is the cheque-rolls or muster rolls of her household and retainers; and he says, ' Let me not for mere form's
sake have my name inserted in ostentatious and vain muster-
roll of your attendants: "I hate dead names," ' &c.—such a
roll as flatterers make when they describe their king by giving
him sway over realms he does not possess; *e.g.* still our mon-
archs are called king or queen of France.

The badness of the simile lies in this, that the acts of the flatterers are put in connection with her acts, and this state with that of the Prince; and so it seems to liken her to the flatterers, and himself to the Prince. (So in next Elegy, lines 29-30, he makes 'her' his mistress='him,' a colt growing up to a male horse.) The ms. reading gets rid of this, but at the expense of the thought involved, that he does not wish to be a nominal attendant, nor be nominally enrolled as one, without being really subject to her.

Line 6, '*realms :*' 1669 'names.'
,, 7, '*where :*' 1669 'bear.'
,, 9, '*dead names :*' see note on Satire i. lines 17-18.
,, 24, '*there,*' 1669; usually 'then,' and so our ms. wrongly.
,, 26, '*utmost :*' 'upmost' in 1633, wrongly.
,, 38, '*with disdain*'=compared with disdain. At first blush the expression is ambiguous, for it suggests that the meaning is=armed, with disdain for armour; while the form of the sentence, and the words 'ne'er so wise,' show that this cannot be. The meaning is, 'A Lover dull'd with despairing pain is not so wise nor so well armed as one whetted with scorn;' or *poeticè*, 'Love dull'd with pain is not, &c. as Disdain.' I accept the ms. in preference to 'as Disdain,' with our explanation.

Line 39, '*thee :*' 1669 drops 'thee.'
,, 45, '*Recusant.*' Donne was originally a Roman Catholic. G.

VIII.

AMOROUS DELICACIES.

Nature's lay-ideot, I taught thee first to love,
And in that sophistry, oh ! how thou didst prove
Too subtill ! Fool, thou didst not understand
The mistique language of the eye nor hand :
Nor could'st thou judge the difference of the ayre 5
Of sighs, and saie this lies, this sownds dispaire :·

Nor by the eye's water cast a malady
Desperately hot, or changing feverouslye.
I had not taught thee then the alphabett
Of flowers, how they, devisefully being sett   10
And bownd up, might with speechles sècresie
Deliver errands mutely 'and mutually.
Remember, since all thy words vsde to bee
To every suytor, ' I, if my freinds agree ;'   Ay
Since howshold charms, thy husband's name to teach, 15
Were all thy love-tricks that thy witt could reach ;
And since an howr's discourse cold scarse have made
One answer in thee, and that ill-aray'd
In broken proverbes and torne sentences.
Thou art not by so many dutyes his,   20
(That, from the world's common havinge sever'd thee,
Inlayd thee, neither to be scene nor see,)
As myne, who have with AMOROUS DELICACYES
Refynde thee into a blysfull paradice.
Thy graces and good works my creatures bee,   25
I planted knowledge and life's tree in thee ;
Which, oh ! shall strangers tast? Must I, alas !
Frame and inamel plate, and drinke in glas ?
Chafe wax for other's seals? break a colt's force,
And leave him then being made a ready horse ?   30

NOTES AND ILLUSTRATIONS.

Our text is from Stephens' MS. as before, where it is numbered ' Elegia Decima tercia :' in Haslewood-Kingsborough MS.

'Elegy 3ᵘᵒ.' It appeared originally in the 4to of 1633 (pp. 55-6), and in all after-editions.

Line 1, '*lay:*' used perhaps in the sense in which it is used by the painters—layman, or a lay figure, which has no motion in itself. But Donne seems to use it elsewhere as laic, not cleric, and therefore ignorant. Cf. Second Ep. to Countess of Bedford, line 50, 'On these I cast a *lay* and country eye.'

Ib. '*first:*' usually dropped; and so line 2, 'how.'

Line 7, '*cast:*' in 1633 'call;' 1639, &c. 'know.' The word '*cast*' proves our ms. of this Elegy to be later and revised, because it is evidently an alteration from and improvement on '*know.*' It is here used medically. It was the technical term for diagnosing the disease by other water than eye-water. Cf. Macbeth (v. 3):

'If thou couldst, doctor, *cast*
The water of my :and, find her disease,
And purge it to a sound and pristine health.'

Line 13, '*since*'=remember [all that has passed between you and me, all my teachings] since all thy words, and since, &c.; *i.e.* remember and compare both times, since and the time when.

Line 22, '*Inlayd,*' as a composite, not a compound word= laid thee in, or sequestered thee.

Line 23, '*delicacyes:*' 1633 onward: our ms. 'delightes,' wrongly.

Line 25, '*works:*' 1633 and onward 'words;' but 1669 'works.'

I have headed this Elegy from line 23. G.

IX.

THE COMPARISON.

As the sweet sweat of roses in a styll,

.As that, which from chaf'd musket's pores doth trill,

As the almightie balm of the 'orient East,

Such are the sweat-drops on my mistres' brest;

And on her neck her skyn such lustre setts,   5
They seeme no sweat-dropps, but pearle carkanets.
Ranck sweatie froth thy mistresse' brow defyles,
Like spermatique issue of ripe menstruous byles ;
Or like that scum, which, by Need's lawles law .
Enforc'd, Sancerra's starvèd men did draw   10
From parboyl'd shoos and bootes, and all the rest,
Which were with any soveraigne fatness blest ;
Or like vyld stones lying in saffron'd tynn,
Or warts, or wheals, it hangs upon her chynn.
Round as the world's her heade, on every syde,   15
Like to that fatal ball which fell on Ide :
Or that, whereof God had such jealosy,
As for the ravishing thereof we dy.
Thy head is like a rough-hewen statue of jett,   .
Where markes for eyes, nose, mouth, ar yet scarse sett ;
Like the first chaos, or flatt-seeminge face   21
Of Cynthia, when th' Earth shadows her imbrace.
Like Proserpine's white bewty-keeping chest,
Or Jove's best fortune's vrne, is her faire brest.
Thyne, like a worm-eaten trunck cloth'd in seal's skin ;
Or grave, that's durt without, and stench within.   26
And like the slender stalk, at whose end stands
The woodbyne quivering, are her arms and hands :
Like rough-barkt elme-boughes, or the russet skin
Of men late scourg'd for madness, or for sinne ;   30
Like sun-parcht quarters on the citie's gate,
Such is thy tan'd skinne's lamentable state ;

And like a bunch of ragged carrets stand
The scurfe-swollen fingers of the gowty hand.
Then like the Chimick's masculine-equal fire,   35
Which in the lymbeck's warme womb dothe inspire
Into th' earth's worthles durt a sowle of gold,
Such cherishinge heat her best-worst part doth hold.
Thine's like the dread mouth of a fyrèd gunn,
Or like hot liquid mettals newly runn   40
Into clay mowlds, or like to that Ætna,
Where round about the grasse is burnt away.
Are not your kysses then as filthie and more,
As a worme suckinge an envenom'd sore?
Doth not thy fearfull hand in feeling quake,   45
As one which gathering flowers, still fears a snake?
Is not your last act harsh and vyolent,
As when a plowgh a stony ground doth rent?
So kisse good turtles, so devoutly nyce
Are preists in handlinge reverent sacrifize,   50
And such in searching wownds the surgeon is,
As we, when we embrace, or touch, or kisse;
Leave her, and I will leave comparinge thus,
Shee and COMPARISONS are odyous.

NOTES AND ILLUSTRATIONS.

Our text is from Stephens' MS. as before, where it is numbered ' Elegia Quarta :' in Haslewood-Kingsborough MS. ' Elegy
6ᵈᵒ.' It appeared originally in 1635 edition, and since in after-
editions.
    Line 2, 'chaf'd :' our MS. 'chas'd;' but so far as I can

judge, 'chas'd' is a clerical error. This is the more probable,
in that if it 'trilled' from chased animals, it could hardly be
'gathered.'   'Chaf'd' is also supported by a curious quotation
by Sir Thomas Browne in Pseudod. (b. iii. c. 4); and as matter
of fact civet-cats must be fretted and vexed before the civet is
taken out of the bag; 'for the more the animal is enraged, the
musk is the better' (Horne, Essays and Thoughts; as in Richardson's Dict. *s. v.* civet). See also Lovell's History of Animals and
Minerals (1661) for quaint lore.

Line 2, '*trill :*' see our full note in HENRY VAUGHAN, *s. v.*

  ,, 3, '*orient :*' usually 'early :' perhaps the former is
tautological, and as such may have been altered by Donne to
'early.'

Line 6, 'carkanets :' usually 'coronets.'

  ,, 8. In this horrible line, 'menstruous' is probably=
polluting or filthy, a latinate sense. The old medical writers
yield elucidations, but I mind not quoting.

 · Line 10, '*Sancerra :*' the allusion is to the siege of Sancerre
near Bourges, in which the besieged suffered the extreme of
famine, in 1573. It was held by the Protestants against the Ca-
tholics, and the siege lasted nine months.

Line 13, '*Or*,' usually '*And :*' 'vyld,' usually 'vile ;' 'saffron'd tynn'=coloured tinfoil.

Line 14, '*wheal :*' a pimple, vesicle, or pustule. It is curious
that Johnson gives this sense under 'wheal ;' but quotes this
very passage under 'weal' for the mark of a stripe.

Ib. '*chynn :*' usually 'skinn.' I accept the usual 'it hangs'
for 'they hang' of MS. Cf. line 7.

Line 19, a curious change to apostrophising the friend's
mistress, which continues to line 37.

Line 22, '*Earth :*' usually 'Earth's.'

  ,, 26, '*durt :*' usually 'dust.'

  ,, 34, '*scurfe :*' usually 'short ;' 'the gowty,' 1669 'mistress :' 'the gouty' is preferable, being rare in women.

Line 38, '*best-worst :*' usually 'best-loved.'

  ,, 51, '*such :*' usually 'nice.'

  ,, 54, '*comparisons are odyous :*' an accepted 'household'
phrase ; but I find it earlier in 'The most horrible murther of
John Lord Bourgh, 1591' (p. 5, Collier's reprint)—'scornefull
tearmes and *odious comparisons.*' G.

X.

THE AUTUMNAL.

No Springe nor Somer's bewty hath such grace,
As I have scene in one AUTUMNALL FACE.
Yonge beutyes force our loues, and that's a rape ;
This doth but counsaile, and you canot 'scape.
If 'twere a shame to love, here 'twere no shame :   5
Affectyon here takes Reverence's name.
Were her first years the Golden Age? that's true ;
But now she's gold oft tryde and ever newe.
That was her torrid and inflaming tyme ;
This is her tolerable tropique clyme.   10
Faire eies, who askes more heat then comes from hence,
He in a fever wisheth pestilence.   [than
Call not these wrinckles graves : if graues they were,
They were Love's graves ; for else he is nowhere.
Yet lyes not Loue dead here, but heere doth sitt   15
Vow'd to this trench, like an anachorytt.
And here, till her's (which must be his) death, come,
He doth not dygg a grave, but buyld a tombe.
Heere dwells he ; though he sojourns everywhere
In progresse, yet his standinge-howse is here ;   20
Heere, where still evening is, nor noon nor night,
Where's no voluptuousnes, yet all delight.
In all her words, unto all hearers fytt,
You may at revels, you may at councells sytt.

This is Love's tymber, Youth, his underwood ;   25
There he, as wyne in June, enrages blood,
Which then comes seasonablest, when our tast
And appetyte to other things is past.
Xerxes's strange Lydian loue, the platan tree,
Was lov'd for age, none beinge so old as shee,   30
Or els because, beinge young, Nature did blesse
Her youth with age's glory, barrennesse.
If we loue thinges long sought for, age is a thing,
Which we are fiftye years in compassinge ;
If transitorie things, which soone decay,   35
Age must be loveliest at the latest day.
But name not wynter-faces, whose skyn is slacke,
Lank as an unthrifte's purse,—but a sowle's sacke ;
Whose eyes seeke light within, for all heere's shade ;
Whose mouths are holes, rather worne out then made ;
Whose every tooth to a severall place is gone   [than
To vex their sowle at the Resurrectyon ;
Name not these living death's-heads unto mee,
For these not ancyent but antiques bee :
I hate extreams : yet I had rather stay   45
With tombes then cradles, to weare out a day.   than
Since such Love's naturall station is, may still
My love descend, and journey downe the hyll ;
Not panting after growinge bewtyes ; soe
I shall ebb on with them, who homewards goe.   50

NOTES AND ILLUSTRATIONS.

Our text is from Stephens' MS. as before, where it is numbered 'Elegia Viscessima quarta,' and headed 'A Paradox of an ould Woman.' It appeared originally in 1635 edition, and since in all after-editions, under our heading.

Line 2, '*one :*' so 1635 and usually: our MS. misreads 'an.'
  ,, 3, '*our :*' so usually: our MS. 'your.'
  ,, 4, '*and :*' 1635 'yet,' and usually.
  ,, 6, '*Affectyon :*' usually 'affections;' but while affections =all the affections of one mind, as well as the affection of all, is expressive, the double personification of Affection and Reverence vindicates our MS. reading.

Line 10, '*tolerable :*' usually 'habitable.' Either seems an odd word to express that feeling which would lead one to live with another as in a pleasant place; and to say that the tropic clime is only 'tolerable' is a strange way of expressing how pleasant it is to dwell with her; but (1) Donne abounds in such oddities; (2) 'tolerable' is=habitable; and conversely (3) there is the usual and inevitable sarcastic touch.

Line 16, '*anachorytt :*' so 1635, &c.: the more Greek form, ἀναχωρητής.

Line 18, '*tombe*'=the raised part of the wrinkle, beautiful as a mausoleum.

Lines 23-4. Usually the reading is 'You may . . . you at.' Our MS. 'You may . . . you may,' means that one sits at the same time at revels and council, *i. e.* hears jocose and cheerful conversation, which is at the same time full of wisdom. Thus it answers to the first clause, 'In all her words.' 'You may . . . you at' means, Some you or some of you may enjoy revels, and other you may sit at council with her. This answers rather to the second clause, 'unto all hearers fit,' that she can fit all.

Line 26, '*There*'=this of previous line=her.
  ,, 29, '*platan tree :*' Pliny, N. H. xii. 1-3; xvi. 44.
  ,, 37-8. Our MS. reads 'whose skyn slacke, Lookes like.' This is not idiomatic but foreign English. Moreover our text, which is that of 1635 and usually, is stronger by dwelling on it. First comes the general enunciation, 'whose skyn is slacke;' then the variation and simile, 'Lank as an unthrift's purse—but [=yet] a sowle's sack.'

Line 39, '*heere*'=outside in the sunken cavity and lack-lus-
tre eye.

Line 42, '*their*.' I accept 'their' instead of the usual 'the'
(which is also in our MS.), as it agrees better with 'wynter-
faces,' 'mouths,' 'death's-heads and tombs.'

Line 47, '*station:*' so usually; and I accept it. Our MS.
has 'acyon'=action, seemingly a clerical error. 'Station' agrees
with what is said of her in line 20, that she is Love's home.

At line 37 he digresses to explain what he does not love;
and at line 45 he says he hates extremes, though, had he to
choose one extreme, he would, &c. Then he returns to the
subject of his song, and closes his eulogy with, Since such
autumnal face and person is Love's palace, let my love, &c. G.

XI.

THE DREAM.

IMAGE of her, whome I loue more then she,   than
Whose faire impression in my faithfull hart   heart
Makes me her medall, and makes her love mee,
As kings do coynes, to which their stamp imparts
The valew: goe, and take my hart from hence,   5
Which now is growne too great and good for mee.
Honors oppresse weake spirits, and our sence
Strong objects dull: the more, the lesse wee see.
When you are gone, and Reason gone with you,
Then Fantasie is queene, and sowle, and all;   10
Shee can present joyes meaner then you doe;   than
Convenient, and more proportionall.

Soe, if I DREAME I have you, I have you ;
For all our joyes are but fantasticall.
And soe I 'scape the paine, for paine is true ;   15
And Sleepe, which locks upp sense, doth lock up all.
After such a fruition, I shall wake,
And, but the wakinge, nothing shall repent ;
And shall to Loue more thankfull sonets make,
Then if more honours, tears, and pains were spent. than
But dearest hart, and dearer image, stay,   21
Alas! true joyes at best are dream enough ;
Though you stay here, you passe too fast away :
For even at first Life's taper is a snuffe.
Fil'd with her love, may I be rather growne   25
Madd with much heart, then idiot with none.   than

NOTES AND ILLUSTRATIONS.

Our text is from Stephens' MS. as before, where it is numbered 'Elegia Decima.' It appeared originally in 1635 edition,
and since in after-editions. This Elegy is written of one somewhat obdurate : hence in line 21 he calls the more yielding
image of his dream the dearer, and in line 1 calls her one
whom he loves more than she [loves him].

. Line 16, ' up :' usually ' doth lock out.'

„ 22, 'dream :' I accept this from '35 rather than the
usual ' dreams' (which is also in our MS.), as the plural is more
readily ambiguous and the singular more forceful = all joys,
the whole of them, are but one short dream.

Line 24, ' snuffe :' see note on Satire ii. line 82.

„ 26, ' heart :' our MS. ' hurt,' wrongly.   G.

XII.

VPON THE LOSSE OF HIS MISTRESSE'S CHAINE,

FOR WHICH HE MADE SATISFACTION.

Not that in colour it was like thy hayre,
For armelets of that thou maist let me weare ;
Nor that thy hand it oft embrac't and kist,
For soe yt had the good, which oft I mist ;
Nor for that sillie old morallity,   5
That ' *as these links are tyde, our loves shold bee ;*'
Mourne I, that I the SEAVENFOLD CHAYNE haue lost.
Nor for the lucke-sake, but the bytter cost.
Oh, shall twelue righteous angels, which as yett
No leaven of vile soder did admitt ;   solder   10
Nor yet by any faults haue strai'd or gone
From the first state of their creatyon ;
Angels, which Heaven commanded to provide
All things to mee, and be my faithfull guyde ;
To gayne new frends, t' appease great enemyes,   15
To comfort my sowle, when I ly or rise :
Shall these twelue inocents, by thy severe
Sentence (great judge) my syn's great burthen bear ?
Shall they be damn'd, and in the furnace thrownc,
And punisht for ofences not their owne ?   20
They saue not me, they doe not ease my paines,
When in that hell they are burnt and tyde in chaines :

Were they but crownes of France, I carèd not,
For most of them, their natural country rott
I think possesseth, they come here to vs,   25
So leane, so pale, so lame, and ruynous ;
And howsoere French kings ' *most Christian*' bee,
Their crownes are circumcised most Jewishly ;
Or were they Spanish stamps, still travailing,
That are become catholique as their king,   30
Those unlickt bear-whelps, unfyl'd pistolets,
That (more then cannon-shots) avayles or letts,
Which, negligently left vnrounded, looke
Like many-angled fygures in the booke
Of some great conjurer, which wold enforce   35
Nature (as thay do Justice) from her course,
Which, as the sowle quickens head, foot, and hart, heart
As stream-like vaines run through the Earth's every part,
Visit all countryes, and haue slylie made
Gorgeous France, ragged, ruyned, and decay'd ;   40
Scotland, which knew noe state, prowd in one day ;
And mangled seventeen-headed Belgia :
Or were it such gold as that wherewithall
Almightye chimicks from each mynerall,
Having by subtle fyre a sowle out-pul'd,   45
Are durtily and desperately gul'd ;
I wold not spit to quench the fyre they are in,
For they are guylty of much haynous sin.
But shall my harmles angels perish ? shall
I loose my guard, my ease, my food, my all ?   50

Much hope, which they shold nourish, wilbe dead ;
Much of my able yowth and livelie-head
Will vanish, if thou, Loue, let them alone,
For thou wilt loue me less when they are gone.
Oh! be content, that some lowd-squeakinge cryer,   55
Well pleas'd with one leane threed-bare grot for hyer,
May like a divill roare through every street,
And gall the fynder's conscience if they meet :
Or let me creep to some dread conjurer,
Which with fantastique schemes fils full much paper ;
Which haue devided heaven in tenements,   .   61
And with whores, theeves, and murtherers stuft his rents
Soe full, that though he passe them all in synne,
He leaves himselfe no roome to enter in.
     But if, when all his art and time is spent,   65
He say 'twill ne're be found ; oh! be content ;
Receive the doome from him ungrudgeingly,
Because he is the mouth of Destiny.
     Thou sai'st, alas! the gold doth still remain,
Though it be chaung'd, and put into a chayne.   70
Soe in the first falne angels, resteth still
Wisdom and knowledg, but 'tis turnd to ill :
As these shold doe good works, and shold provide
Necessities, but now must nurse thy pryde.
And they ar still badd angels ; myne ar none,   75
For forme gives being, and their forme is gone.
Pitty these angels, yet their dygnities
Pass Virtues, Powres, and Principalities.

But thou art resolute: Thy will be done !
Yet with such anguish, as her only sonne   80
The mother in the hungry graue doth lay,
Unto the fyre these marters I betray.
Good sowles, (for you give life to every thing.)
Good angels, (for good messages you bringe,)
Destin'd you might haue been to such an one,   85
As wold haue lov'd and worshipt you alone :
One that wold suffer hunger, nakednes,
Yea death, e're he would make your number less.
But I am guyltie of your sad decay :
May your few-fellowes longer with me stay !   9c
    But, oh ! thou wretched fynder, whom I hate
Soe much that I almost pyttie thy estate :
Gold being the heavyest metall amongst all,
May my most heaviest curse upon thee fall :
Here fettred, manacled, and hang'd in chaynes,   95
First mai'st thou bee, then chain'd to hellish paines ;
Or be with foraigne gold brib'd to betray
Thy contry, and faile both of that and thy paye.
May the next thing thou stoop'st to reach, containe
Poyson, whose nymble fume rott thy moist braine ;
Or lybells, or some interdicted thinge,   101
Which, negligently kept, thy ruyne bring.
Lust-bred diseases rott thee ; and dwell with thee
Itchy desire, and no abilitye.
May all the hurt which ever gold hath wrought,   105
All mischiefs which all devills ever thought,

Want after plenty, poore and gowty Age,
The plague of travailers ; love and marryage,
Afflict thee ; and at thy live's latest moment
May thy fowle syns to thee themselues present.   110
  But I forgive thee ; repent, thou honest man !
Gold is restoratiue, restore it than ;   then
But if from yt thou beest loath to depart,
Because 'tis cordiall, wold 'twere at thy hart.   heart

NOTES AND ILLUSTRATIONS.

Our text is Stephens' MS. as before, where it is numbered
' Elegia Decima sexta.' It appeared originally in 1635 edition,
and since in all the after-editions. Our heading is first found
in '35 : but 'Chaine' is scarcely the right word, seeing it is
clear from the description that it was a (seven) chain-bracelet.
Hence the heading in Haslewood-Kingsborough MS. is more
accurate : ' Upon the Loss of a Bracelet.' See our Essay for
Ben Jonson's 'Conversation' with Drummond of Hawthornden
on this Elegy.
  Line 2, 'For . . . let :' usually 'Armelets . . . still let.'
  ,,   5, 'morallity :' I know no other example of this word
used to denote a moral saying or posy.
  Line 6, 'are tyde :' usually 'were knit.' It is most likely
that the chain-bracelet bore the morality.
  Line 8, 'Nor . . . the.' I adhere to the usual printed text
here, rather than accept our MS. 'Not . . . they.' ' Not' sepa-
rates the thought unnecessarily and unpleasantly from the
rest, whereas there is an enumeration, Not, nor, nor, nor, &c.
Farther, as it is evident that Donne took the ' chain-bracelet'
from her arm and wore it, that ' he might have something that
had embraced her,' and by misadventure lost it, it seems impossible that he could write ' they.' The omen would be as to his
luck—that as he had lost, so the loss of her love would follow.
  Line 11, 'fault :' usually ' way.'
  ,,   13, 'Heaven :' so usually, and I accept it : our MS.
badly 'Heavens'=Heaven has ; but 'had' would be needed, not
' has.'

Line 15, '*great :*' 'old' usually.
„   16, '*rise :*' so usually : our MS. misreads ' raise.'
„   18, '*great :*' 'dread' usually : and so line 35.
„   23, '*crownes of France :*' a new application of the common equivoque with regard to the *morbus gallicus :* crowns of
less value (6*s.* 8*d.*) than angels (10*s.*).
Line 24, '*natural country rott :*' '35 'countrey's naturall
rot.'
„   26. Usually ' So pale, so lame, so lean, and ruinous :'
our MS. yields a better climax in describing the observer's per-
ception of the progress of the disease.
Line 29, '*Spanish stamps.*' On account of the influx of silver
from Mexico, Spanish silver coins had become a universal or
catholic medium of exchange, and all purchases in China and
the Moluccas are still paid in dollars : ' stamp'= coin bearing
the Spanish stamp.
Line 31, '*pistolets :*' see former note :=26 ryals, 14*s.*
„   32, '*cannon :*' so usually : our MS. ' comon.' I prefer
the former, because as in a similar passage (Satire ii. line 20)
there is an equivoque on pistolets as money and as small pistols;
such small-bore shots, he says, are of more avail as artillery
for my purpose than great cannon-shot.
Line 38. See note in our SOUTHWELL, *s. v.*
„   52, ' *livelie-head :*' usually ' lusty.'
„   60, ' *schemes.*' As in another case (noted in its place),
where ' scenes' has been miswritten for ' schemes,' I have ventured to adopt it here instead of the usual ' scenes' and ' sheawes'
of our MS. The reference is not to cabalistic and other decora-
tions or hangings, but, as the words ' fils full much paper' show,
to astrological ' schemes,' drawn out with the constellations,
&c. or persons and the like.
Line 62, ' *rents*'=not the rending, but the divisions or parts
so divided or rent.
Line 72, ' *Wisdom :*' a contemporary annotator of 1639 edit.
has put in margin ' cunning.'
Line 74, ' *thy :*' so usually : our MS. has the not uncommon
clerical error of ' their' for ' thy' [Shakespeare, Sonnets xxvi.
l. 12 : xxvii. l. 10 : xxxv. l. 8 (*bis*): xxxvii. l. 7 : xlv. l. 12 : xlvi.
(*ter*)]. Her saying ends at line 70. His answer begins with
the simile (ll. 71-2), and ends with the application (ll. 73-4).
The virtues of the fallen angels remain, but turned to ill, like
as these [angels of mine], which should do good works for me

(ll. 13-16), by procuring me food, &c.; but now, having passed
into the hell of the goldsmith's fire, must as a bracelet nurse
'thy' pride.

Line 78 The angelic Hierarchy is divided into three ter-
nions, and each ternion into three classes or orders. Reckoning
downwards there are: 1. Seraphim; 2. Cherubim; 3. Thrones
(Throni); 4. Dominations; 5. Principalities; 6. Powers (Potes-
tates); 7. Virtues (Virtutes); 8. Archangels; 9. Angels. Hence,
as in his reference to pistolets, Donne humorously says, though
made the lowest of the heavenly hierarchy, yet here they surpass Virtues, Powers, and Principalities. For the qualities and
offices of the angelic orders, see Batman on Bartholomew (b. xi.
cc. 6-18); and Heywood's Hierarchie of the Blessed Angels,
book iv. &c. Note that in Holy Scripture, only one 'Archangel'
occurs.

Line 96, 'chain'd :' so usually, and I prefer it to 'chaung'd'
of our MS.

Line 105. Usually 'May all the evils that gold ever wrought :'
'evils' here is, as usual, monosyllabic, and is perhaps the wider
and stronger word.

Line 109, 'latest :' usually 'late.'

„ 110, 'fowle :' usually 'swoln.' 'Swoln' is = sins which
have gone on increasing in number and enormity, according
to the saying that one ill leads to another and another, each
greater than the last.

Line 112, 'restoratiue'= as a medicine. 'Gold . . . sove-
raign it is for green wounds if it be outwardly applied; and
if young children weare it about them, lesse harme that they
have by any sorcery, witchcraft' (Pliny, N. H. by Holland). See
also for much quaint lore, Batman on Bartho omew; and for a
grotesquely-serious account of the results of swallowing a pill
of gold, Richard Baxter's 'Life,' in his noble folio 'Reliquiœ
Baxterianœ,' s. v.

XIII.

LOVE-MEMORIES IN ABSENCE.

Come, Fates! I feare you not.   All, whome I owe,
Are paide but you.   Then 'rest mee e're I goe.
But Chance from yow all soueraignty hath gott,
Loue woundeth none but those whome Death dares not:
Else if you were, and just in equity,   5
I should haue vanquisht her, as you did mee.
Else louers should not braue Death's pains, and liue:
But 'tis a rule, Death comes not to relieue.
For pale and wann Death's terrors, are they laide
Soe deep in louers, they make Death affraide?   10
Or, (the least comfort) haue I companny?
Orecame she Fates, Loue, Death, as well as mee?
      Yes, Fates doe silke unto her distaffe pay
For ransome, which tax they on us do lay.
Love giues her youth, which is the reason why   15
Youths, for her sake, some wither and some dye.
Poore Death can nothing giue; yet for her sake,
Still in her turne, he doth a louer take.
And if Death should proue fals, she fears him nott,
For our Muse, to redeeme her, she hath got.   20
That last and fatal night wee kist, I thus praide,
(Or rather thus despair'd, I should haue saide.)
Kisses, and yet despaire!   The forbidden tree
Did promiss (and deceaue) no more then she.   than

Like lambs that see their teats, yet must eat hay,   25
A food, whose tast hath made me pine away:
Diues, when thou sawst bliss, and crauest to touch
A drop of water, then thy great pains were such.
Heere greif wants a fresh wit, for mine being spent,
And my sighes weary, grones are all my rent;   30
Unable longer to endure the paine,
They breake like thunder, and doe bring downe raine.
Thus, till drye tears soder mine eyes, I weepe: solder
And then I dreame, how you securly sleepe,
And in your dreams doe laugh at me.   I hate,   35
And pray Loue, all may: He pittyes my estate,
But sayes, I therin no reuenge shall find;
Tho sun would shine, though all the world were blind,
Yet, to try my hate, LOUE SHEW'D MEE YOUR TEARE;
And I had dyde, had not your smile been there.   40
Your froune undoes mee; your smile is my wealth;
And as you pleas to looke, I haue my health.
Methought Loue, pittying mee, when he saw this,
Gaue me your hands, the backs and palmes, to kiss.
That cur'd me not, but to beare pain gaue strength;
And what it lost in force, it took in length.   46
I call'd on Loue againe, who fear'd you soe,
That his compassion still prou'd greater woe:
For then I dream'd I was in bedd with you,
But durst not feele, for fear 't should not proue true.
This merritts not your angar, had it been;   51
The Queen of Chastity was naked seene:

And in bed, not to feele, the paine I tooke,
Was much more then for Actæon not to looke. than
And that breast, which lay ope, I did not knowe 55
But for the clernes, from a lump of snowe :
Nor that sweet teat which on the top it bore
From the rose-bud which for my sake you wore.
These griefs to issue forth, by verse I proue,
Or turne their course by trauell or new loue. 60
All would not do, the best at last I tryde,
Unable longer to hold out I dyide.
And then I found I lost lif's death by flying ;
Where hundreds liue, are but so long in dying.
Charon did lett me pass ; I him requite 65
To walke the groues or shade, wronging my delight :
Ile speak out of those ghosts I found alone,
Those thousand ghosts, wherof my self made one,
All images of thee : I askt them whie ;
The Iudge told mee, they all for thee did dye, 70
And therefore had for their Elizian bliss
Another, their owne loues to kisse.
O here I myst, not blisse, but being dead
(For loe I dreampt) I dreamt, and waking sed,
Heauen if whoe are in thee ther must dwell, 75
How is't I now was there, and now I fell ?

NOTES AND ILLUSTRATIONS.

Our text in this instance is from Haslewood-Kingsborough
MS. as before, as this Elegy does not appear in the Stephens'

MS. But we for the fi st time print ll. 57-76, deriving them
from our British-Museum MS. This Elegy (as far as l. 56)
originally appeared in 1635 edition, and since in the after-
editions. The heading is ours.

Line 4, '*these :*' so usually : our MS. ungrammatically reads
'them.'

Line 5, 'Else :' so in '35, but usually 'True,' as in '69. The
former is preferable, because stronger; the meaning being,
Else if you were [sovereigns], sovereigns being taken out of
sovereignty in l. 3.

Line 9, '*pale and wann.*' Cf. Suckling's 'Why so pale and
wan, fond lover?'

Line 12, '*Orecame she :*' usually 'Or can the Fates love
Death,' to the confusion of the sense : but I accept the usual
order, 'Fates, Loue, Death,' because they so appear in the other
copies, and because they so enumerated in the poem : Fates,
l. 13; Love, l. 15; Death, l. 17.

Line 14, '*tax :*' so usually, and I prefer it to 'taske' of our
MS. because they take our thread of life to add to her distaff
for ransom for themselves. Our MS. also misreads '*they* lay,'
from the common error of inadvertently rewriting a word that
has caught the eye and memory. Similarly 'their' is mis-
inserted before 'ransom' in l. 14, and 'true' before 'reason'
in l. 15; which make the scansion irregular, as well as lessen
the neatness of the wording, without adding to the strength.
So too in l. 24 our MS. by reading 'Did not promise,' and eras-
ing 'no,' turns the line into mere prose, and throws the words
out of accent.

Line 20, '*Muse :*' usually 'Muses,' badly.

„ 21. Usually 'That fatal night we last kiss'd ... thus
praide,' *i. e.* as above from l. 1.

Line 25, '*yet :*' usually 'and,' badly.

„ 28. Our MS. reads here 'A small little drop.' This
shows it to have been a transcription from a MS. in which the
author had been in doubt which epithet he would decide on,
and had written both. So writing 'A small little drop,' the
epithet 'great' was erased : but on revision it became clear
that the size of the drop was wholly irrelevant, and therefore
took away from his meaning, while 'pains' expressed that in
which he would say Dives and he were alike. Hence he struck
out the epithet from 'drop,' and added one (*i.e.* 'great') to pains,
as usually.

Line 30, '*are all*:' so usually: our MS. misreads 'all are.'
,, 36, 'all may:' so usually: our MS. 'alway.' I accept
the former=I hate and pray to Love that all 'may,' so that
all others may hate her too. Not only is this stronger, but it
agrees with Love's answer (1. 38), 'The sun would shine, though
all the world were blind' = She would be the same beauty
whatever might be the world's opinion of her. The MS. 'way'
is not unlikely the error of w for m, of which we have noted
another example in 'wench' for 'month.' So in l. 37, I accept
the usual 'shall,' instead of 'should' of our MS.=Even if I
grant it, that shall be no revenue to you.

Line 46. He being weak through sight of the tear, wanted
force to kiss as he would, but made up for this by the duration
of the kiss.

Line 50. Cf. Elegy ix. (The Comparison), l. 45, Doth not,
&c.

,, 65. I have ventured to read 'I' for 'he him:' and l.
66 'walke' for 'make'—the common clerical error of m for w,
as before. So too in l. 72 'Another' for 'In other;' the conceit being that for or in recompense for that Elizian bliss of
dying for her [probably an Eliza], they were granted that
other, viz. of having their own loves to kiss.

Lines 73-6 are somewhat obscure; but as a (too characteristic) equivoque underlies them, I am not careful to elucidate
here. G.

XIV.

PARTING.

Since she must goe, and I must mourne, come Night,
Enuiron me with darknes, whilst I write :
Shadowe that hell unto mee, which alone
I am to suffer, when my loue is gone.
Alas, the darkest magick cannot doe itt,   5
And thow great hell to boot are shadows to it.

Should Cinthia quit thee, Heauen, and each starre,
It would not forme one thought darke as mine are ;
I could lend them obscurenes now, and say
Out of myselfe, there should be no more day.   10
Such is already my felt want of sight,
Did not the fyer within me force a light.
O Loue, that fire and darknes should be mixt,
Or to thy triumphs such strange torments fixt !
Is 't because thou thyselfe art blinde, that wee,   15
Thy martirs, must noe more each other see ?
Or tak'st thou pride to breake us on thy wheele,
And view ould Chaos in the paine we feele ?
Or haue we left undone some mutuall rite
That thus with parting thou seek'st us to spight ?   20
No, no. The fault is mine, impute it to me,
Or rather to conspiring Destenye ;
Which, since I lou'd, in jeast before, decreed,
That I should suffer, when I loved indeed,
And therefore now sooner then I can say   than   25
I saw the goulden fruite, its rapt away.
Or as I had watcht one drop in a vast streame,
And I left wealthy only in a dreame.
Yet, Loue, thou'rt blinder then thyselfe in this, than
To vex my doue-like freind for my amiss :   30
And, where one sad truth may expiate
Thy wrath, to make her fortune runn my fate.
Soe blinded Justice doth, when fauorites fall,
Strike them, their house, their freinds, their fauorites all.

Was't not enough that thou didst dart thy fyors 35
Into our blood, inflaming our desires,
And madest us sigh and blow, and pant, and burne,
And then thyselfe into our flames did'st turne ?
Was't not enough, that thou did'st hazard us
To paths in loue so darke and ruinous : 40
And those so ambushte round with houschould spyes,
And ouer all thy husband's two red eyes
That flam'd with ugly sweat of jealousy :
Yett went wee nott still on with constancy ?
Haue wee for this kept guards, like spy on spy ? 45
Had correspondence, when the foe stood by ?
Stoln (more to sweeten them) our manny blisses
Of meetings, conference, imbracements, kisses ?
Shadow'd with negligence, our most respects ?
Varyed our language through all dialects 50
Of becks, winks, lookes, and often under-boords
Spoke dialougs with our feet farr from our woords ?
Haue we prou'd all the secrets of our art,
Yea, the pale inwards att thy panting hart ?   heart
And after all this passèd purgatorye 55
Shall sad diuorce make us the vulgar story ?
First let our eys be riueted quite through
Our turning braines, and both our lips grow too :
Let our arms clasp like iuys, and our feare   ivy's
Freez us together, that we may stick here ; 60
Till Fortune, that would ruen us with the deed,
Straine his eyes open, and yet make them bleed.

For Loue it cannott be, whom hithertoo
I haue accus'd, should such a mischiefe doe.
Oh Fortune, thou'rt not worth my least exclaime,　65
And plague enough thou hast in thy own shame :
Doe thy great worst, my frend, and I haue charmes
('Though not against thy stroakes) against thy harmes.
Rend us in sunder, thou can'st not deuide
Our bodyes soe, but still our soules are tyde ;　70
And we can loue by letters still, and guifts,
And thoughts, and dreams : Loue neuer wanteth shifts.
I will not looke upon the quickening sone,　　sun
But streight her beauty to my sence shall runn ;
The aire shall noate her soft, the fire most pure ;　75
Waters suggest her clear, and the Earth sure ;
Time shall not loose our passages ; the Spring
Shall tell how fresh our love was in 'beginning ;
The Summer, how it ripned in the yeare ;
And Autumn, what our goulden harvests wore.　80
The Winter I'le not thinke on to spight thee,
But count it a lost season, soe shall shee.
And, dearest frend, since wee must part, drown Night
With hope of Day ; (burthens well born are light.)
The cold and darknes longer hang somewheere,
Yett Phœbus equally lights all the spheare.　85
And what he cant in like proportion pay,
The world enjoyes in mass, and soe we may.
Be then euer yourselfe, and let no woe
Winn on your health, your youth, your beauty : soe　90

Declare yourself base Fortune's ennemy,

No less be your contempt then constancy :   than

That I may grow enamored on your mind,

When mine own thoughts I there neglected finde.

For this to th' comfort of my deare I vowe,   95

My deeds shall stilbe what my deeds are now;

The poles shall moue to reach me when I start,

And when I change my Loue, I'll change my hart; heart

Nay, if I but wax cold in my desire,

Thinke, heauen hath motion lost, and the world fyer :

Much more I would; but many woords haue made   101

That oft suspected, which men would perswade : ·

Take therefore all in this ; I loue so true,

As I will neuer look for less in you.

NOTES AND ILLUSTRATIONS.

Our text here is again from Haslewood-Kingsborough ms. as before : as neither does this Elegy appear in Stephens' ms. It originally appeared in 1635 edition, and since in all after-editions. 1669 has considerable additions in agreement with our ms.

Line 4, ' loue :' '35 ' soule.'

  ,, 7, ' *Heauen :*' '69 ' Venus' = the brightest star and leader of the host of heaven.

Line 11, ' *felt :*' '69 ' self-want.'

  ,, 23, ' *in jeast :*' our ms. here is specially good : usually ' for me before.'

Line 40, ' *ruinous :*' '69 ' dangerous.'

  ,, 42-3. 1669 ' husband's towring :' query, lowering ? *i. e.* for ' two red :' and for ' That flam'd' reads ' Inflam'd with th' ouglie.'

Line 49, ' *most :*' '69 ' best.'

  ,, 66, ' *shame :*' '69 ' name :' and l. 67 reads ' armes' for ' charmes.'

Line 78. Usually ' How fresh . . . the . . .' and l. 79 ' un-
ripen'd.'
Line 87, ' he' and ' proportion :' '69 ' we' and ' portion ;' an
example of how our collation of MSS. rewards all the toil.   So
l. 97 ' reach' in '69 is ' teach :' and ' ere' for ' when.'   G.

XV.

JULIA.

HARKE, newes, O Enuy, thou shalt hear discry'd
My JULIA ; who as yett was ne'er enuide.
To vomitt gaulle in slaunderss, swels her vaines
With callumny, that hell itself desdaines,
Is her continuall practice, to doe her best,   5
To teare oppinion euen out of the brest
Of nearest frends, and (which is worse then vild)
Stick jealousy in wedlock ; her own child
'Scapes not the showers of enuy : To repeate
The monstrous fashions how, were aliue to eate   10
Dear reputation ; would to God she were
But halfe so loath to act vice, as to heare
My milde reproof : Liued Mantuan now agen
(That femall-Mastix) to lim out with his penn
This shee Chimera, that hath eyes of fire,   15
Burning with angar (angar feeds desire),
Tongud like the night-crowe, whose ill-boading cryes
Giue out for nothing but new iniuryes.

Her breath like to the aire of Tennarus,

That blasts the springs, though ne're so prosperous. 20

Her hand, I know not how, usd more to spill

The food of others, then herself to fill.   than

But of her mind, that Orcus, which includes

Legions of mischeif, countles multitudes

Of former curses, proiects unmade up,   25

Abuses yet unfashoned, thought corrupt,

Misshapen cauels, palpable untreaths,

Ineuitable errors, selfe-accusing oathes :

Thes, like those attoms swarming in the sun,

Throng in her bosome for creation.   30

I blush to giue her half her dew ;· yet say,   due

No poyson's halfe so bad as Julia.

NOTES AND ILLUSTRATIONS.

Again our text is from Haslewood-Kingsborough MS., as before. This Elegy appeared originally in 1635 edition, and since
in all after-editions.

    Line 3, ' her:' so 1635. Our MS. 'in.'

    ,, 5, ' to doe:' 1635 ' does.'

    ,, 8. Here our MS. misinserts ' yᵉ sheets of ;' and in line
31 ' only this I' for ' yet say.'

    Line 13, ' Mantuan.' I presume the poet Baptista Spagnolus,
' the good old Mantuan' of Holofernes in Love's Labour Lost;
so called from his birthplace.

    Line 19, ' aire :' 1635 ' juice.'

    Ib. ' Tennarns'=Teneriffe.

    Line 28, ' oathes :' 1635 ' loathes.' G.

XVI.

THE EXPOSTULATION.

To make the doubt cleare, that no woman's true,
Was it my fate to prove it stronge in you?
Thought I, but once had breathèd purest ayre,
And must she needs be false, because she's faire?
Is it your beawtie's markes or of your yowth,   5
Or your perfectyon not to study truth?
Or thinke you heaven is deafe? and hath no eyes?
Or those she hath smyle at your periuries?
Are vowes so cheape with women, or the matter
Whereof they ar made, that they 'are writ in water?
And blowne away with wynd? Or doth their breath
(Both hott and cold) at once make life and death?
Who could have thought so many accents sweet
Formd into words, so many sighs shold meet,
As from our hart, soe many oaths, and teares   15
Sprinkled amonge (all sweetned by our feares)
And the devine impression of stolne kisses,
That seald the rest, shold now prove empty blisses?
Did you draw bonds to forfeit? signe to break?
Or must we read you quight from what you speak,   20
And find the truth out the wronge way? or must
He first desire you false, wold wish you just?
Oh, I prophane: though most of women bee
This kynd of beast, my thoughts shall except thee,

My dearest Lou'd ; though froward jealousie 25
With circumstance might urg thy 'inconstancye,
Sooner I'le think the sun will cease to cheere
The teeming earth, and that forget to beare :
Sooner that rivers will run backe, or Thames
With ribbs of ice in June will bynd her streams ; 30
Or Nature, by whose strength the world endures,
Wold change her course, before you alter yours.
But oh ! that treacherous breast, to whom weak you
Did trust our cownsels, (and we both may rue,
Havinge his falshood fownd too late,) 'twas hee 35
That made me cast you guilty, and you mee ;
Whilst the black wretch betraid each symple word
We spake, unto the cunninge of a third ;
Curst may he bee, that so our loue did stayne,
And wander on the earth, as cursed as Caine, 40
Wretched as he, and not deserue least pitty ;
In plagueing him let Miserie be wytty.
Let all eyes shun him, and he shun each eye,
Till he be noysom as his infamie ;
May he without remorse deny God thrice, 45
And not be trusted more on his sowl's price ;
And after all selfe-torment when he dyes,
May wolues tear out his hart, vultures his eyes ; heart
Swyne eat his bowels ; and his falser toungue
That uttered all, be to some raven flunge ; 50
And let his carion corse be a longer feast
To the King's doggs, then any other beast. than

Now I have cursed, let us our loue revive ;
In me the flame was never more alive ;
I could begin againe to court and praise,   55
And in that pleasure strengthen the short dayes
Of my life's lease.   Like painters that do take
Not in made workes delight, but whilst they make,
I cold renew those tymes, when first I sawe
Love in your eyes, that gaue my toungue the lawe   6o
To like what you likt ; and at maskes and plaies
Comend the selfe-same actors, the same waies ;
Ask how you did, and often, with intent
Of beinge officious, bee impertinent ;
All which were such soft pastimes, as in these   65
Love was as subtilie catcht as a disease ;
But, beinge gott, it is a treasure sweet,
Which to defend is harder then to get :
And ought not to be prophande on eyther part ;
For though 'tis got by chance, 'tis kept by art.   7o

NOTES AND ILLUSTRATIONS.

Our text is from Stephens' MS., as before, where it is headed
'Elegia Decima quarta.'   This Elegy appeared originally in
1633 edition, and since in all the after-editions.   It is the
more important to keep in mind that the dates 1633 and 1635
inform us that it had twice appeared during Ben Jonson's lifetime—for he did not die until 1637 ; a fact quite sufficient to
set aside its introduction into his *posthumous* ' Underwoods'—
than which a more uncritical and illiterately-edited book it is
scarcely possible to imagine.   Besides, I have not met with any
edition of DONNE not containing this Elegy, and in all the MS.
collections—and they are very numerous—it is found ; while in

no ms. is it over assigned to Jonson, notwithstanding that there are many of his poems in such ms. collections. Internally the whole sentiment, colouring, turns, and wording of the Elegy is Donne's, and the antithesis of Jonson. Lieut. Cunningham in his edition of Ben Jonson (3 vols. 8vo), while retaining this Elegy in the 'Underwoods,' notes its resemblance to Donne, and suggests that probably other two of the Elegies belong to Donne. My answer is, that while the present Elegy is found in all the printed editions of Donne, and similarly in all the mss., those other two never have been found assigned to Donne. Cunningham's idea of the present Elegy springing out of another Elegy, certainly Jonson's, is a mere fancy unsupported by evidence external or internal. See more on this in our Essay.

Line 3, 'Thought:' so usually: our ms. miswrites 'Thoughe.'

„ 8, 'smyle at your periuries:' a saying quoted by Shakespeare:

> 'at lovers' perjuries
> They say Jove laughs.'
> Romeo and Juliet, ii. 2.

Usually it is 'it,' not 'she,' the latter quaintly making heaven feminine.

Line 10, 'writ in water.' Was the dying Keats thinking of this? See our Essay on the place.

Line 25, 'lou'd'=others had been loved. Usually 'love.'

„ 33, 'breast:' our ms. 'beast;' but I prefer the former, because it implies he was one to whose supposedly faithful 'breast' she confided her secrets.

Line 36, 'cast.' See former note.

„ 39, 'stayne:' 1669 'so our loue hath slain:' and line 40 usually 'wretched.' I adopt our ms., although some may think 'revive' of line 53, and line 55 'I could begin againe,' agree better with 'hath slain' in line 40.

Line 49, 'falser;' so usually: our ms. inadvertently 'false.'

G.

XVII.

A TALE OF A CITIZEN AND HIS WIFE.

I sing no harme, good sooth, to any wight,
To lord or foole, cuckold, beggar, or knight,
To peace-teaching lawyer, proctor, or brave
Reformèd or reducèd captaine, knave,
Officer, jugler, or iustice of peace,   5
Iuror or iudge; I touch no fat sowe's grease;
I am no libeller, nor will be any,
But (like a true man) say there are too many:
I fear not *ore tenus*, for my tale
Nor count nor counsellour will looke red or pale.   10
    A citizen and his wife the other day,
Both riding on one horse, upon the way
I overtooke; the wench a pretty peate,
And (by her eye) well fitting for the feate;
I saw the lecherous citizen turne backe   15
His head, and on his wife's lip steale a smacke,
Whence apprehending that the man was kinde,
Riding before to kisse his wife behinde;
To get acquaintance with him, I began
To sort discourse fit for so fine a man;   20
I ask'd the number of the Plaguing Bill,
Ask'd if the custome-farmers held out still;
Of the Virginian plot, and whether Ward
The traffique of the Iland seas had marr'd;

Whether the Brittaine Burse did fill apace,   25
And likely were to give th' Exchange disgrace ;
Of new-built Algate, and the Morefield crosses,
Of store of bankerouts and poore merchants' losses,
I urgèd him to speake ; but he (as mute
As an old courtier worne to his last suite)   30
Replies with onely yeas and nayes ; at last
(To fit his element) my theame I cast
On tradesmen's gaines ; that set his tongue agoing,
Alas, good Sir (quoth he), there is no doing
In court nor city now.   She smil'd and I,   35
And (in my conscience) both gave him the lie
In one met thought.   But he went on apace,
And at the present times with such a face
He rail'd, as fray'd me ; for he gave no praise
To any but my Lord of Essex dayes :   40
Call'd those the age of action : true (quoth he)
There's now as great an itch of bravery
And heat of taking up, but cold lay-downe ;
For put to push of pay, away they runne ;
Our onely city trades of hope now are   45
Bawds, tavern-keepers, whores, and scriveners ;
The much of priviledg'd kinsmen, and the store
Of fresh protections make the rest all poore :
In the first state of their creation
Though many stoutly stand, yet proves not one   50
A righteous paymaster.   Thus ranne he on
In a continued rage : so void of reason

Seem'd his harsh talk, I sweat for feare of treason.
And (troth) how could I lesse? when in the prayer
For the protection of the wise Lord Major,　　　55
And his wise brethren's worships, when one prayeth,
He swore that none could say amen with faith.
To get him off from what I glowed to heare,
(In happy time) an angel did appeare,
The bright signe of a lov'd and well-try'd.inne,　　60
Where many citizens with their wives had been
Well-us'd and often; here I pray'd him stay,
To take some due refreshment by the way;
Looke, how he look'd.that hid the gold (his hope),
And at returne found nothing but a rope;　　　65
So he at me; refus'd and made away,
Though willing she pleaded a weary day :
I found my misse, struck hands, and prai'd him tell
(To hold acquaintance still) where he did dwell;
He barely nam'd the street, promis'd the wine;　　70
But his kinde wife gave me the very Signe.

NOTES AND ILLUSTRATIONS.

This tale appeared originally in 1635 edition. Our text is that of 1639.

Line 4, 'Reformèd Captain,' or Reformado. Said by Nares to be an officer who for some disgrace had been deprived of his command, but not of his rank, nor perhaps of his pay. Some of the uses of the word, however, do not seem to agree with this, and I rather think it was eventually, if not originally, applied to any officers who had no present command, and who, awaiting vacaucies or the like, were formed into a company by themselves. With this Bullaker, Dyche, and Kershaw agree, though not Coles.

Line 6, '*fat sowe's grease:*' evidently a proverbial saying.

  ,, 9, '*ore tenus*'=by word of mouth, a law term.

  ,, 10, '*looke:*' not in 1669.

  ,, 20, 'To:' 1669 'And.'

  ,, 21, 'Plaguing:' 1669 'Plaguy'=Bill of Mortality for the Plague.

Lines 22-3 : these are date-marks if we could get at them.

  ,, 23, '*Ward.*' There was printed in 1612 a play by R^d. Daborne, 'A Christian turn'd Turk, or the tragical Lives and Deaths of the two famous Pirates, *Ward* and Dansiker;' and Halliwell says it is taken from an account of the overthrow of these two pirates by Andrew Barker (1609, 4to). This gives the (probable) date of this tale. The Iland seas are those around the West Indian and other islands. The Midland seas (as in 1669) were probably the Gulf of Mexico and Caribbean Seas.

Line 25, 'Brittaine Burse :'=(now) British.

  ,, 34. This unseemly equivoque is frequent in the writers of that day.

Line 41, '*quoth he :*' a notable correction in 1669 of the 'Quoth I' of 1635, 1639, &c.

Line 47, '*kinsmen :*' 1669 'kingsmen.'

  ,, 57, '*say amen:*' because neither Mayor nor Brethren were wise.

Line 58, '*him off:*' i.e. to get from him, [and] from what I glowed to hear.

   Line 62, '*Well-us'd and often,*' may refer to the inn; but it is simpler to take these words as referring to citizens and wives.

Line 65, '*rope :*' an old story found in many forms, of a man who saw another hide some stolen money in a hole in a barn, and took it, and replaced it by a rope.

Line 68, '*misse*'=I found my failure. This is no equivoque, as 'miss' in that sense was not used till later. See our MAR-VELL, *s.v.*

Line 71, '*Signe,*' i.e. of their shop. ·G.

XVIII.

LOVE'S PROGRESS.

WHOEVER loves, if he doth not propose
The right true end of loue, hee's one that goes
To sea for nothinge but to make him sicke :
Love is a beare-whelpe borne, if we ore-licke
Our loue, and force it newe strange shapes to take,　5
We erre, and of a lump a monster make.
Were not a calf a monster, that were grown
Faced like a man, though better than his own?
Perfection is in vnity : preferr
One woman first, and then one thing in her.　　　10
I, when I valew gold, may thinke uponn
The ductilness, the applicatyon,
The wholsomenes, the ingenuctye,
From rust, from soile, from fire for ever free :
But if I loue it, 'tis because 'tis made　　　　　15
(By our new nature) use, the sowl of trade.
　　All this in woman we might think upon
(If women had them), and yet loue but one.
Can men more iniure women then to say　　. than
They love them for that, by which they're not they?　20
Makes virtue woman? must I coole my blood
Till I both be, and fynd one, wise and good?
Let barren angels loue soe, but if wee
Make love to woman, virtue is not shee,

As bewtie's not, nor wealth; he that strais thus,   25
From her to her's, is more adulterous
Then if he tooke her mayd.   Serch every sphære   than
And firmament, our Cupid is not there :
He's an infernall god, and undergrownd,
With Pluto dwolls, where gold and fyro abound;   30
Men to such gods their sacrifizing coles
Did not on altars lay, but in pytts and holes:
Although we see cælestiall bodyes move
Above the earth, the earth we tyll and loue :
So we her aires contemplate, words, and hart,   heart 35
And virtues ; but we love the centrique part.
    Nor is the sowle more worthy, or more fytt
For love, then this, as infinyte as it.   than
But in attayning this desirèd place
How much they err, that set out at the face !   40
The hayre a forrest is of ambushes,
Of springges, snares, fetters, and manacles :
The browe becalms us, when 'tis smooth and plaine ;
And when 'tis wrinkled, shipwracks us againe.
Smooth, 'tis a paradice, where we wold haue   45
Immortal stay ; but wrinkled, 'tis our grave.
The nose (like to the first meridian) runns
Not betwixt east and west, but 'twixt two sunns ;
It leaves a cheeke, a rosie hemispheare
On eyther syde, and then directs us where   50
Upon the islands Fortunate wee fall,
Not faint Canaries, but ambrosiall

And swelling lipps to which when we are come,
We anchor there, and thinke ourselves at home,
For they seeme all: there syrens' songes, and there 55
Wise Delphique oracles, doe fill the care ;
There in a creeke, where chosen pearls do swell,
The Remora, her cleaving toungue, doth dwell.
These and the glorious promontory, her chynn,
Being past, the straits of Helespont, between   60
The Sestos and Abidos of her brests,
(Not of two lovers, but two loves, the nests)
Succeeds a bowndless sea, but yet thyne eye
Some island moles may scattred there discry,
And sayling towards her India, in the way   65
Shall at her faire Atlantique navill stay,
Though thence the current be thy pylot made,
Yet ere thou be where thou would'st be embaide,
Thou shalt vpon another forrest sett,
Where many shipwrack and no further gett.   70
When thou art there, consider thou thy chace
Maskt longer by beginninge at the face.

    Rather sett out belowe; practize my art;
Some simmetrie the foot hath with that part,
Which thou dost seek, and is as mapp for that ;   75
Lovely enough to stopp, but not stay att :
Least subject to disguise and change it is ;
Men say the Devil never can change his.
It is the embleme, that hath figurèd
Firmnes ; 'tis the first part that comes to bedd.   80

Civilitie we see refyned : the kisse
(Which at the faee begun) transplanted is,
Since to the hand, since to the imperiall knee,
Now at the Papall foote delights to bee :
If kings thinke that the nearer way, and doe   85
Rise from the foot, lovers may doe so too.
For as free sphæres move faster farr then can   than
Byrds, whom the ayre resists; so may that man,
Which goes this emptie and ethireall way,
Then if at bewtie's enemies he stay.   than   90
Rich Nature hath in woman wisely made
Two purses, and their mowths aversly laid :
Then they, which to the lower tribute owe,
That way, which that exchequor looks, must goe :
He who doth not, his error is as great,   95
As who by clyster gives the stomack meate.

NOTES AND ILLUSTRATIONS.

Our text is from Stephens' ms., as before, where this Elegy
is numbered 'Elegia Nona,' and headed, as we have done,
'Love's Progresse,' and so too in ms. 4955, as before. It appeared originally in 1669 edition (pp. 94-97), but very incor-
rectly, as a collation will show. We have silently put right
from our ms. and other mss.

Line 4, 'ore-licke :' a reference to the belief that animals
licked their young into shape, whence the phrase 'lick into
shape.'

Line 12, 'the :' our ms. misreads ' of.'

  ,, 13, 'ingenuetye :' Latinate, free-born or noble descent,
untaintedness.

Line 16. The reference is to the proverb, 'use is second

nature,' and I accept the usual text rather than ' By use of our
new nature,' as in our MS.

Line 20. Our MS. inserts badly ' That' before ' they,' and
reads ' they are' for ' they're :' I accept the usual printed text.
So in line 21 our MS. misreads ' Make.'

Line 22, ' be :' so usually. Our MS. misreads ' see'=Must
I cool my blood both till I ' be' wise and good, and till I find a
woman equally so?

Line 25. Our MS. reads badly ' As bewtie nor wealth is.'

,,   27, ' if he tooke :' our MS. misreads ' then he that tooke.'
There is no woman spoken of in particular, but only ' woman'
generically.   I therefore accept the usual printed text, ' if he
tooke,' as it agrees with this, while ' he that tooke' makes a reference to one that has not been referred to.

Line 42, ' *springges*,' &c.   Cf. MARVELL, *s.v.*

,,   60. The construction here is elliptical, or requires a
double use of the verb : ' These and . . . her chin being past,
and the straits being passed.'   There is a similar phrase (lines
3-4) in the ' Funeral Elegy' commencing ' Language, thou art
too narrow' (hitherto erroneously included in this Series). ' If
we could sigh out our accents, and weep words, grief wears and
lessens [grief wears and lessens] that affords breath [to] tears.'
See also note on next Elegy, line 40.   Cf. too Elegy on Julia,
line 5, where ' Is her continual practice' has to do double duty.

Lines 71-2. 1669 reads ' what this chase Misspent, by thy.'

,,   88, ' whom :' so usually. Our MS. reads ' when ;' ' when'
gives the first sense, ' free spheres move faster when the air
resists than birds :' ' whom' frees the sentence from that absurd-
sounding ambiguity.

One mourns that ever Donne wrote in this vein of Carew at
his worst. G.

XIX.

TO HIS MISTRESS GOING TO BED.

Come, Madam, come, all rest my powres defic,
Untill I labour, I in labour lye.
The foe ofttymes, havinge the foe in sight,
Is tir'd with standinge, though he never fight.
Off with that gyrdle, like heavn's zone glysteringe,   5
But a farr fayrer world incompassinge.
Unpin that spangled brestplate, which you weare,
That the 'eyes of busy fools might be stopt there;
Unlace yourselfe, for that (your woman's chyme)
Tells me from you, that now 'tis your bedtime.   10
Off with that happy busk, which I envyc,
That still can bee, and still can stand so nigh.
Your gowne goeing off such bewteous state reveales,
As when from flowry meads th' hill's shadowe steals.
Off with your wirie coronett, and showe   15
The hairye diadems which on you doe growe :
Off with your hose and shooes, then safely tread
In this Love's hallow'd temple, this soft bedd.
In such white robes heaven's angels use to bee
Perceiv'd by men ; thou angell bring'st with thee   20
A heaven-like Mahomet's paradice ; and though
Ill spirits walke in whyte, we easily know
By this, these angels from an evill sprite ;
Those sett our hayre, but these our flesh upright.

    Licence my roaving hands, and let them goe   25
Behynd, before, betweene, above, belowe.
Oh my America! my Newfoundland!
My kingdom, safest when with one man man'd.
My myne of precious stones! my emperie!
How blest am I, in thus discoveringe thee!   30
To enter in those bonds is to be free;
That where my hand is sett my seale shalbee.
    Full nakednes! all joyes are due to thee;
As fowles unbodyed boydes uncloth'd must bee,
To tast whole joyes. Gems, which you women use,
Are, as Atlanta's balls, cast in men's viewes;   36
That when a foole's eye lighteth on a gemm,
His earthly sowle might covrt those, not them:
Like pictures or like books' gay coverings made
For lay-men, are all women thus arraide.   40
Themselves are only mistique books, which wee
(Whome their imputed grace will dignifie)
Must see revail'd. Then since that I may know,
As liberally as to a midwife showe
Thyselfe; cast all, yea ye white lynen hence;   45
There is no penance due to inocence.
To teach thee, I'le be naked first; why, than
What needs thou haue more covering then a man?   <small>than</small>

NOTES AND ILLUSTRATIONS.

    Our text is from Stephens' MS., as before, where it is num-
bered 'Elegia Decima octava.' This Elegy, the most sensual

ever written by English poet of the genius of Donne, originally
appeared in 1669 edition (pp. 97-9).

Line 7, '*spangled brestplate*.' Those who have seen the
Corfeot women in their gala dresses, Venetian fashions of two
or three hundred years ago, will recognise the 'spangled' and
sometimes 'gold' plate, breast-plate, or stomacher of the text.

Line 12. The first 'still'=quiet; the second=yet or continuously.

Line 13, 'bewteous:' so usually : our MS. reads 'beautie's
state,' not so good.

Line 15, '*wirie coronett:*' on which the hair and added hair
and head-gear were built up.

Line 40, '*lay-men:*' in the sense of ignorant laics, not admitted into the inner precincts. 'For laymen' is to be used
with both the preceding and following clause ; a kind of ellipse
already noted in Donne. G.

XX.

OPINION.

THE heavens rejoice in motion ; why should I
Abjure my so beloued varyety,
And not with many, youth and loue deuide ?
Pleasure is none, if not diversifide.
The sun, that sitting in the chaire of light,   5
Sheds flame into what else soe'er seemes bright,
Is not contented att one Sign to inn,
But ends his yeare, and att a new begins.
All things doe willingly in chang delight,
The fruitfull mother of our appetite :   10

Riuers the clerer and more pleasing are,   [clear;
Wheere their faire-spreading streams run wide and
And a dead lake, that no strange barque doth greete,
Corrupts itself and what doth liue in itt.
Let no man tell me such a one is faire   15
And worthy all alone my loue to sheire.   share
Nature hath done in her the liberall part
Of a kind mistress, and emploide her art
To make her loueable; and I auerr
Him not humane, that would return from her;   20
I loue her well; and could, if need weer, dye   were
To doe her seruice.   But followes itt that I
Must serue her only, when I may haue choice?
The lawe is hard, and shall not haue my voice.
The last I saw in all extreames is faire,   25
And houlds me in the sunnbeams of her haire;
Her nymphlike features such agreements haue,
That I could venture with her to the graue :
Another's broune, I like her not the worse;
Her toungue is soft, and takes me with discourse; 30
Others, for that they well descended are,
Doe in my loue obteine as larg a share;
And though they be not faire, 'tis much with me
To winn their loue only for their degree;
And though I faile of my requirèd ends,   35
The attempt is glorious, and ittself comends.
How happy weer our sires in ancient time,   were
Who held plurality of loues no crime !

With them it was accounted charroty
To stirr up race of all indifferently;   40
Kindred were not exempted from the bands,
Which with the Persians still in usage stands.
Women were then no sooner askt then won;   than
And what they did was honest, and well done.
But since this title honnour hath been used,   45
Ower weake credulety hath been abusde;   .
The goulden lawes of nature are repeald,
Which our first fathers in such reuerence held;
Our libertye's reverst, and chartar's gone,
And we made servants to OPINION;   50
A monster in no certeine shape attird,
And whose originall is much desired;
Formless at first, butt growing on, itt fashions,
And doth prescribe manners and laws to nations.
Here Loue received immedicinable harmes,   55
And was despoilèd of his daring armes;
A greater want then is his dareing eyes,
He lost those awfull wings with which he flyes;
His sinewy bow, and those imortal darts,
Wherewith hee's wont to bruise resisting harts.   hearts
Only some few, strong in themselues, and free,   61
Retaine the seeds of ancient liberty;
Following that part of loue, although deprest,
And make a throne for him within their brest;
In spite of modern censures, him avouïng   65
Their soveraigne, all seruice him allowing.

Amongst which troope, although I am the least,
Yet equall in affections with the best,
I glory in subjection of his hand,
Nor neuer did decline his least comaund ;   70
For in whateuer form the message came,
My heart did open, and receaue the flame.
But time will in its course a point descrye,
When. I this lovèd seruice must denye ;
For our allegience temporary is ;   75
With firmer age returne ower libertyes.
What time, in grauer judgement, wee repos'd,
Shall not soe easily be to change disposed ;
Nor to the art of several eyes obeying,
But beauty with true worth soe rarely weying ;   80
Which being found assembled in some one,
Wee'll loue her euer, and loue her alone.

NOTES AND ILLUSTRATIONS.

Our text is Haslewood-Kingsborough ms., as before. This
Elegy appeared originally in 1669 edition (pp. 411-414).
Line 2, '*beloued:*' 1669 'much lov'd.'
  ,,   3. 1669 badly reads 'many youth and lov'd.'
  ,,   5. Usually 'soever'=soe'er, which accordingly I have
ventured to give; but even thus there is a syllable which will
not come into scansion, and 'soe'er doth seem bright' is un-
metrical prose. From other instances it is plain Donne did not
always at once detect that he had written an Alexandrine instead of an ordinary five-foot verse. I correct by reading 'seemes'
for 'doth seem.'
Line 7, '*inn.*' See our PHINEAS and GILES FLETCHER, *s. v.*
  ,,   8, '*att:*' 1669 'with.'
  ,,   12, '*clear:*' our ms. 'faire:' I accept 1669.

Line 16, 'sheire' = (as in margin) share: so usually, but
our MS. reads 'to inheire.'
Line 36. See our Essay on this line and Addison.
  ,, 45, 'title:' 1669 'little,' badly.
  ,, 50, '*Opinion:*' so 1669: our MS. badly 'Oppression;'
and so line 52 'desired' is in MS. 'admird.'
Line 55, '*immedicinable:*' 1669 'immedicable.'
  ,, 77. 1669 reads 'in years and judgement.'
  ,, 82, 'loue:' 1669 badly 'leaue.' G.

XXI.

A PARADOX OF A PAINTED FACE.

Not kisse! by Jouve I must, and make impression!
As longe as Cupid dares to hould his scessyoun session
Within my flesh and blood, our kisses shall
Out-minvte tyme, and without number fall.
Doe I not know these balls of blushinge redd   5
That on thy cheeks thus amorously are spread,
Thy snowie necke, those vaines vpon thy browe
Which with their azure twinklinge sweetly bowe,
Are artificiall, borrowed, and no more thyne owne
Then chaynes which on St. George's day are showne
Are propper to their wearers; yet for this   11
I idole thee, and begge a luschyous kisse.
The fucus and ceruse, which on thy face
Thy cuninge hand layes on to add new gráce,
Deceive me with such pleasinge fraud, that I   15
Fynd in thy art, what can in Nature lye.

Much like a paynter that vpon some wall
On which the cadent sun-beames vse to fall
Paynts with such art a guylded butterflie
That sillie maids with slowe-mov'd fingers trie   20
To catch it, and then blush at their mistake,
Yet of this painted flie most reckoninge make :
Such is our state, since what we looke vpon
Is nought but colour and proportionn.
Take we a face as full of frawde and lyes   25
As gipsies in your common lottereyes,
That is more false and more sophisticate
Then are saints' reliques, or a man of state ;
Yet such beinge glosèd by the sleight of arte
Gaine admiration, wininge many a hart.   30
Put case there be a difference in the mold,
Yet may thy Venus be more choice, and hold
A dearer treasure.   Oftentimes we see
Rich Candyan wynes in wooden bowles to bee;
The odoriferous civett doth not lye   35
Within the pretious muscatt's eare or eye,
But in a baser place ; for prudent Nature
In drawinge us of various formes and feature,
Gives from y⁰ envious shopp of her large treasure
To faire partes comlynesse, to baser pleasure.   40
The fairest flowres that in y⁰ Springe do grow
Are not soe much for vse, as for the showe ;
As lyllics, hyacinths, and your gorgious byrth
Of all pied-flowers, which dyaper the Earth,

Please more with their discoulered purple traine 45
Then holsome pot-hearbs which for vse remayne.
Shall I a gawdie-speckled serpent kisse
For that the colours which he wears be his ?
A perfum'd cordevant who will not weare
Because ye sent is borrowed otherwhere? 50
The robes and vestments which do grace vs all
Are not our owne, but adventitiall.
Tyme rifles Nature's bewtie, but slie Art
Repaires by cuninge this decayinge part;
Fills here a wrinckle and there purls a vayne, 55
And with a nymble hand runs ore againe
The breaches dented in by th' arme of Tyme,
And makes deformitie to be noe cryme ;
As when great men be grypt by sicknes' hand
Industrious phisick pregnantly doth stand 60
To patch vp fowle diseases, and doth strive
To keepe their totteringe carcasses alive.
Bewtie's a candle-light, which euery puffe
Blowes out, and leaves naught but a stinking snuff
To fill our nostrills with.   This boldly thinke, 65
The clearest candle makes ye greatest stinke ;
As your pure food and cleanest nutriment
Getts the most hott and most strong excrement.
Why hang we then on things so apt to varye,
So fleetinge, brittle, and so temporarie, 70
That agues, coughs, the tooth-ake, or catharr
(Slight howses of diseases) spoyle and marr ?

But when old age their bewty hath in chace,
And ploughes vpp furrowes in their once smooth face,
Then they become forsaken, and doe shewe   75
Like stately abbies ruyn'd longe agoe.
Nature but gives the modell and first draught
Of faire perfection, which by Art is taught
To make itselfe a compleat forme and birth
Soe, stands a coppie to these shapes on Earth.   80
Jove grant me then a repairable face,
Which whil'st that coulors are, can want noe grace;
Pigmalion's painted statue I wold loue,
Soe it were warme or soft, or could but move.

NOTES AND ILLUSTRATIONS.

This Elegy was first printed by Sir John Simeon in his
tractate of Donne poems from MSS. for the Philobiblon Society (on which see our Preface); but as throughout Sir John
modernised the orthography, I take our text in preference from
the Stephens' MS. as before. In the Simeon copy the heading
is simply 'To a Painted Lady.' These variations, taken from
Simeon's copy, may be recorded (orthographical not noted):
Line 1, ' will.'
  „   3, ' Within :' our MS. ' vpon :' the former accepted.
  „   5, ' Do not I . . . white and red.'
  „   8, ' wrinkles.'
  „   9, ' borrowed' dropped.
  „   10, ' showne :' our MS. ' worne :' the former accepted.
  „   11, ' the.'
  „   13, ' fucus and the ceruse on :' ' fucus,' Latin, counter-
feit painting, deceit: used in those days as the name for the
preparations employed in colouring the skin.
Line 14, ' more.'
  „   15-16. First printed by us.
  „   19, ' such gilded art a.'

Line 21, 'it' and 'then' dropped.
  ,, 22, 'more.'
  ,, 23, 'Such:' our MS. miswrites 'Sure,' and 'estate' for 'state,' and 'that' for 'what;' 'what' being preferable, as making what it is a general reflection, there being probably an allusion to the philosophic idea of the day that we see the accidents, colours, and proportion, but not the true *substantia* of anything.
Line 25, 'Make.'
  ,, 26, 'their cunning'st flatteries.' I do not remember any other allusion to this custom (except as below), nor do I know whether the gipsies were real or 'stage' gipsies:

> 'He's a scurvy informer; has more cosenage
> In him than is in five travelling lotteries.'
> Middleton, Anything for a Quiet Life, act i.

Line 29, 'thus.'
  ,, 31-34 first printed by us.
  ,, 37, 'baser,' wrongly; and so in line 38, 'use' for 'us.'
  ,, 39, 'Gives unto them the shop,' which is nonsense.
  ,, 43, 'the.'
  ,, 47-8 in Simeon copy follow our lines 49-50, but run thus:

> 'A gaudy speckled serpent who would kiss
> Because the colours that he wears are his?'

Line 51, 'do' I insert from Simeon copy.
  ,, 53, 'rifles:' our MS. badly 'rifled;' but I retain 'bewtie' for 'bountie.'
Line 54, 'decayed.'
  ,, 55, 'here:' I accept this for 'there,' but not 'pearls' for 'purls:' purls=makes a vein ripple or run wavingly. Cf. 'winding meanders,' El. xxv. line 24.
Line 58, 'Making.'
  ,, 61, 'old.'
  ,, 64, Simeon reads badly 'stuff.' See our note on 'snuff' in Satire ii. line 6.
Line 67, 'pure:' spelled oddly 'poare.'
  ,, 74, 'wrinkles.' I accept 'once' for 'owne' of our MS.
  ,, 77, 'or.'
  ,, 78, 'wrought.'
  ,, 79. Our MS. 'Speak to y^t selfe . . . breath.' I accept the Simeon copy.
Line 81, 'you' for 'then.'

Line 82, 'are' dropped in MS. from the common cause of error, alliterative letters and similar syllables: 'colours are.'
Line 83, 'image . . . could.'
  ,, 84, 'and soft and;' 'could' is spelled 'cold.'
  ,, 49, 'cordevant' is Spanish leather, so named from Cordova, once famous for its manufacture. G.

XXII.

LOVE'S WAR.

Till I have peace with thee, warr other men ;
And when I haue peace, can I leave thee then ?
All other warrs are scrupolous, only thou
A faire free cyttie, maist thy selfe allowe
To any one. In Flanders, who can tell   5
Whether the master 'press, or men rebell ?   oppress
Onely we knowe, that which all ideots say,
They beare most blowes that come to part the fray.
France in her lunatique giddines did hate
Even our men, yea and our God of late ;   10
Yet she relies vpon our angells well,
Which n'ere returne no more then they that fell.
Sicke Ireland is with a strange warr possesst,
Like to an ague, now raging, now at rest,
Which tyme will cure : yet it must doe her good   15
If she were purg'd, and her head-vaine let blood.
And Midas joyes, our Spanish jorneys give,
We touche all gold, but fynd no food to live.

And I shold be in the hot parchinge clyme
To dust and ashes turnd before my tyme.　　20
To mewe me in a shipp is to inthrall
Me in a prisonn, that were like to fall;
Or in a cloister, save that there men dwell
In a calme Heav'n, here in a swayring Hell.
Long voiages are long consumptions,　　25
And shipps are carts for executyons;
Yea, they are deaths : It is all one to flye
Into another world, as 'tis to die.
Heere let me warre, in these arms let me lye;
Here let me parley : better bleed then dye.　　30
Thyne arms imprison mee, and myn arms thee;
Thy hart thy ransom is, take myne for mee.
Other men warr, that thay their rest may gaine;
But we will rest that we may fight againe.
Those warrs th' ignorant, these the experienct love; 35
There we are alwais vnder, heere aboue;
There engines farr of[f] breed a iust true feare;
Neere thrusts, pickes, stabbs, yea bullets, hurt not heere.
There lyes are wronges, here safe vprightly lye;
There men kill men, wee'le make one by and by.　　40
Thou nothinge, I not halfe soe much to doe
In these warrs, as they may which from vs two
Shall springe.　Thowsands we see which travail not
To warr, but stay, swords, arms, and shott
To make at home; and shall not I do then　　45
More gloriovs service, staying to make men ?

NOTES AND ILLUSTRATIONS.

This Elegy was first printed by Waldron (on whom see our Essay), and, ignorant thereof, by Sir John Simeon, as before; but again, and for the same reasons, I follow the Stephens' MS., where it is headed simply 'Elegia Decima quinta.' These variations from our MS. are noteworthy:

Line 1. Characteristically Donne writes in our MS. 'I warr with,' oblivious of scansion, &c. 'Warr other men'=let other men warr—second and greatly-improved thought. So in like manner 'The present wars devour him' (Coriol. i. 1); a phrase surprisingly puzzling to some, even after Warburton had pointed out its true meaning.

Line 6, ''press'= oppress (as in margin). Our MS. reads 'master-peers.'

Line 8, 'who,' and line 12, 'which.' The allusion is to the assistance at various times given to the Provinces in their War of Independence.

Lines 10-11. Perhaps referring to the force which was sent to the assistance of Henry of Navarre under Essex in 1591. The Queen, who had given him and the Dutch money and other secret assistance before, then sent him 20,000*l.* in gold.

Line 15, 'straying;' and line 15, 'must' for 'will.'
  ,, 16, 'dead-vaine.'
  ,, 18. I accept 'touche' for the first 'fynd.'
  ,, 24, 'swaggering.'
  ,, 27, 'is't not.'
  ,, 30, 'batter, bleed, and.' The explanation of such a phrase can be found in Sir Thomas Browne's Pseudod. b. iii. c. ix.; and the computation has been usefully—for their purpose—employed by quacks in the present day.

Line 32. I accept 'for' instead of 'from' of our MS.; and 'thy' for '*the* ransom,' as the context demands.

Line 35. Our MS. 'unexperienct.'
  ,, 37. Our MS. 'their:' Simeon 'these:' accepted.
  ,, 41, 'shall do.'

Waldron has this footnote: "'Than they which fell' (line 14). The MS. from which this and the following Elegy were printed reads, 'then they,' &c., the common orthography of the time. It is dated 1625. For the sake of perspicuity, some other trifling variations have been made—as bear for bare, vein for vaiuc—and a few commas inserted. The distinction between *angels*, coin so-called, and the Fallen Angels scarcely needs being pointed out." All the references go to show that this Elegy was written in the reign of Elizabeth. G.

XXIII.

LOVE'S POWER.

Shall Love, that gave Latona's heire the foile,   · Apollo
(Proud of his archerie and Pethon's spoile,)   Python's
And so enthral'd him to a nimph's disdaine
As, when his hopes were dead, hee, full of paine,
Made him above all trees the lawrell grace,   5
An embleme of Loue's glory, his disgrace;
Shall he, I say, be termed a foot-boy now
Which made all powers in Heauen and Earth to bowe?
Or is't a fancy which themselves doe frame,
And therefore dare baptize by any name?   10
A flaming straw! which one sparke kindles bright,
And first hard breath out of itselfe doth fright;
Whose father was a smile, and death a frowne,
Soon proud of little and for lesse cast downe?
'Tis so! and this a lackie terme you may,   lackey 15
For it runs oft, and makes but shortest stay.
But thou, O Love! free from Time's eating rust,
That sett'st a limite unto boundles lust,
Making desire grow infinitely stronge,
And yett to one chast subiect still belong;   20

Bridling self-love, that flatters us in ease,
Quick'ning our witts to striue that they may please ;
Fixing the wand'ring thoughts of straying youth,
The firmest bond of Faith, the knott of Truth :
Thou that did'st never lodge in worthles hart,   heart 25
Thou art a master, whersoe're thou art.
Thou mak'st food loathsome, sleep to be unrest,
Lost labor easeful, scornefull lookes a feast ;
And when thou wilt, thy ioyes as farr excell   joys
All elce as, when thou punish'st, thy Hell.   else 30
Oh make that rebell feele thy matchles power,
Thou that mad'st Jove a bull, a swan, a showre.
Give him a love as tirannous as faire,
That his desire goe yoakèd with despaire ;
Live in her eyes, but in her frozen heart   35
Lett no thaw come that may have sence of smart.
Lett her a constant silence never breake,
Till he doe wish repulse to heare her speake ;
And last, such sence of error lett him haue
As he may never dare for mercy crave.   40
Then none will more capittulate with thee,
But of their harts will yield the empire free.   hearts

NOTES AND ILLUSTRATIONS.

First printed by Sir John Simeon, as before ; but through a friend who collated this and others in our Vol. II. at Sir John's sale, I have been enabled to give the original ortho-graphy. I regret that there was no time to do the same for

Nos. xxiv. and xxv. that follow, which I am obliged to give as
in the Simeon tractate.

Who the rebel was that represented Love as a post-boy, and
so gave rise to the present poem, it is probably impossible now
to discover. Ben Jonson in his Cynthia's Revels (1600) introduces Cupid as a gamesome boy-deity, who disguises himself
as a page or foot-boy in the Court of Cynthia, and is foiled in
his attempts, in part through those who may be likened to
'themselves' of line 9, &c. having drunk of the fountain of
'self-love' (line 21). Line 11, 'proud'=when proud; line 30,
'thy Hell' [excels all other Hells]. G.

XXIV.

LOVE AND REASON.

Base Love, the stain of youth, the scorn of age,
The folly of a man, a woman's rage;
The canker of a froward will thou art,
The business of an idle, empty heart;
The rack of Jealousy and sad Mistrust,   5
The smooth and justified excuse of lust;
The thief which wastes the taper of our life;
The quiet name of restless jars and strife;
The fly which dost corrupt and quite distaste
All happiness if thou therein be cast;   10
The greatest and the most concealed impostor
That ever vain credulity did foster;
A mountebank extolling trifles small,
A juggler playing loose, not fast with all;
An alchymist, whose promises are gold,   15
Payment but dross, and hope at highest sold.

This, this is Love, and worse than I can say
When he a master is, and bears the sway.
He guides like Phaeton, burns and destroys,
Parches and stifles what would else be joys. 20
But when clear Reason, sitting in the throne,
Governs his beams,—which otherwise are none
But darts and mischiefs,—oh, then, sunlike, he
Doth actuate, produce, ripen, and free
From grossness, those good seeds which in us lie 25
Till then as in a grave, and there would die.
All high perfections in a perfect lover
His warmth does cherish, and his light discover.
He gives an even temper of delight
Without a minute's loss; nor fears affright 30
Nor interrupt the joys such love doth bring,
Nor no enjoying can dry up the spring.
Unto another he lends out our pleasure,
That—with the use—it may come home a treasure.
Pure link of bodies where no lust controuls, 35
The fastness and security of souls!
Sweetest path of life, virtue in full sail,
Tree-budding hope whose fruit doth never fail!
To this dear love I do no rebel stand,
Though not employed, yet ready at command. 40
Wherefore, oh Reason high, thou who art king
Of the world's king, and dost in order bring
The wild affections, which so often swerve
From thy just rule, and rebel passions serve;

Thou without whose light love's fire is but smoke, 45
Which puts out eyes and mind's true sense doth choak;
Restore this lover to himself again,
Send him a lively feeling of his pain,
Give him a healthy and discerning taste
Of food and rest, that he may rest at last, 50
By strength of thee, from his strange strong disease,
Wherein the danger is that it doth please.
Grant this, oh Reason, at his deep'st request
Who never loved to see your power supprest.
And now to you, Sir Love, your love I crave, 55
Of you no mastery I desire to have.
But that we may, like honest friends, agree,
Let us to Reason fellow-servants be.

NOTES AND ILLUSTRATIONS.

From Sir John Simeon's tractate, as before. But while Sir
John assures us very earnestly that he had well weighed the
evidence furnished in the different mss. of his own and of (now)
Lord Houghton of the authorship of all printed by him being
Donne's, a critical perusal of the present Elegy suggests that
it cannot have been written by, though probably it was addressed to, him. Line 39 (to notice only it)—

'To this dear love I do no rebel stand'—

seems plainly the poetic rejoinder of the person whom Donne
had addressed in Elegy xxiii. This grows plainer still when we
find that in reply to Donne's humorous curses he gives as 'a
soft answer turning away wrath' the prayer beginning line 41;
and then applying to Donne the title of SIR LOVE, clearly applies
to him the phrase Donne had applied to Love: 'Thou art a
master' (El. xxiii. line 26), and concludes with, 'of you, Sir
Love:'

'Of you no mastery I desire to have,
But that we may, like honest friends, agree.' (ll. 55 et seqq.)

The same is also referred to, line 18, 'When he a master is,'
&c. And again [Reason],

> 'Give him a healthy and discerning taste
> Of food and rest, that he may rest at last' (ll. 49-50.)

refers to Donne's

> 'Thou [Love] mak'st food loathsome, sleep to be unrest.'

So line 35 refers to Donne's line 18, and lines 41-3 to Donne's
lines 23 and 26; for reason, king of the world's king, is reason
king of man. I am indebted to the insight of Dr. Brinsley
Nicholson for above line of detection.

On line 7 see former note on the opinion of philosophers on
this; line 34, 'use'=usury, interest. G.

XXV.

TO A LADY OF DARK COMPLEXION.

If shadows be the picture's excellence
And make it seem more lively to the sense ;
If stars in the bright day are lost from sight
And seem most glorious in the mask of Night ;
Why should you think, rare creature, that you lack   5
Perfection, cause your eyes and hair are black ;
Or that your heavenly beauty, which exceeds
The new-sprung lilies in their maidenheads,
The damask colour of your cheeks and lips
Should suffer by their darkness an eclipse ?   10
Rich diamonds shine brightest being set
And compassèd within a field of jet ;
Nor were it fit that nature should have made
So bright a sun to shine without some shade—

It seems that Nature, when she first did fancy   15
Your rare composure, studied nigromancy :
That when to you this gift she did impart
She used altogether the black art,
By which infused powers from magic book
You do command, like spirits, with a look.   20
She drew those magic circles in your eyes,
And made your hair the chains with which she ties
Rebelling hearts. Those blue veins, which appear
Winding meanders about either sphere,
Mysterious figures are ; and when you list,   25
Your voice commandeth as the exorcist.
O, if in magic you have power so far,
Vouchsafe to make me your familiar.
Nor hath dame Nature her black art revealed
To outward parts alone, some lie concealed.   30
For as by heads of springs men often know
The nature of the streams which run below,
So your black hair and eyes do give direction
To think the rest to be of like complexion ;
That rest where all rest lies that blesseth man,   35
That Indian mine, that straight of Magelan,
That world-dividing gulph, where he who ventures
With swelling sails and ravisht senses, enters
To a new world of bliss. Pardon I pray,
If my rude Muse presumeth to display   40
Secrets unknown, or hath her bounds o'erpast
In praising sweetness which I ne'er did taste. .

Starved men do know there's meat, and blind men may,
Though hid from light, presume there is a day.
The rover, in the mark his arrow strikes   45
Sometimes as well as he that shoots at pricks ;
And if that I might aim my shaft aright,
The black mark I would hit and not the white.

NOTES AND ILLUSTRATIONS.

From Sir John Simeon, as before, as printed by him from
his MSS. The queen [Elizabeth] being fair, all beauties were
golden-haired, and gray eyes were esteemed the loveliest; and
as we have seen in our own day, those who had dark hair
used auricome dyes. This explains the heading and treatment
generally.

Line 6, '*nigromancy*.' This is not a punning coinage of
Donne's ; for both forms — nigromancy=the black art=German
man Schwarzkunst ; and necromancy=divination by calling up
the deceased—existed in English, Italian, and French. As
necromancy in its general sense is a misnomer—for it can only
be applied to such arts as that of the Witch of Endor—it may
be that nigromancy, as having to do with spirits of blackness,
was a mediæval coinage, suggested by *necromantia*, and this is
supported in some degree by the Teutonic forms. The evidence,
however, seems stronger for the belief that nigromancy is but
a corruption of the modern Latin race pronunciation of the
former *necro*, assisted by the evident fitness of the word *niger*
so compounded. Thus the Italian pronunciation of *necro* would
be *negro*, and this would glide, with the assistance mentioned,
into *nigro*. In Spanish also there is, so far as I can find, but
one form—*negromancia* (negro being also=black in Sp.); and
it confirms this view, that the dictionary compilers of those
days, and especially such a one as Minsheu, make no distinction between the two forms.

Line 46, ' pricks :' miswritten ' picks :' the rover shot at
any casual mark, the other at a ' prick,' or established and
measured mark. Minsheu gives ' prick' as = butt, though
sometimes it would appear to be used preëminently of its

centre. From the use of the verb 'pricking' in Ascham it would seem that a 'butt' was called a 'prick,' because, it being for instruction and exercise in accuracy, the arrow was not shot with a long or strong flight so as to pierce, but for a short distance, with moderate strength (and even with a weaker bow), so as only to 'prick' the mark. I commend this to my admirable and erudite friend Rev. J. E. B. Mayor, who has edited with such scholarliness Ascham's 'Scholemaster.' G.

XXVI.

AN ELEGIE TO MRS. BOULSTRED.

SHALL I goe force an elegy? abuse
My witt? and breake the hymen of my Muse
For one poore hower's love? descrues it such
Which scrues not mee to doe on her as much?
Or if it would, I would that fortune shunn—   5
Who would be rich to be soe soon vndone?
The beggar's best that wealth doth never know,
And but to shew it him increaseth woe.
But we two may enioy an hower, when never
It returns, who would have a losse for ever?   10
Nor can soe short a loue, if true, but bring
A half-hower's feare with thought of loosing.
Before it all howers were hope, and all are,
That shall come after it, yeares of dispaire.
This ioy brings this doubt, whether it were more   15
To haue enioyed it, or haue dy'de before.

'Tis a lost Paradize, a fall from grace,
Which I think Adam felt more than his race;
Nor need these angels any other Hell,   .
It is enough for them from Heaven they fell.   20
Beside, conquest in love is all in all,
That when I list shee under me may fall;
And for this turne, both for delight and view
I'll haue a Succuba as good as you.
But when these toyes are past, and o' blood ends,   our
The best injoying is, wee still are freindes.   26
Loue can but be friendship's outside, there two   their
Beauties differ as minds and bodyes do.
Thus I this good still fayne would be to take,
Vnles one hower another happy make;   30
Or that I might forgett it instantly;
Or in that blest estate that I might dye.
But why doe I thus trauaile in the skill
Of dispos'd Poetry, and perchance spill
My fortune, or undoe myself in sport   35
By hauing but that daungerous name in Court?
I'll leaue, and since I doe your poet proue,
Keepe you my lines as secret as my loue.

NOTES AND ILLUSTRATIONS.

This Elegie as published by Sir John Simeon (as before,
pp. 13-14) differs in several places from his own ms. (exclusive of
modernised spelling), as a collation thereof by my scrupulously-
accurate friend Colonel Chester reveals. I exactly reproduce
the original ms. Sir John seems to have made up his text from

some other copies; but as he does. not adduce these, it seems
better to adhere to the MS. itself. These departures from the
MS. being important, it is deemed expedient to record them:
Line 7, 'his wealth he doth not know;' line 25, 'hast' for 'our'
—the former better certainly, yet unauthentic; line 29, 'this
great good still would;' line 30, ' but a poet's name;' line 34, ' Of
deeper mysteries.' With reference to our heading, which is that
of the MS., it is noticeable from the after-elegies ' on,' and not
' to,' the Lady. Sooth to say, this Elegy is obscure and unsatisfactory. G.

XXVII.

LOVE AND WIT.

TREW love fynds wytt, but he whose witt doth move
Him to love, confesseth he doth not love;
And from his wytt, passions and true desire
Are forc't as hard as from the flynnt is fyre.
My Love's all fyer, whose flames my sowle doth nurs,
Whose smoakes are syghs, whose euery spark's a vers.
Doth measure win women? Then I know the why
Most of our ladyes with the Scots doe lye.
A Scot is measured, in each syllable, terse
And smooth as a verse, and like that smooth verse   10
Is shallow, and wants matter cut in bands,
And they're rugged. Her state better stands
Whom dawncinge measures tempted, not yᵉ Scott;
In briefe their out of measure cost, so gott.
Greene-sicknes wenches (not needs must, but) may   15
Looke pale, breathe short: at Court none so long stay.

Good wit never dispairèd there, or ay me sayd, ah me
For never wench at Covrt was ravishèd.
And she but cheats on Heav'n whom soe you wynn,
Thinkinge to share the sport, but not the synn. 20

.NOTES AND ILLUSTRATIONS.

We print this for the first time from the Stephens' ms.,
where it is headed simply ' Elegia Vndecima.' In the Haslewood-Kingsborough ms. (624, p. 165) there is another copy,
with the name ' John Done' appended. It offers these various
readings :
 Line 1, ' Trew :' our ms. miswrites ' Even.' Cf. this line
with Elegy xxiii. Love's Pow'r.
 Line 9, ' A Scott measure :' both our text and this seem
corrupt here. I have ventured to read ' A Scott is measured'
for ' A Scot's ;' the meaning=a Scot is measured [in his pro-
nunciation] terse in each syllable. As may be seen by comparison of Shakespeare's later writings, it became the fashion to
run words and syllables together, and to pronounce them as it
were blurringly. The Scots were seemingly behind the fashion,
besides having naturally that pronunciation which gave the
spelling qhair and the like—a difference which led to great dis-
puting. So much for ' measured and terse ;' but ' smooth' I do
not understand, except that, to myself a Scot, our vernacular
seems liquid and musical as Italian in much of it. Possibly
Raleigh, and the fashionable maritime expeditions, might have
brought into vogue a more Devonian pronunciation.
 Line 10. I take the ' And' before ' smooth' from Haslewood-
Kingsborough ms.
 Line 11, ' writt in his hands :' ibid. Both texts obscure.
 Ib. ' Is shallow and wants matter, but [=except] in his
hands, [which have the itch] ; and are also, unlike his smooth
speech, rugged.'
 Lines 12-13. Possibly said with some remembrance of Queen
Elizabeth, whom Sir C. Hatton pleased by his dancing, and who
hated the Scots.
 Line 14, ' she's out of measure lost :' ibid.
 Ib. ' Her state,' &c. being a comparison, he now returns,

and says, In brief, those so obtained by Scots and by measure, that is, not by force of burning affection, are out of measure, or wholly lost.

Line 16. *Id est*, none long stay so or such.

,, 17, 'or (aymer) sed:' ibid.: meaningless. 'Ay me'= ah me: restores sense. The meaning seems to be, that true forceful love was never known at Court, but that 'wit,' which moved one to love fancifully, or in a measured way, never became disconsolate through ill success; for the women were enver ravished, but loved, as they ever did, by measure, and gave themselves up measuredly and willingly, without being forced either by their lovers' forceful love or by their own.

Line 18, 'mingled:' ibid. G.

XXVIII.

A LOVE-MONSTER.

Behold a wonder such as hath not bene
From Pirrhus age vnto this present seene!
Six fingers, two heads, and such rarieties
Which sometyme haue been thought as prodigies
May passe as common things. No monster there   5
Compar'd with this which I about me beare.
Sporting with Calda as I oft before
Had done with her, and many of them more,
When in few dayes somthinge began t' appeare
The thought whereof amazèd me with feare.   10
I 'had thought that I 'had plundyred a sandy shore,
For what's more barren then a comon whore?
But now I see the signes, feele them and handle,
And know, alas, I 'am in for sope and candle.

But heer's the wonder, that noe Oedipus　　　　15
Nor sphinx can ere vnryddle without vs.
The father and the mother are the same,
And I the agent both and patient am.
I gott the chyld and beare it, she is free,
The care of being delivered lyes in mee.　　　　20
My belly swells and cannot be conceald,
The poyson is gone too farr to be heald.
All men that see me [do] faint, halt and shrinke,
Wonder to see't, but know not what to think.
Now is the tyme of my deliverance neare,　　　　25
And now I labour betwixt hope and feare.
Hopinge ye best, yet euermore in doubt
How this Cæsarian bratt can be cut out.
A barber is my mydwife, and a knyfe
That cuts the infant's throat doth give it life.　　　　30
One such a chance acruid to Jove, when hee
Slylie on earth stole secret leacherye.
When Vulcan launc't him and so drest ye sore
That from that tyme he never felt it more.
The chyld he Pallas call'd, because, quoth hee,　　　　35
Hereafter I do meane wyser to bee.
So call I myne as aptly and as fytt,
For I'me resolvèd, myne shal teach me wytt.

NOTES AND ILLUSTRATIONS.

From the Stephens' ms. (for the first time), where it is
headed simply 'Elegia Vicesima pryma.' The conceits of the
age and of Donne were often so far-fetched, that a satisfactory

solution of the subject of this poem is, as he says, impossible
without his own aid. Perhaps he had a Winchester goose or
poulain, or possibly, from the expressions in line 30, paraphi-
mosis.

Line 2, 'Pirrhus age:' when the Romans were affrighted
by his elephants.

Line 14: probably used to facilitate delivery and to wash
the child, &c. Cf. Middleton's Chaste Maid in Cheapside,
where a 'promoter' looking out for those who sold or ate meat
in Lent is left with a new-born baby in a basket of meat, and
says (ii. 2, vol. iv. p. 37, ed. Dyce):

> ' Half our gettings
> Must run in sugar-sops and nurses' wages now,
> Besides many a pound of *soap and tallow;*
> We've need to get loins of mutton still, to save
> Suet to change for candles.'

Line 28 refers to the Cæsarian operation. G.

IV.

EPITHALAMIUMS, OR MARRIAGE SONGS.

NOTE.

Our text of this division of Donne's poetry is that of 1669, with the results of collation of all the printed editions and MSS. in Notes and Illustrations. These in this case are slight, as the variations are almost wholly in orthography, and so not demanding record. See our Essay (Vol. II.) for critical remarks on these Epithalamiums and the class to which they belong: also our edition of Donne's friend CHRISTOPHER BROOKE (in Fuller Worthies' Miscellanies, Vol. IV.) for his Epithalamium. G.

AN EPITHALAMION.

ON FREDERICK COUNT PALATINE OF THE RHENE AND THE
LADY ELIZABETH
BEING MARRIED ON ST. VALENTINE'S DAY.

I.

HAIL, Bishop Valentine, whose day this is,
   All the air is thy diocis,
   And all the chirping choristers
And other birds are thy parishioners :
   Thou marryest every year
The lyrique larke, and the grave whispering dove,
The sparrow, that neglects his life for love,
The household bird with the red stomacher ;
   Thou mak'st the blackbird speed as soon
As doth the goldfinch or the halcion ;
The husband cock looks out, and straight is sped,
And meets his wife, which brings her feather-bed ;
This day more cheerfully than ever shine,
This day, which might inflame thyself, old Valentine.

II.

Till now, thou warm'dst with multiplying loves
   Two larks, two sparrows, or two doves :

All that is nothing unto this,
For thou this day couplest two phœnixes.
   Thou mak'st a taper see
What the sun never saw ; and what the ark
(Which was of fowl and beasts the cage and park)
Did not contain, one bed contains, through thee ;
   Two phœnixes, whose joynèd brests
Are unto one another mutual nests ; .
Where motion kindles such fires, as shall give
Young phœnixes, and yet the old shall live :
Whose love and courage never shall decline,
But make the whole year through thy day, O Valentine.

III.

Up then, fair phœnix bride, frustrate the sun ;
   Thyself from thine affection
Tak'st warmth enough, and from thine eye
All lesser birds will take their jollity.
   Up; up, fair bride, and call
Thy stars from out their several boxes, take
Thy rubies, pearls, and diamonds forth, and make
Thyself a constellation of them all :
   And by their blazing signifie
That a great princess falls, but doth not die ;
Be thou a new star, that to us portends
Ends of much wonder ; and be thou those ends.
Since thou dost this day in new glory shine,
May all men date records from this day, Valentine.

IV.

Come forth, come forth, and as one glorious flame,
   Meeting another, grows the same,
   So meet thy Frederick, and so
To an unseparable union go ;
   Since separation
Falls not on such things as are infinite,
Nor things, which are but one, can disunite,
You are 'twice inseparable, great, and one.
   Go then to where the bishop stays,
To make you one, his way, which divers wayes
Must be effected ; and when all is past,
And that y' are one, by hearts and hands made fast,
You two have one way left yourselves t' entwine,
Besides this bishop's knot of Bishop Valentine.

V.

But oh ! what ayles the sun, that here he staies
   Longer to-day than other daies ?
   Stayes he new light from these to get ?
And finding here such stores, is loath to set ?
   And why do you two walk
So slowly pac'd in this procession ?
Is all your care but to be look'd upon,
And be to others spectacle and talk ?
   The feast with gluttonous delays
Is eaten, and too long their meat they praise ;

The masquers come late, and I think will stay,
Like fairies, till the cock crow them away.
Alas, did not antiquitie assign
A night, as well as day, to thee, old Valentine?

VI.

They did, and night is come : and yet we see
     Formalities retarding thee.
     What mean these ladies, which (as though
They were to take a clock in peeces) go
     So nicely about the bride?
A bride, before a good-night could be said,
Should vanish from her clothes into her bed,
As souls from bodies steal, and are not spy'd.
     But now she is laid : what though she be?
Yet there are more delayes ; for where is he?
He comes, and passeth through sphear after sphear ;
First her sheets, then her armes, then anywhere.
Let not this day, then, but this night be thine,
Thy day was but the eve to this, O Valentine!

VII.

Here lies a she sun, and a he moon there ;
     She gives the best light to his sphear,
     Or each is both, and all, and so
They unto one another nothing owe ;
     And yet they do, but are
So just and rich in that coin which they pay,
That neither would, nor needs, forbear, nor stay ;
Neither desires to be spar'd, nor to spare :

They quickly pay their debt, and then
Take no acquittances, but pay again ;
They pay, they give, they lend, and so let fall
No such occasion to be liberal.
More truth, more courage in these two do shine,
Than all thy turtles have, and sparrows, Valentine !

VIII.

And by this act of these two phœnixes
   Nature again restorèd is ;
   For since these two are two no more,
There's but one phœnix still, as was before.
   Rest now at last, and we
(As Satyrs watch the sun's uprise) will stay
Waiting when your eyes opened let out day,
Only desir'd, because your face we see ;
   Others near you shall whispering speak,
And wagers lay, at which side day will break,
And win by observing then, whose hand it is,
That opens first a curtain, hers or his ;
This will be tryed to-morrow after nine,
Till which hour we thy day enlarge, O Valentine !

NOTES AND ILLUSTRATIONS.

Our text of this 'Epithalamium' is from 1669 edition, with collation of the others, as explained in the general note prefixed. It originally appeared in the 4to of 1633 (pp. 118-122), and since in all the after-editions.
The Marriage celebrated took place at Whitehall on 14th

February 1612-13. Frederick V. Duke of Bavaria and Elector
Palatine of the Rhine (spelled as usual 'Rhene' in the inscription), afterwards elected king of Bohemia, was driven from his
dominions by the Emperor Ferdinand, and died at Mentz 29th
November 1632. The Princess Elizabeth, eldest and only sur-
viving daughter of James I. by Anne of Denmark, was born
19th August 1596, at the palace of Falkland in Fifeshire, Scotland. She — the unfortunate Queen of Bohemia in history—
died at Leicester House, in London, 13th February 1661-2, and
was buried in Westminster Abbey on the 17th of the same
month. They were the parents of 'Prince Rupert.'

The texts of printed editions and MSS. are nearly identical,
but these variants may be recorded in 1635 edition :

St. iv. last line has ô (MS. 'our') ; probably an error for o' =
of (1669, &c.).

St. v. last line reads O Val. for 'old :' the latter agrees better with context, 'Antiquity,' &c.

St. vii. line 1 reads 'Moon here' for 'Moon there ;' the
latter preferable.

Then in st. vii. line 12, 1669 omits 'such' by mistake ; or
possibly the author, discontented with the word, struck it out,
without deciding on another. Several of the MSS. (especially
the Stephens') similarly drop words, to loss of metre.

On the other hand, the Stephens' MS. offers variations worth
record :

St. i. l. 12, 'his wife, and brings his feather bed' (MS.).
　　　　　which　　　　　　　her

Both the sense and allusion make the latter preferable. In
human marriages the man does not 'bring' furniture ; and there
is reason to believe that a bed was sometimes a gift with the
bride.

Ib. line 13, 'than others shine' (MS.).
　　　　　　　　ever

As the poet is speaking not of other days, but of past Valen-
tines, the latter is preferable.

St. ii. line 7. Cf. Progress of the Soul, st. iii. line 1, and
note that the words 'cage' and 'park,' used in both, confirm
the view expressed there, that Janus is=Noah.

St. iii. line 9, 'this blazing' (MS.).
　　　　　　　　their

'This blazing' makes it an act of the princess ; and by context,
'their meteor portents' gives the better reading.

St. iv. line 4, 'grow' (ms.).

go

Here the ms. may be said to be equally good; yet 'go' might be defended, because he is speaking of before the marriage ceremony, and of 'going' to it. Haslewood-Kingsborough ms. 'growe.'

St. vi. is not in the ms.

,, vii. line 6, 'their' (ms.).

that

'That' seems preferable; as also in these: line 7, 'or stay' for 'now stay;' and line 11, 'and' for 'they;' and line 13, 'and' for 'more;' and st. viii. line 10, 'at whose side' (ms.) for 'which.' I prefer the printed texts. Other differences, mainly in spelling, do not call for notice. From whatever cause, the printed texts of the Epithalamiums are unusually good and accurate. This point requires notice :

St. viii. line 12. A strange custom this of visiting the yesterday-married couple in their chamber at morn, and while yet asleep or not risen. G.

ECLOGUE.

December 26, 1613.

ALLOPHANES *finding* IDIOS *in the Country that Chrismas time, reprehends his absence from Court at that Marriage of the Earl of Summerset;* IDIOS *gives an account of his purpose therein, and of his actions there.*

ALLOPHANES.

UNSEASONABLE man, statue of ice,
What could to countrie's solitude entice
Thee, in this yeare's cold and decrepit tyme?
Nature's instinct drawes to the warmer clyme

Ev'n smaller birds, who by that courage dare   5
In numerous fleets sayle through their sea, the ayre.
What delicacy can in fields appeare,
Whil'st Flora herself doth a freez jerkin wear?   frieze
Whil'st winds do all the trees and hedges strip   .
Of leaves, to furnish rods enough to whip   10
Thy madness from thee, and all springs by frost
Have taken cold, and their sweet murmurs lost?
If thou thy faults or fortunes would'st lament
With just solemnity, do it in Lent :
At Court the Spring already advancèd is,   15
The sun stayes longer up ; and yet not his
The glory is ; far other, other fires :
First, zeal to Prince and State ; then Love's desires
Burn in one breast, and like heaven's two great lights,
The first doth govern daies, the other nights.   20
And then that early light, which did appear
Before the sun and moon created were,—
The prince's favour,— is diffus'd o'er all,
From which all fortunes, names, and natures fall ;
Then from those wombes of stars, the Bride's bright eyes,
At every glance a constellation flies,   26
And sows the Court with stars, and doth prevent
In light and power the all-ey'd firmament.   [anticipate
First her eyes kindle other ladies' eyes,
Then from their beams their jewels' lusters rise,   30
And from their jewels torches do take fire ;
And all is warmth and light and good desire.

Most other Courts, alas, are like to hell,
Where in dark plots, fire without light doth dwell:
Or but like stoves, for lust and envy get   35
Continual but artificial heat;
Here zeal and love, grown one, all clouds disgest,
And make our Court an everlasting East.
And canst thou be from thence?

IDIOS.

                              No, I am there:
As heaven, to men dispos'd, is ev'ry where,   40
So are those Courts, whose princes animate,
Not only all their house, but all their State.
Let no man think, because he's full, he hath all ;
Kings (as their pattern, God) are liberal
Not only in fulness but capacity,   45
Enlarging narrow men to feel and see,
And' comprehend, the blessings they bestow.
So reclus'd hermits oftentimes do know
More of heaven's glory, then a worldling can. than
As man is of the world, the heart of man   50
Is an epitome of God's great book
Of creatures, and man need no farther look ;
So's the country, of Courts where sweet peace doth,
As their own common soul, give life to both.
And am I then from Court?

ALLOPHANES.

                              Dreamer, thou art. 55
Think'st thou, fantastique, that thou hast a part

In the Indian fleet, because thou hast
A little spice or amber in thy taste?
Because thou art not frozen, art thou warm?
Seest thou all good, because thou seest no harm?   60
The earth doth in her inner bowels hold
Stuff well dispos'd, and which would fain be gold:
But never shall, except it chance to lye
So upward, that heaven gild it with his eye;
As for divine things, faith comes from above,   65
So, for best civil use, all tinctures move
From higher powers; from God, religion springs;
Wisdom and honour, from the use of kings;
Then unbeguile thyself, and know with me,
That angels, though on earth employ'd they be,   70
Are still in heaven; so is he still at home
That doth abroad to honest actions come.
Chide thyself then, O fool, which yesterday
Might'st have read more than all thy books bewray:
Hast thou a history, which doth present   75
A Court, where all affections do assent
Unto the king's, and that, that kings' are just?
And where it is no levity to trust,
Where there is no ambition but t' obey,
Where none need whisper anything, yet may;   80
Where the king's favours are so plac'd, that all
Finde that the king therein is liberal
To them in him, because his favours bend
To virtue, to the which they all pretend?

Thou hast no such; yet here was this, and more,—
An earnest lover, wise then, and before.　　　86
Our little Cupid hath sued livery,
And is no more in his minority;
He is admitted now into that brest
Where the king's councels and his secrets rest.　　90
What hast thou lost, O ignorant man!

IDIOS.

　　　　　　　　　　　　　　　I knew
All this, and only therefore I withdrew.
To know and feel all this, and not to have
Words to express it, makes a man a grave
Of his own thoughts; I would not therefore stay　95
At a great feast, having no grace to say.
And yet I 'scaped not here; for being come
Full of the common joy, I uttered some.
Read then this nuptial song, which was not made
Either the Court or men's harts to invade;　hearts 100
But since I'm dead and buried, I could frame
No epitaph, which might advance my fame,
So much as this poor song, which testifies
I did unto that day some sacrifice.

I. THE TIME OF MARRIAGE.

Thou art repriev'd, old year, thou shalt not die,　105
Though thou upon thy death-bed lie,
　　And should'st within five days expire.
Yet thou art rescu'd from a mightier fire,

Than thy old soul, the sun,
When he doth in his largest circle run: 110
The passage of the West or East would thaw,
And open wide their easie liquid jaw
To all our ships, could a Promethean art,
Either unto the northern pole impart   114
The fire of these inflaming eyes, or of this loving heart.

II. EQUALITY OF PERSONS.

But undiscerning Muse, which heart, which eyes,
      In this new couple dost thou prize,
      When his eye as inflaming is
As hers, and her heart loves as well as his?
      Be tryed by beauty, and than   then   120
The bridegroom is a maid, and not a man;
If by that manly courage they be tryed,
Which scorns unjust opinion, then the bride
Becomes a man: should chance or envie's art
Divide these two, whom nature scarce did part,   125
Since both have the inflaming eye, and both the loving
            heart?

III. RAISING OF THE BRIDEGROOM.

Though it be some divorce to think of you
      Single, so much one are you two,
      Let me here contemplate thee
First, chearful bridegroom, and first let me see,   130
      How thou prevent'st the sun,
And his red foaming horses dost outrun;

How, having laid down in thy sovereigne's brest
All businesses, from thence to reinvest
Them, when these triumphs cease, thou forward art 135
To show to her, who doth the like impart,
The fire of thy inflaming eyes and of thy loving heart.

IV. RAISING OF THE BRIDE.

But now to thee, fair bride, it is some wrong,
   To think thou wert in bed so long :
      Since soon thou liest down first, 'tis fit   140
Thou in first rising should allow for it.
   Powder thy radiant hair,
Which if without such ashes thou would'st wear,
Thou who, to all which come to look upon,
Wert meant for Phœbus, would'st be Phaeton.   145
For our ease give thine eyes the unusual part
Of joy, a tear ; so quencht, thou mai'st impart,
To us that come, thy 'inflaming eyes ; to him, thy lov-
        ing heart.

V. HER APPARELLING.

Thus thou descend'st to our infirmity,
   Who can the sun in Winter see ;   150
      So dost thou, when in silk and gold
Thou cloud'st thyself ; since we, which do behold,
   Are dust and worms, 'tis just
Our objects be the fruits of worms and dust.
Let every jewel be a glorious star ;   155
Yet stars are not so pure as their sphears are.

And though thou stoop to appear to us in part,
Still in that picture thou intirely art,   [heart.
Which thy inflaming eyes have made within his loving

VI. GOING TO THE CHAPPEL.

Now from your Easts you issue forth, and we,   160
    As men, which through a cypres see
    The rising sun, do think it two,
So, as you go to church, do think of you :
    But that vail being gone,
By the church-rites you are from thenceforth one. 165
The Church Triumphant made this match before,
And now the Militant doth strive no more.
Then, reverend priest, who God's Recorder art,
Do from his dictates to these two impart   [heart.
All blessings which are seen or thought by angel's eye or

VII. THE BENEDICTION.

Blest pair of swans, O may you interbring   171
    Daily new joys, and never sing :
    Live, till all grounds of wishes fail,
Till honor, yea till wisdom grow so stale,
    That new great hights to trie,   175
It must serve your ambition, to die ;
Raise heirs, and may here to the world's end, live
Heirs from this king, to take thanks ; you, to give.
Nature and grace do all, and nothing Art ;
May never age or errour overthwart   [heart.
With any West these radiant eyes, with any North this

VIII. FEASTS AND REVALS. <small>revels</small>

But you are over-blest. Plenty this day
   Injures; it causeth Time to stay;
   The tables groan, as though this feast
Would, as the flood, destroy all fowl and beast.   185
   And were the doctrine new
That the earth mov'd, this day would make it true;
For every part to dance and revel goes,
They tread the ayr, and fall not where they rose.
Though six hours since the sun to bed did part,   190
The maskes and banquets will not yet impart
A sunset to these weary eyes, a center to this heart.

IX. THE BRIDE'S GOING TO BED.

What mean'st thou, bride, this company to keep?
   To sit up, till thou fain would sleep?
   Thou maist not, when thou'rt laid, do so.   195
Thyself must to him a new banquet grow,
   And you must entertain,
And do all this day's dances o're again.
Know, that if sun and moon together do
Rise in one point, they do not set so too.   200
Therefore thou maist, faire bride, to bed depart;
Thou art not gone being gone; where're thou art,
Thou leav'st in him thy watchfull eyes, in him thy
      loving heart.

X. THE BRIDEGROOM'S COMING.

As he that sees a starr fall, runs apace
   And finds a gelly in the place,   jelly   205 ·
So doth the bridegroom haste as much,
Being told this starre is faln, and finds her such.
And as friends may look strange
By a new fashion, or apparel's change,
Their souls, though long acquainted they had been,   210
These clothes—their bodies—never yet had seen.
Therefore at first she modestly might start,
But must forthwith surrender every part   [heart.
As freely, as each to each before gave either hand or

XI. THE GOOD-NIGHT.

Now, as in Tullia's tomb one lamp burnt clear,   215
   Unchanged for fifteen hundred year,
   May these love-lamps we here enshrine,
In warmth, light, lasting, equall the divine.
   Fire ever doth aspire,
And makes all like itself, turns all to fire,—   220
But ends in ashes; which these cannot do,
For none of these is fuell, but fire too.
This is joye's bonfire, then, where Love's strong arts
Make of so noble individual parts   224
One fire of four inflaming eyes and of two loving hearts.

IDIOS.

As I have brought this song, that I may do
A perfect sacrifice, I'll burn it too.

ALLOPHANES.

No, Sir, this paper I have justly got,
For in burnt incense' the perfume is not
His only that presents it, but of all ;   230
Whatever celebrates this festivall
Is common, since the joy thereof is so.
Nor may yourself be priest : but let me go
Back to the Court, and I will lay't upon
Such altars as prize your devotion.   235

NOTES AND ILLUSTRATIONS.

This 'Eclogue' and Epithalamium appeared originally in
the 4to of 1633 (pp. 123-129), and has since been reprinted in
all the editions. Our text is that of 1669, as before. There
are no variations calling for record. It was fitting that Ben
Jonson should write his delicious Masque of ' Hymenæi' at the
marriage of the Lady Frances Howard (in her fourteenth year)
with the Earl of Essex (in his fifteenth year) ; for there was
then scope and warrant for all ' Pleasures of Imagination' and
' Pleasures of Hope ;' but it is deplorable to read his verses ' To
the most noble and above his titles, Robert, Earle of Somerset,
sent to him on his Wedding-day, 1613' (Cunningham's Jonson,
vol. iii. pp. 465-6; from Notes and Queries, 1st series, vol. v. p.
193), and equally so to have Donne celebrating the same vilely
adulterous second marriage of the divorced ' Countess' of Essex
with the minion of James, Robert Carr, Viscount Rochester
(created just before it Earl of Somerset). This infamous marriage led to the murder of Sir Thomas Overbury, and the trial
and condemnation of the earl and countess—whose lives, re-
prieved by the king, were dragged out in mutual recrimination
and loathing. Somerset died obliviously; his devilish wife the
object of national horror. I fear that as Bacon got Campion to
write his Masque for the present occasion, he too over-persuaded
Donne to prep\ire his Eclogue and Epithalamium. Be this as
it may, it is saddening to find the great names of Bacon and

Jonson and Donne mixed-up with a marriage so disgraceful.
The 'Insatiate Countess,' whether by Marston or not, probably
reproduces (though founded on an older story) the popular
opinion of our ' Countess,' spite of her beauty and fascination.
On these see ll. 25, &c., and st. ii. iv. v. &c.: on the public
opinion of her, ll. 122-4: l. 167, again, refers to the differences
of opinion among those who tried the case of divorce. Arch-
bishop Abbot gave against it, notwithstanding the king's reproof,
and three out of the five doctors of law went with him; but
some of the bishops took the king's view, and the divorce was
decreed by seven against five: ll. 121, 142, and 222 remind us
that the plea of divorce being that she forcedly remained a
virgin, she was married as a virgin-bride, with 'untrimmed
locks,' that is with loose and flowing hair.

Line 5, ' that :' Haslewood-Kingsborough ms. ' their.'

„   6, ' fleets:' cf. MARVELL, and our relative note.

„   12. The construction ' having taken' is colloquial and
irregular : and I accept the ' have taken' of 1633.

Line 21, ' then :' Haslewood-Kingsborough ms. ' show.'

„   37, ' disgest'=separate in a reflective sense, tend to
dissolve as things digested in a retort or in the stomach : ' disgest' accepted from 1635 edition.

Line 39, ' from thence :' this reduplication is now a forbidden
colloquialism.

Line 40, ' dispos'd.' This and the example line 62 show how
' dispos'd' came (like ' procative') to have the particular meaning first noticed by Dyce, and how the particular disposition is
to be deduced from the context. See Jonson's Tale of a Tub
(act iv. sc. 5), where out of three uses, the second, like the example in Love's Labour Lost (ii. 1), seems to show that it
sometimes stood merely for disposed [to be merry].

Lines 54-5. Haslewood - Kingsborough ms. 'I am not then
from court.'

Line 57. Ibid. ' East Indian.'

„   62-3. If this be a piece of mediæval natural science, it
is unknown to me.

Line 67, ' powers :' Haslewood-Kingsborough ms. ' points.'

„   77, ' and [doth present this] that kings' are just.'

„   80. I accept here Haslewood-Kingsborough ms. instead
of 1669 ' Where men need whisper nothing . . .'

Line 83, ' to them in him :' the particular one favoured, the
bridegroom.

Line 86, '*wise then, and before:*' the allusion is to the saying that one cannot love and be wise.

Line 87, '*livery*'=release from wardship.

,, 89, '*into:*' Haslewood-Kingsborough 'within.'

,, 116. Ibid. reads 'undeserning . . . what eyes.'

,, 131, '*prevent'st the sun.*' This, and the wording of lines 5-8, vi. line 1, vii. line 2, and the opening of the Epith. at Lincoln's-inn, have greater point and appropriateness when we remember the customs of the period. In more than one old play the people rise before sunrise to be ready for a bridal; and in one the father is surprised at the girls not being up; but not surprised when from their absence he supposes that they rose before him, and slipped off to church.

Line 145, '*Phaeton*' [and scorch them].

,, 150, '*Winter.*' I accept this reading from Addl. mss. 18647, Plut. 201 H. In 1633, 1635, 1639, 1649, and 1669 'water:' in Stephens' ms. 'waters:' but line 152 'cloud'st' shows Winter to be the true reading, because the thought. It is no question of non-viewing the direct splendour of the sun.

Line 161, '*cypres*'=crape.

,, 172, '*never sing,*' and therefore never die; the allusion being to the myth that swans sing [only] before they die.

Lines 205-6, 'gelly'=jelly. One of those popular beliefs which in all probability arose from a coincidence, some gelatinous matter having been found where an aerolite had buried itself and been lost, or where a star had seemingly fallen.

Line 211, '*These clothes*' = their bodies, and so I punctuate (—).

Line 215, '*lamp.*' The ever-burning light in Tullia's tomb and in another are mentioned by Sir Thomas Browne in his Pseudodoxia Epid. l. iii. c. 21: 'Why some lamps included in close bodies have burned many hundred years, as that discovered in the sepulchre of Tullia, the sister of Cicero, and that of Olibius many years after, near Padua?' The belief is supposed to have arisen from the taking fire of pent-up gases at the moment of opening. G.

EPITHALAMION : MADE AT LINCOLN'S INN.

I.

THE sun-beams in the East are spred,
Leave, leave, fair Bride! your solitary bed ;
   No more shall you return to it alone,
It nurseth sadness ; and your bodie's print,
Like to a grave, the yielding downe doth dint :   5
   You and your other you meet there anon :
   Put forth, put forth, that warm balm-breathing thigh,
Which when next time you in these sheets will smother
There it must meet another,
   Which never was, but must be, oft' more nigh.   10
Come glad from thence, go gladder then you came, than
To-day put on perfection, and a woman's name.

II.

Daughters of London ! you which be
Our golden mines and furnish'd treasurie ;
   You which are angels, yet still bring with you   15
Thousands of angels on your marriage dayes,
Help with your presence, and devise to praise
   These rites, which also unto you grow due ;
   Conceitedly dress her, and be assign'd

By you fit place for every flower and jewel ;   20
Make her for Love fit fuel
        As gay as Flora, and as rich as Indie ;
So may she, fair and rich, in nothing lame,
To-day put on perfection, and a woman's name.

III.

And you, frolic Patricians,   25
Sons of those senators, wealth's deep oceans ;
        Ye painted Courtiers, barrels of others' wits ;
Ye countrymen, who but your beasts love none ;
Ye of those fellowships, whereof he's one,
        Of study and play made strange hermaphrodits,   30
        Here shine ; this bridegroom to the Temple bring.
Loe, in yon path, which store of strew'd flowers graceth,
The sober virgin paceth ;
        Except my sight fail, 'tis no other thing.
Weep not, nor blush, here is no grief nor shame ;   35
To-day put on perfection, and a woman's name.

IV.

Thy two-leav'd gates, fair Temple 'unfold,
And these two in thy sacred bosome hold,
        Till, mystically joyn'd, but one they be ;
Then may thy lean and hunger-starvèd womb   40
Long time expect their bodies, and their tomb,
        Long after their own parents fatten thee.
        All elder claims, and all cold barrenness,

All yielding to new loves, be farre forever,
Which might these two dissever;   45
    Alwayes all th' other may each one possess;
For the best bride, best worthy of praise and fame,
To-day puts on perfection, and a woman's name.

V.

Winter dayes bring much delight,
Not for themselves, but for they soon bring night; 50
    Other sweets wait thee then these diverse meats, than
Other disports then dancing jollities,   than
Other love-tricks then glancing with the eyes,   than
    But that the sun still in our half-sphear sweats;
    He flies in winter, but he now stands still;   55
Yet shadows turn; noon-point he hath attain'd,
His steeds will be restrain'd,
    But gallop lively down the western hill:
Thou shalt, when he hath run the heaven's half-frame,
To-night put on perfection, and a woman's name.   60

VI.

The amorous evening starre is rose;
Why then should not our amorous star inclose
    Herself in her wish'd bed? Release your strings,
Musitians, and dancers, take some truce
With these your pleasing labours, for great use   65
    As much wearines as perfection brings.

You, and not only you, but all toyl'd beasts,
Rest duly; at night, all their toyles are dispenced;
But in their beds commenced
    Are other labors, and more dainty feasts.   70
She goes a maid, who, lest she turn the same,
To-night puts on perfection, and a woman's name.

VII.

Thy virgin's girdle now vntie,
And in thy nuptial bed (love's altar) lie
    A pleasing sacrifice; now dispossess   75
Thee of these chains and robes, which were put on
T' adorn the day, not thee; for thou alone,
    Like virtue and truth, art best in nakedness;
    This bed is only to virginitie
A grave, but to a better state a cradle.   80
Till now thou wast but able
    To be what now thou art; then that by thee
No more be said, *I may be,* but *I am,*
To-night put on perfection, and a woman's name.

VIII.

Even like a faithful man, content   85
That this life for a better should be spent,
    So she a mother's rich stile doth prefere,
And at the bridegroom's wish'd approach doth lie,
Like an appointed lamb, when tenderly
    The priest comes on his knees t' imbowel her.   90

Now sleep, or watch with more joy; and, oh, light
Of heav'n! to-morrow rise thou hot and early,
This sun will love so dearly
　　Her rest, that long, long, we shall want her sight.
Wonders are wrought; for she which had no name 95
To-night puts on perfection, and a woman's name.

NOTES AND ILLUSTRATIONS.

This Epithalamium appeared originally in the 4to of 1633
(pp. 135-138), and since in all the editions. Our text is that
of 1669, as before. The variations are of no importance.

St. i. line 1. See note on previous poem (iii. 5).

Ib. line 6, '*meet*'=do meet=will meet.

St. iii. line 1 (line 25), 'Patricians:' Addl. mss. 18647 reads
'Puritans . . . Come of . . .'

Ib. line 6. The students of the Law constantly supple-
mented 'study' with masques and plays, either acting themselves or hiring others to act before them.   One very magnificent entertainment was given to Queen Elizabeth by those of
the Inner Temple at Christmas 1561-2, when they performed
Ferrex and Pollux; and the Four Inns combined in February
1634 to present before the court Shirley's Masque of the Triumph
of Peace, the music of which cost 1000*l.*, and the clothes of the
horsemen were valued at 10,000*l.*, and the whole charges 20,000*l.*
See Collier, Ann. of Stage, i. 179, and iii. 59, and authorities
there noted.

St. iv. line 9 (line 45); ms. 18647 reads ' Never night . . .'

　,, vi. line 8 (line 68), '*dispenc'd :*' a license for ' dispensed'
[with].

St. viii. line 9 (line 93), ' This sun . . .'=the bridegroom:
a thought reversed from Psalm xix. 4-5.

END OF VOL. I.

.

London : Robson & Sons, Printers, Pancras Road.